Does Civil Society Matter?

Does Civil Society Matter?

Governance in Contemporary India

Edited by

Rajesh Tandon
Ranjita Mohanty

SAGE Publications
New Delhi • Thousand Oaks • London

First published in 2003 by

Sage Publications India Pvt Ltd
B-42, Panchsheel Enclave
New Delhi 110 017

Sage Publications Inc
2455 Teller Road
Thousand Oaks, California 91320

Sage Publications Ltd
6 Bonhill Street
London EC2A 4PU

Published by Tejeshwar Singh for Sage Publications India Pvt Ltd, typeset by InoSoft Systems in 11 pt Calisto MT and printed at Chaman Enterprises, New Delhi.

Library of Congress Cataloging-in-Publication Data

Does civil society matter?:governance in contemporary India/edited by Rajesh Tandon, Ranjita Mohanty.
     p.   cm.
Includes bibliographical references and index.
1. Civil society—India. 2. Civil society. I. Tandon, Rajesh.
II. Mohanty, Ranjita.

JQ281.D64   306.2⎯0954—dc21   2003   2003006732

ISBN: 0–7619–9684–2 (US-Hb)   81–7829–148–7 (India-Hb)
      0–7619–9685–0 (US-Pb)   81–7829–149–5 (India-Pb)

Sage Production Team: Sarita Vellani, Praveen Dev, Sushanta Gayen and Santosh Rawat

Contents

Section II

Preface and Acknowledgements

This book grew out of a research project that the Society for Participatory Research in Asia (PRIA) undertook on civil society and governance in India as part of a multi-country study co-ordinated at the Institute of Development Studies (IDS), Sussex, UK that aimed at exploring and analysing the way civil society initiatives address and impact on issues of governance. We are thankful to the Ford Foundation for providing us the financial support to carry out the study.

It would not be an exaggeration to say that the interest in the idea of civil society and the association of good governance with it has become a sort of a rage among academics, in national and international development policy debates and in development aid circles. This is confusing because such an interest may well be a passing fad; but it also generates hope, because the debate relating to the role of civil society in promoting good governance has both academic merit and implications for actual improvement in the lives of people. We have therefore attempted to bring in diverse views, in the hope that they may set off something like a ripple effect.

As part of the study, a set of theoretical papers, which now form part of this volume, were contributed by both scholars in academia as well as on-the-ground practitioners. In addition, a number of empirical studies were conducted to answer the questions that the study posed—questions ranging from governance issues that civil society addresses, to the nature of the relationship that evolves between the state and civil society during the course of their interface and the implications that such interface holds for both spheres. Each of the case studies has its own merit in exploring the nuances of the interface between civil society and the state. However, due to con-straints of space, only five representative cases are included in this volume.

We have benefited immensely from the team of authors who worked independently but shared their thoughts collec-tively in many meetings that were organised in connection with this study. Among our academic colleagues, who were the source of an uninterrupted supply of ideas, we are most thank-ful to Neera Chandhoke, Bishnu Mohapatra and T.K. Oommen. Mark Robinson, in his dual role as an academic from IDS and as Ford Foundation's representative, took keen interest in the study. James Manor and his team from IDS kept us in touch, through the Internet and through face-to-face meetings, with other country researchers and we benefited from their thoughts and writings.

We have been involved in this study for over two years, trying to analyse the results of our endeavour. To pass this on to the reader is hence a relief—we can only hope that the ideas contained in this book not only generate more ideas, but also help those who are involved with actual struggles taking place in civil society to make human life a little more dignified.

March 2003   Rajesh Tandon
                                             Ranjita Mohanty

Introduction

Civil Society and Governance

Issues and Problematics

Rajesh Tandon and *Ranjita Mohanty*

The recent upsurge of interest in the idea of civil society can be attributed to two parallel, yet somehow interrelated shifts in the way societies would prefer to organise their affairs in relation to polity and the way economies would like to influence the course of direction that societies take. What is now popularly called the wave of democracy, which swept through hegemonic regimes, both orthodox Marxist and military, in the countries of East-Central Europe, Latin America and Africa, reflected the incongruence between the state and society on desirable political conditions under which people would like to live. The fall of communism and military dictatorship mirrored the aspirations of ordinary men and women to carve out for themselves an autonomous space for collective action and act as a counter to state power. These aspirations drove home two messages—they affirmed the desire and competency of ordinary people to define both political and social good and their terms of engagement with the state in pursuing these; and second, they affirmed the strength of collective action in achieving their desired political and social goals. Thus, the struggle, which began with carving out a space away from the prying eyes of the state, where people could discuss the essence of freedom, autonomy and dignity of human existence, in due course of time became a politically volatile force to bring down the most authoritative regimes.

A simultaneous shift in the economy was also taking place around this time in the form of neo-liberal ideas of the supremacy of the market in delivering to people what the states failed to do. The Reagan–Thatcher initiative in North America and England of withdrawing social sector spending and letting the market take over some of the state's responsibilities of providing service, employment and resources to the people became the basis for promoting the ascendancy of the market in the rest of the world. This space for the market in developing countries, where the states were starved of resources and had become notorious for failing to deliver essential goods and services, was facilitated through the structural adjustment programmes designed by the Bretton Woods institutions.

While the capitalist economies and their international allies were introducing the orthodoxy of neo-liberalism, they were not quite sure how this would actually be achieved. The resurgence of civil society coincided very neatly with the rise of neo-liberalism and provided the necessary insight as well as relief to its promoters. Countries of East-Central Europe not only democratised themselves, they also opened their economies to capitalist ventures, thus signing the death warrant for communism. The failure of communism closed it as an option for the Latin American countries, where a new way of defining the role of state and polity began to be deliberated by radical civil society groups who had previously drawn their inspiration from Marxist ideology. Autonomous associations of people were identified by the capitalist countries of North America and Western Europe as a rich source of energy, which had the potential to be channelled not only towards promoting the idea of the essential goodness of the market but also towards curbing the authoritarian tendencies of the state and creating a democratic environment in which the market could thrive. In addition, civil society was also perceived as providing the necessary buffer to people affected by the structural adjustment programmes, in terms of necessary development support and services. The association of civil society with governance can be traced to these historical shifts.

The critical and uncritical subscription of a large number of actors—academia, policy-makers, international aid agencies, social activists and non-government organisations (NGOs)—influenced by the historical shifts towards the idea of civil society, has made the concept complex, ambiguous and, to a large extent, fluid. Worse, it has flattened the concept so much that it has come to mean all sorts of things to its followers. The conceptualisations of civil society that vest it with the task of democratisation are rooted in two traditions. The revolutionary imagery of civil society makes it a site for contestation, where people counterpose themselves against state power and in the process either replace or reform it (Keane 1988a, 1988b, 1998; Chandhoke 1995). A second stream of conceptualisation, which links civil society to the state, is the Tocquevillean interpretation of civic associations performing the role of watchdogs in a democracy (Tocqueville 1990). This linkage of civic associations with democracy is further supported by Putnam who, drawing on his experience in North Italy, advocates strong civic associations for establishing a strong democratic tradition (Putnam 1999).

A conceptualisation that completely divorces civil society from the state is provided by Walzer, who refers to it as the uncoerced realm of society where social affairs are conducted without any reference to or interference by the state or market (Walzer 1992). The voluntary groups who serve the poor and the needy fall into this Walzarian conceptualisation of civil society.

The spread of liberalisation of the economy has furthered the conceptualisation of civil society as a separate 'sector', different from the state and the market (Cohen and Arato 1992). The conceptualisation of civil society as a third sector[1]—the state being the first and market the second—has been effected in recent times by clubbing together various actors such as NGOs, non-profit organisations, community-based organisations, social movements and charitable trusts under the umbrella of the third sector.

The recent shift in emphasis from government to governance indicates that addressing the concerns of society cannot be left only to the goodwill of the state; it must include other actors, including the people, who can together ensure that managing the affairs of society reflects fulfilling the needs and aspirations of ordinary people. Historically, particularly after the Second World War, it was assumed that the job of governing nation-states was the responsibility of governments. Democratic political frameworks of governments suggested three independent but interrelated functions: legislative, executive and judiciary. Over the past 50 years, different societies have organised these functions differently, although the underlying aspiration has been the same. However, with the growing disenchantment of ordinary people in many countries with institutions of government, the declining capacity of these institutions to respond to the diverse interests and expectations of populations, the increasing gap between government policies and their practical elaboration, the growing alienation of the poor and the marginalised from the elite-dominated government institutions, the continued persistence of problems of poverty, exclusion and marginalisation, and the growing importance of national and transnational private business interests, the concept of government has now begun shifting to the concept of governance.

While governance in its broader sense embraces the wider concerns of society, the problematic of governance lies in the way multilateral and bilateral aid agencies conceptualise it and associate civil society with good governance to further the promotion of neo-liberal ideas. The World Bank, one of the leading institutions promoting neo-liberalism, is, in fact, the first to have used the term governance in this context (World Bank 1989, 1991). Drawing from its sub-Saharan experience, where structural adjustment efforts failed due to an inefficient and corrupt state, the Bank associated good governance with administrative efficiency, transparency in public institutions and maintenance of the law and order situation. Following its policy of not taking any political stands, the Bank avoided associating good governance with any political regime. That is, it was regime-neutral in its promotion of good governance. This gap was filled by other bilateral donor agencies, which established in no uncertain terms the link between good governance and democracy. Operationally, they sought to establish this by making aid conditional to the promotion of democracy in the form of free and fair elections, promotion of civil rights and transparency in the dealings of state institutions.

Civil society has fitted into this framework in three important ways: first, civil society organisations[2] have been targeted as effective via media to channel aid for development to poor countries, so that the gap opened by the rolling back of the state is filled through the delivery of development directly to the poor. Second, as recipients of aid, civil society organisations are also under obligation to fulfil their funder's agenda of furthering neo-liberalism by providing safeguards to people who are adversely affected by the onslaught of the market. And third, following the tradition of Tocqueville and Putnam, civil society is viewed as an effective watchdog that can curb any authoritarian tendencies of the democratic state. This, in turn, would provide a suitable environment for the promotion of neo-liberalism, leading to the unquestioned triumph of the market.

This linkage of civil society with good governance results from the way civil society and governance are conceptualised. It therefore rests on certain questionable premises. To begin with, the conceptualisation of governance appears to be highly administrative and assumes that once elections are held, public institutions perform their tasks and corruption is checked, good governance will be assured. It thus views governance as a separate realm that can be improved without any reference to what is happening in other spheres of human existence. The wider social context, in which polity operates and by which it is vitiated, and which in turn it vitiates, is not taken into account. The conceptualisation therefore very naively assumes a link between a vibrant civil society and good governance.

Closely related to this is the assumption of civil society as a harmonious space where affairs are conducted peacefully and with consensus. That civil society is itself fractured from within is ignored by this concepualisation. It therefore associates good governance only with the democratisation of the state and does not take into account the fact that achieving good governance would also require the simultaneous democratisation of society. Part of the problem with straightforwardly associating civil society with good governance results from the way the former is viewed as a separate realm between the household and the state, or as an autonomous 'third' sphere, different from the state and the market. In fact, the boundaries between the three spheres are not watertight but highly porous. Not only does the state define the playing field for civil society through its legal framework, it also creates enabling policies and environment for the market. And there is no reason why civil society must always further the interest of the market and not question it.

The problem of conceptually linking civil society with governance becomes apparent when applied to India. For one, the relationship between state and society is not simple or straightforward: it is complex, dialectical and dynamic. In the wake of its formation, the Indian democratic state reflected the aspiration of its nationalist leaders to undo all that colonial subjugation had done to the society. This aspiration manifested itself in four ways: (a) the framing of a constitution that guaranteed the fundamental rights and freedoms essential for people to live with dignity; (b) the adoption of a multiparty parliamentary democracy which made people sovereign in deciding who they wanted to be governed by; (c) the adoption of a developmental path designed to accelerate economic growth through increase in agricultural productivity and industrialisation; and (d) the passing of legislations that would end the unequal distribution of land, the social exclusion of lower castes and the evils of untouchability.

With all these measures, the state assumed complete responsibility for fulfilling the political, social and economic aspirations of the people. Centralised planning by experts and a protectionist economy to benefit the public sector became the hallmarks of the Nehruvian model of development. Dams, mines and industries were set up in quick succession to change the social and economic landscape. It was hoped that with economic prosperity, which would trickle down to the lowest rung in the socio-economic hierarchy, all social inequalities would automatically be wiped out. But the ruling elite soon realised that there were forces within society that, for their own benefit, wanted to perpetuate the status quo. The landed elite tried to sabotage the progressive land legislations, the economic elite tried to appropriate the benefits of capital for themselves, and the upper castes resisted the abolition of untouchability. The caste–class nexus, which had made upper castes the rural bourgeoisie, became difficult to deal with and required compromise in many instances. In time, the cracks in development planning and the ideals of social transformation began to show. Through their nexus with the ruling elite, the dominant and influential sections of society appropriated the benefits of development, while the disadvantaged sections continued to suffer poverty and deprivation. Indeed, development seemed to further increase their misfortune: thousands of families were displaced by dams, mines and industries without adequate resettlement and had to migrate to urban centres where they ended up in urban slums. Social services, employment opportunities and fulfilment of basic needs for vast sections of Indian society remained unachievable.

This reflects laxity in the way the state dealt with its people. In many cases the policies made to benefit the deprived sections were not implemented; often, the absence of policy itself became a cause for concern. In other instances, policies meant to benefit the poor did not take their needs into consideration. The state institutions also showed considerable apathy and high-handedness in their dealings with the people. Hence, in many instances, people could not exercise the democratic rights and freedoms guaranteed to them under the constitution. This was particularly evident in the case of lower castes, women and tribals.

All this resulted in the gradual erosion of people's faith in the state and the space claimed by civil society began to be filled with voluntary associations committed to renewing the Gandhian tradition of social reconstruction and providing basic services to the poor. At the same time, the marginalised raised their voice against the state with the help of social movements. A prime example of this is the Self-Employed Women's Association (SEWA), which was established during the early 1970s. Simultaneously, a plethora of social movements against dams, industries and mines began to emerge in different regions of India. These movements questioned the logic of development and demanded that the state recognise people's ownership and control over their sustenance resources. The Chipko movement in the hills of the western Himalayas to save the forest from commercial exploitation, the movement in Narmada valley to stop the gigantic multipurpose Sardar Sarovar project, the movement in Chilika to save the lake from the commercial culturing of prawns, and the movement against the nuclear power plant in Kaiga are some instances of people questioning the state's developmental logic and actions.

As the marginalised sections became alienated from the processes of governance, state institutions began to lose their legitimacy. Also, while dealing with subaltern voices, the state frequently turned violent. The benevolent nature of the state, which was already beginning to tarnish in the 1960s, was shattered when the state proclaimed a national emergency in 1975. This demonstrated that the democratic state does possess the potential to turn outright authoritarian and that constant vigilance is required to check its authoritarian tendencies.

The nature of civil society's interface with governance in India reiterates the argument made earlier in this chapter that the problem of governance has to be located both within the state and the wider society. The state is not a neutral actor that can be taken to task and brought back to play its role more efficiently without any reference to the social setting in which it operates. Therefore, in instances where civil society raises its voice against the state, it invariably attracts the wrath of not only the ruling political elite but also the dominant forces within society itself. Besides, civil society is not inherently virtuous; it is also fractured from within. The divisiveness of society that vitiates the state also vitiates civil society. The marginalised and the poor do not fall into a homogeneous category; there are further stratifications among them that lead them to compete and contest for scarce resources. Civil society, therefore, has to contend with both state and society and hence the problems of governance need to be addressed in relation to both. Good governance thus does not only mean reforming the state; the reformation of society also needs to be simultaneously undertaken.

The fact that civil society is not as autonomous as it is assumed to be determines not only the style civil society adopts in addressing issues of governance but also the extent to which it, by itself, can contribute towards good governance. There are many angles from which this argument can be pursued.

First, civil society does not plan its actions independently of the state. The Constitution of India guarantees the freedoms of association and speech, thereby legitimising the role of civil society in independent India. The democratic system, through the rights and freedoms it grants to the people, provides a framework for civil society to operate in. In other words, it is the state that draws the boundaries of political permissibility and renders acts falling beyond these boundaries as 'uncivil', thereby denying them state protection. This does not mean that the boundaries of political permissibility cannot be extended. From time to time, civil society not only challenges but extends these boundaries as well. But it does so within the limits prescribed by the state, suggesting that the state has the upper hand in controlling the initiatives of civil society. When challenged, the state does not hesitate to use violence; civil society, however, cannot afford to respond in the same way if it is to survive. Hence, civil society initiatives have been largely carried out through peaceful demonstrations and dialogue that challenge the actions of the state but do not threaten its existence.

Second, in conceptualising the association of civil society with the state, particularly in the Indian context, the state cannot be treated as a monolith. Even within a repressive government structure, there are always individuals willing to provide support to civil society. In situations where this happens, despite the overall conflictive relationship with the state, civil society does collaborate with it. This conflict and collaboration, with various shades and degrees, determines the overall relationship of civil society with the state and its impact on governance. However, this does not imply that every instance where civil society interfaces with the state affords the possibility of forging a collaboration. As many examples of collective mobilisation, including the Chhattisgarh Mukti Movement, reveal, the state can be overridingly repressive. Since there is no protective cushioning from the wrath of the state available to civil society in such instances, it takes a long time for civil society to make its mark.

The Indian state does not have a universal character: there are different levels at which it operates. The character of the state at the provincial level can be different from the state at the national level and the character of the state at the local level may be different from that of the state at the provincial level. It follows that in any instance of civil society interface with governance, the nature of the state at different levels plays a crucial role. The state at the local level might be oppressive, but if the state at the provincial level is supportive, it can create space for civil society to make an impact. Similarly, if the state at the provincial level is oppressive and the state at the national level is supportive, the directives travel downwards, allowing for the voice of civil society to be heard.

The different instruments and functions of the state have captured the attention of civil society interventions. Most of them have focused on the *executive function* of the state, and therefore on public officials, ministries and departments. In recent years, the *use of the judiciary* through public interest litigation has served as an instrument of civil society interventions in demanding appropriate action by the executive branch of the state. Civil society intervention in *legislative processes*, in particular with political parties, has been less pronounced, though it has been increasing in recent years.

In this context, it must be mentioned that mainstream politics in India has usually shied away from supporting civil society initiatives. However, when in opposition, political parties do support such initiatives. This can be seen as a consequence of electoral politics to gain votes by extending sympathy to the struggling masses, and the inherent compulsion of parties, when they come to power, to discontinue support. The alliance with political parties thus works both to the advantage and disadvantage of civil society. When the party not-in-power extends its sympathy, civil society does make a dent in the legislature—a domain that is not usually open to it—through a mediator who is close to power. The 'backtracking' by parties when they come to power makes it doubly difficult for civil society to influence governance.

The assertions of civil society vis-à-vis the state forcefully drive home the message that the state cannot be let off the hook. It needs to be reformed and brought back to perform its task of responsible governance. The empirical case studies included in this book suggest this—the struggle in Chhattisgarh to provide a dignified environment for the people to live in, the struggle of the Kol tribals in Chitrakoot to get the benefit of land redistribution, the struggle of fishermen in Chilika to save their livelihood resources, the struggle of pavement dwellers for housing rights, and the Dalit protest in Shergarhi against the violations of their fundamental rights to life and freedom of expression—all point to people's dissatisfaction with the state. But this dissatisfaction does not manifest in undermining the existence of the state; rather, it proposes to make the state respond to people's demands.

These instances of collective action also rescue governance from the narrow definition given to it by neo-liberal ascendancy and provide a broader and fuller understanding wherein governance is not the sole responsibility of the state, but something in which people participate to decide what is good for them. In the context of the liberalisation of the economy, the market has also become an important actor in the arena of governance. However, the agenda for good governance has thus far been hijacked by the state and market without the recognition that ordinary people are also capable of defining their own version of governance, which might be different from that of the state, and whose logic might be different from the logic of the market. Many contemporary social movements, particularly those against state-led development, are critical of both state-led and market-determined governance. The assertions in civil society vis-à-vis the state therefore reflect the need for incorporating people's agenda in the scheme of governance and in situations where there is incongruence between the people's and the state's version of what constitutes the elements of a desirable society and polity, privileging people's definition over the that of the state.

The chapters in this volume both implicitly and explicitly make the case for broadening the conceptualisation of governance and emphasise plead that while civil society can play the role of reforming the state, the relationship between civil society and good governance needs to be problematised to prevent us from romanticising it, since more often than not such romanticisation only blurs our understanding of actual civil societies.

The chapters are organised in two sections. Five chapters in Section I deal with the conceptual and theoretical debate relating to the interface of civil society with governance. The chapters in Section II substantiate the debate with empirical insights drawn from the study of assertions taking place in the space of civil society.

Neera Chandhoke's chapter extends a critique of the concept of civil society as the third sphere which, she says, would help restore some insights that should logically attend any understanding of the concept. Her critique is built up by problematising the concept and interrogating some of the dominant conceptualisations. Her central argument is that civil society is part of a complex of other concepts and any conceptualisation of it must take cognisance of this understanding.

The chapter by Rajesh Tandon provides an Indian perspective to the interface between civil society and governance. He begins with a description of the roots of contemporary discourses on civil society and goes on to provide a brief conceptual understanding of civil society and governance. He then delineates five analytical strands to capture the interface between the two in contemporary India.

T.K. Oommen's chapter moves the civil society–state debate from its confrontational orientation to a cooperative engagement. Reflecting that good governance is related to the liberal conception of the state and therefore to the market, he suggests that good governance should be viewed as a conjoined effort of the citizen, customer and communitarian. Through his argument, he attempts to establish a balance between the state, the market and civil society.

Harsh Mander's chapter looks at the phenomenon of corruption in India, particularly among the civil servants, its causes, dynamics and the methods and dilemmas associated with its possible control. Taking the instance of the movement for the right to information in India, he argues that citizen vigilance and assertion can play a critical role in checking the corrupt and arbitrary exercise of state power.

'Save the Chilika Movement' by Ranjita Mohanty talks about the Chilika Bachao Andolan in the early 1990s. The movement, led largely by the fishermen of the Chilika lake area in Orissa, resulted in successfully resisting the Integrated Shrimp Farming Project (ISFP)—a joint venture of the Tata Iron and Steel Company and the Government of Orissa for prawn cultivation and export. The project posed a direct threat to the livelihood of fishing communities living around the lake. Mohanty's chapter focuses on the collective resistance, which raised important governance issues pertaining to policy formulation, resource use and control and socio-economic equity with regard to not only the specific instance but also the broader question concerning the prevalent paradigm of development.

The chapter on the Chhattisgarh Mukti Movement (CMM) by Neera Chandhoke depicts the struggle of workers in the informal sector against the lack of governance. The government had shown itself to be profoundly indifferent to the plight of the people living in and around Chhattisgarh. Before the launch of the movement, large numbers of people were living under conditions of oppression and exploitation. This was despite the fact that the area, which is rich in minerals, contributes in large measure to the productive resources of the country. The movement reflected the determination of the people, who had been sidelined from the structures of governance, to recover their dignity through sustained political mobilisation and struggle.

Sudha Pai and Ram Narayan's chapter on Dalit assertion in Shergarhi, Meerut, examines two related issues of violence and justice—key themes in defining the relationship between civil society and the state. For generations now, the Dalits or the ritually unclean low castes, have been suffering the atrocities unleashed on them by the higher castes. After independence, the state has, through the constitutionally guaranteed right to equality and the principles of protective discrimination, sought to bring the Dalits on a par with others. However, assertion by Dalits in various parts of India indicates that they are still struggling to improve their situation. In this study, the authors highlight key governance issues identified by the Dalits and show how the Rashtriya Soshit Morcha, a collective of Dalits, has fought for the restoration of the rights to life and freedom.

The chapter by Bishnu Mohapatra explores the lives of the pavement dwellers in Mumbai and problematises the notion of citizenship and civility and its link with the process of governance. There are several non-state organisations in Mumbai that have tried to intervene in the process in order to enhance the capacity of the pavement dwellers vis-à-vis the state, a process that was and is still full of challenges and possibilities. A significant part of the study is devoted to critically analysing and evaluating the various intervention strategies adopted over the years. In this context, the role of Society for the Promotion of Area Resource Centre (SPARC), an organisation involved primarily with the urban poor in Mumbai, is taken up for rigorous analysis.

B.K. Joshi's chapter on distribution of land *pattas* to the Kol tribals highlights the subversion of an emancipatory legislation, which vests the tribals with the right to land-ownership, by high caste people and local revenue officials. To improve the lot of the Kols, the government, as part of its land reform legislation in the 1960s and 1970s, gave them rights over ceiling surplus land under the purview of the village panchayat. The fact that, despite these rights and preferences, the exploitation of the Kols continues, reveals that the policies have merely remained on paper and that the feudal powers, in collusion with the local administration, have manipulated the legal provision in their favour. It is in this context that the Akhil Bharatiya Samaj Seva Sansthan (ABSSS) has taken up the issue of the Kols and has engaged them in a relentless struggle to actualise what has been provided to them by the state.

Notes

1. In recent times, the International Society for Third Sector Research, a network of scholars catalysed by America, is promoting the idea of third sectors through research and publication.
2. In fact, the development aid literature has equated civil society organisations with the conventional aid-receiving developmental NGOs.

SECTION I

1

A Critique of the Notion of Civil Society as the 'Third Sphere'

Neera Chandhoke

The main objective of this chapter is to interrogate some of the dominant conceptualisations that have come to cluster around the concept of civil society in recent theory. Due to a variety of historical factors, these conceptualisations have tended to romanticise the concept and, in the process, obfuscated any meaningful or politically relevant discussion of civil society. By problematising the notion of civil society as the 'third sphere', I hope to restore some of the insights that should logically attend any understanding of the concept.

Since the 1980s, we have witnessed a dramatic resurgence of the concept of civil society in both political theory and practice. We have also witnessed its almost uncritical celebration, so much so that it has become a somewhat *consensual* concept. And when concepts become consensual, they become problematic. When a variety of dissimilar groups, such as international funding agencies, non-governmental organisations (NGOs) and institutions of the state on the one hand, and left liberals, trade unions and social movements on the other, subscribe equally to the validity of the concept, it is time to worry. For if groups who should otherwise be disagreeing on the concept come to agree on it, it means that the concept has been *flattened* to such an alarming extent that it has lost its credibility. In other words, the concept of civil society may have become flaccid through consensus.

Just because a concept acquires widespread acclaim all over the world, it does not by any means indicate or ensure that it possesses either analytical rigour or conceptual clarity in contemporary theorisation. And when concepts lack these attributes, both their value and validity as politically relevant and worthy categories for action diminish considerably. In the first section of this chapter, I outline the reasons for the flattening out of the concept of civil society. In the subsequent sections, I make the argument that civil society is part of a complex of other concepts and that it cannot be seen as independent of that complex. This recognition may alter our understanding of civil society to some extent. This recognition may alter our understanding of civil society to some extent.

I

Civil Society: The Power of an Idea

The reasons for the widespread consensus that civil society has come to command in recent times are by now well known. In the 1970s and 1980s, East European intellectuals, political activists and trade union leaders turned their back on the two political options that historically had been available to them. The first of these was reform of state power from above. The second was social revolution from below. The efficacy of both these strategies had been ruled out because the Brezhenev doctrine had stipulated that the erstwhile Soviet Union would not hesitate to intervene in any East European country whenever the need arose to defend socialism. Past experience of Soviet intervention in the affairs of East European states had simply foreclosed the options of both reform and revolution.

The third option that presented itself to people reeling under insensitive state power, arbitrary bureaucracies, lack of civil and political rights and the rule of law, was that of the creation and consolidation of a sphere for collective action that would be independent of the state. Here, ordinary men and women would be able to associate and express their sentiments in freedom and without fear under the protection of institutionalised civil rights and the rule of law. Intellectuals theorising in the Tocquevillean mode termed this sphere of social association, based on solidarity and self-help, as civil society. It may be helpful to note at this stage of the argument, that even as political activists concentrated on crystallising a project of social autonomy in a sphere free from state power, they in effect declared an end to revolutionary imagery. Traditionally, radical theory had focused on harnessing political passions to the cause of social and political transformation. Now, it was seeking to yoke these very same passions to the liberal-democratic project. *Civil society began where revolution ended.*

But in the context of 'Stalinist states', even this project proved to earthshaking. The assertion of civil society developed fairly rapidly into a polemic slogan that sharply counterposed the sphere of voluntary and purposive collective action based on solidarity and self-help organisations, to dictatorial state power. Correspondingly, the invocation of civil society in the East European context came to embody three, and possibly more, meanings, all of which led to some sensational consequences.

First, the civil society argument sought to limit the untrammelled power of the state by institutionalising political and, more importantly, civil rights and the rule of law. Second, the argument correspondingly sought to carve out a domain that would function independently of state regulation. Here people, free from state-inspired *diktats*, could engage in projects of all kinds. Third, it propelled an important issue onto the political agenda. It stated that the active engagement of ordinary men and women in groups smaller than the state—family and kinship groups, neighbourhoods, professional and social associations and voluntary agencies—was a good thing in itself. The argument in fact asserted the competence of ordinary men and women to regulate the manner in which they live together in society, and to chart out a discourse on the possible and desirable shape of the present and future of their collective existence.

All these three dimensions gave the civil society argument a critical normative edge inasmuch as it sought to emancipate what Jurgen Habermas has called in another context the 'life world' from the instrumental rationality of the state. What the argument *did not demand*, however, was the emancipation of the life world from the instrumental rationality of the market. For intrinsic to the civil society argument was the demand for property rights and a free market.

The main planks of the civil society argument were thus freedom guaranteed by civil rights and the rule of law, publicity, accessibility, property rights and the free market. In retrospect, it is more than clear that the East Europeans in the 1980s practically re-enacted the bourgeois revolution that, more than 200 years ago, had positioned itself against absolutist state power in countries such as England. Indeed, John Locke, the quintessential liberal thinker, may well have authored the civil society script in this part of the world.

However, matters did not rest here. For in time, an argument that had initially concentrated on carving out a free zone *within* existing state power, rapidly coalesced into a political movement that demanded more than just a space for autonomous action. In other words, the invocation of civil society as a project of social autonomy quickly outstripped its own boundaries as a self-limiting social revolution. By the last year of the 1980s, this purportedly self-limiting social revolution had transformed itself into a highly charged political movement (Pelcynzski 1988: 361–80) that brought down some very awesome states like so many brittle houses of cards. The *civil public* had dramatically transformed itself into a *political public*. In turn, the political public asserted not only its right to hold state power accountable but also its right to dismiss states that failed to respond to the political aspirations of their people. A fourth dimension had been added to the civil society argument: notably, that people had the competence to chart out a *political* discourse on the kind of polity they wanted to live in. The balance of power in those heady last years of the 1980s perceptibly shifted from the state to civil society.

The transformation of the *civil public* into a *political public* concerned with the shape and content of the polity carries an important lesson for states and societies. The lesson simply is that wherever and whenever states pulverise domains of collective action, the assertion of civil society against the state can prove to be politically explosive. Witness how the 1989 Velvet Revolutions were to demonstrate the power of what can be called the 'pressure cooker' effect. In other words, wherever states bottle up freedom of expression through the denial of civil and political liberties, societies explode with some disastrous consequences for state power. Correspondingly, if at some point in history, the paths that states and societies take diverge, or if states fail to keep in touch with popular aspirations, state power becomes vulnerable.

The 1989 revolutions merely substantiated what Gramsci had told us—namely, that states without civil societies are tremendously fragile compared to states that possess civil societies (Gramsci 1971). As far as the state is concerned, the norms of civil society—freedom, publicity, accessibility and the rule of law—howsoever formal they may prove in practice, perform two valuable functions. First, these norms provide a vent for the expression of popular opinion through the institutionalisation of the right of freedom. Second, state power acquires legitimacy through these means. Gramsci, however, conceptualised legitimacy in terms of hegemony, a concept that is deeper than that of legitimacy inasmuch as it gestures towards the creation and consolidation of consent. By relocating the site of consent and thereby of the domination of the ruling classes in civil society, Gramsci theorised this sphere as a site where the state acquires hegemony. Whereas, he suggested, political society disciplines the body through penal codes and prisons, civil society disciplines the mind and the psyche through various social, cultural and pedagogic institutions. Therefore, this sphere functions to reproduce state power in invisible and intangible, but nevertheless very real ways. In contrast, wherever state power is openly and transparently exercised, the dangers of political revolt stalk political power. This is precisely what happened not only in Eastern Europe but also in all those parts of the world where the domain of collective action had been swallowed by structures of militaristic state power. The civil society argument, expectedly, concentrates on resuscitating this domain.

It is not surprising that the argument proved immensely attractive for political activists struggling to free the people from the stultifying grip of the state. In South America in the 1970s and 1980s, the idea of civil society became an important plank in the struggle of urban-based professional groups, intellectuals and political activists, against both military regimes and non-responsive political parties. Brazil, Chile, Argentina—all these countries became important sites for the assertion of civil society against the state. O'Donnell and Schmitter describe how 'trade unions, grassroots movements, religious groups, intellectuals, artists, clergymen, defenders of human rights and professional associations, all support each other's efforts towards democratisation and coalesce into a greater whole which identifies itself as "the people"' (O'Donnell and Schmitter 1986: 54). The recent spectacular success of the Suharto-led mobilisation of civil society against the regime in Indonesia bears testimony to the power of this idea. In effect, the use of the civil society argument to win some spectacular victories against tyrannical elites has sent out an important message about the desirability of civil society.

II

What is Civil Society?

Keeping the preceding discussion in mind, we can with some justifiable reason accept that civil society is desirable in itself. The fact that the civil society argument has won some notable victories against arbitrary state power is unquestionable. What is more problematic is how we characterise civil society— what is civil society? What does it consist of, or what do we fill it with?

At an elementary level, the concept of civil society pin-points and values associational life—interest groups, professional and other associations, voluntary agencies, grassroots organisations, social movements and all other social orders— because it brings people together in networks and shared concerns. All this is important in itself, for modern life is atomised, alienated and fragmented simply because individualism as the hallmark of the modern world breeds self-interested action. However, if self-interested action is allowed to develop to its logical end, society itself disintegrates and dissolves into a host of mutually competing fragments.

The great philosopher Hegel had warned us of precisely this possibility. Civil society, he wrote, is one of the achievements of the modern world because it is here that individuals can realise the self in conditions of freedom. It constitutes, therefore, the 'theatre of history'. Notably, Hegel considered civil society as one of the moments of ethical life—*Sittleichkit*— that regulates the life of the individual, the other two moments being the family and the state. But in contrast to both these institutions, civil society is the site of particularity, of self-seeking individuals concerned with their own gratification and the fulfilment of their private needs. And this poses its own problems, for when individuals are motivated by self-interest and self-aggrandisement, 'civil society affords the spectacle of extravagance and want as well as of the physical and ethical degeneration common to both' (Hegel 1942: para 185). Thus the threat of fragmentation constantly underlies modern life because civil society allows the liberated individuals to be guided solely by their will and to extricate themselves from ethical bonds. They descend, consequently, to 'the level of caprice and physical necessity' (ibid.). In order to achieve his dream of universality in the face of all this, Hegel ultimately subordinates civil society to the state, which in his theory is the embodiment of the universal spirit. The irony is that though Hegel starts with civil society as a precondition of the state, it is ultimately the state that becomes the precondition for the very existence of civil society. For not only civility but the presence of civil society itself depends upon it being vertically organised into the state (Chandhoke 1995).

The option of reconciling the tension between the particularity and universality of civil society in the state has, however, been firmly ruled out by modern democratic theory. For democracy demands as a precondition the limiting of state power, and the limiting of state power means that states cannot be allowed to intrude in domains that are not their provenance. For democrats, therefore, the only site in which self-centredness can be reconciled with universality or concern for others is that of civil society. However, this solution begs the question. For given the general incivility of civil society, how do we ensure the transcendence of self-centredness into what Gillighan has called in another context the 'ethics of care'. The dilemma of bringing together people, who otherwise fiercely safeguard their privacy, was sought to be negotiated by liberal theorists through the creation and sustenance of voluntary social associations. According J.S. Mill, associations manage to transcend private interests and egoism because they bring otherwise self-centred individuals in programmes of social concern:

> Still more salutary is the moral part of the instruction afforded by the participation of the private citizen, if even rarely, in public

function. He is called upon, while so engaged, to weigh interests not his own; to be guided, in case of conflicting claims, by another rule than his private partialities; to apply, at every turn, principles and maxims which have for their reason of existence the common good. He is made to feel himself one of the public, and whatever is for their benefit to be for his benefit. Where this school of public spirit does not exist, scarcely any sense is entertained that private persons, in no eminent social situation, owe any duty to society, except to obey the laws and submit to the government. There is no unselfish sentiment of identification with the public. Every thought or feeling, either of interest or duty, is absorbed in the individual and in the family (Mill 1910: 217).

And Tocqueville was to write that 'an association unites the efforts of minds which have a tendency to diverge in one single channel, and urges them vigorously towards one single end which it points out' (Tocqueville 1900: 1:192). Associations lend 'coherence to public life', cultivate civic virtues and inculcate democratic values. 'Feelings and opinions are recruited, the heart is enlarged and the human mind is developed by no other means than by the reciprocal influence of men upon each other' (ibid.: 2:117). The existence of a plurality of associations was the best means for the reconciliation of the public and private interests, as well as the best guarantee against the unmitigated power of the state. The science of associations, wrote Tocqueville, is the 'mother of sciences', since associations in a differentiated society bring individuals together, teach them civic and political virtues, and thereby act as the 'independent eye of society' where state power is concerned.

For Tocqueville, civil society constitutes the third sphere of society. Whereas the first sphere comprises the state and its institutions, and the second the economy, in the third sphere that is civil society, parties, public opinion, churches, moral crusades, literary and scientific societies and professional and recreational groups possess a superabundant force and energy. Through these associations, the potential excesses of the centralised state can be curtailed: 'There is no other dyke', wrote Tocqueville, 'that can hold back tyranny'.

The formidable impact that Tocqueville had on contemporary theories of civil society, which conceive of associational life as a third sphere of society, is quite evident. It proved to be remarkably apt for all those formulations that seek a free zone for collective action within existing state power. And theorists continue to be fascinated by the notion of civil society as a third sphere, which is counterpoised to the notion of the state and the market. The reasons for this fascination with civil society as a third and an autonomous space for human interaction are understandable. They can be traced to profound disillusionment with and a reaction to the *overreach* of the state. The welfare state that had been brought into being by the Keynesian revolution, the interventionist state that commands the nodal points of the economy, and the developmental state that took shape in countries like India, have been proved to be sadly wanting in the areas of both performance and accountability. Indeed, in popular perception, access to state power has given rise to a new political elite that, concerned with its own reproduction, is supremely insensitive to the needs of the people. It is, therefore, justifiably felt that the dominant need of the day is to hold states accountable for acts of omission and commission through a vibrant and active civil society.

It is widely and correctly believed that state power can be controlled only when groups in civil society exercise constant vigilance and display criticality. Correspondingly, it can only be limited when civil society patrols its borders with the state with care and when it jealously guards its own sphere against encroachment by this power. That such encroachments render otherwise politically vibrant populations passive and quiescent is an uncomfortable fact of our age. Witness how the very same people who had politically mobilised on a massive scale for the cause of political freedom in India have been reduced to consumers of policies and programmes formulated elsewhere. As states have proceeded to monopolise all areas of individual and collective life, agents have been reduced to subjects. More importantly, people have been cut off from each other by the politics of the state. It is only a vibrant and politically aware civil society, suggest theorists, which can mediate and counter these enervating effects of state power.

But a politically vibrant society requires several things as a prerequisite. First and foremost, it requires the coming into being of what Michael Walzer calls the space of uncoerced human association in order to recover sociability. 'The words "civil society",' writes Walzer, 'name the space of uncoerced human association and also the set of relational networks—formed for the sake of family, faith, interest and ideology—that fill this space.' A little later he argues that:

> The picture here is of people freely associating and communicating with one another, forming and reforming groups of all sorts, not for the sake of any particular formation—family, tribe, nation, religion, commune, brotherhood or sisterhood, interest group or ideological movement—but for the sake of sociability itself. For we are by nature social, before we are political or economic beings (Walzer 1998: 7–28).

Civil society, according to Walzer, is the 'setting of settings'; here people associate with each other on various grounds, but notably for the sake of realising their natures as social beings.

In one sense, therefore, civil society goes further than just bringing people together in webs of associational life. For it performs the functions of socialisation and pedagogy. Civil society organisations cultivate care and concern for others, impart citizenship skills and train people in the art of participation. They thus contribute not only to the development of sociability but also to the cultivation of the civic spirit and engagement.

However, in order to grasp the significance of civil society, we may have to venture beyond the idea that civil society performs the functions of social and civic pedagogy. We can only understand why the assertion of an independent civil society is seen as a threat by states struggling to control and lay down agendas when we explore the concept further. And power, we need to remember, is all about laying down agendas, of laying down the parameters of what is politically permissible.

Therefore, I suggest that there is a second and perhaps more important aspect to civil society, that of *being representative*. Civil society is representational inasmuch as it is here—in social associations—that people voice their interests and articulate diverse points of view on how a good society should be arranged. Associational life is important for the many reasons outlined earlier in this section, but above all it is vital because it enables dialogue or the creation, sustenance and expansion of a public discourse on what is desirable for a good society. In other words, associations provide the inhabitants of civil society the means to think of how people belonging to different persuasions or hierarchically ordered groups could live together in some condition of civility if not harmony. Correspondingly, it is here that these diverse interests are reconciled in a public discourse that presses the state to act or not to act in a certain manner. Civil society becomes the staging ground for mounting a challenge to state-given notions of what is politically permissible.

Arguably, it is this aspect of civil society that threatens the state's monopoly of power. For if people begin to talk about and plan the kind of society and polity they want to live in, if they begin to discuss conceptions of the good life, if they begin to lay down agendas, what will the state do? Indeed, the ability of civil society to engage in this kind of discourse asserts the competence of ordinary men and women to delineate their ideas of how a good society should be arranged. Admittedly, discourses on both the desired state of society as well as on the desired state of the polity may by no means be coherent or neatly structured; they may well be discontinuous and fragmented, but they do achieve two things. They announce the political capability of ordinary men and women to think of how they want to live together in historically and geographically bounded spaces, and they challenge the power of the state to do with its people as it wills.

III

The Nature of Civil Society

Upto this stage of the argument, we can discern few faults with the notion of civil society. Civil society, we can suggest, occupies the space—using the concept of space in a purely metaphorical sense—between the household, the market and the state. Here people associate with each other in conditions of relative freedom from unnecessary political regulation; here they come together in various projects that enhance sociability, which is a value in itself; here they learn how to live together; and here they learn political responsibility inasmuch as they relocate the discourse of politics. They relocate the discourse of politics in two senses. One, inhabitants of civil society accept that it is their responsibility to chart out a discourse on the terms and conditions in which people belonging to diverse and perhaps incommensurable persuasions could live together, i.e., the terms and conditions of coexistence. Two, they recognise that they have the responsibility to ensure state accountability when it comes to the implementation of this vision. It is obvious that all this requires relative autonomy from the state and perhaps also from the imperatives of the market.

Therefore, we can believe that, ideally speaking, civil society *should* constitute a relatively separate and autonomous sphere of collective life. But let me now, in the interests of clarity, overturn this assumption and ask the following questions: Can we assume that civil society (*a*) possesses a distinct logic of its own, which is in sharp contrast to the logic of the state or that of the market, and (*b*) that it is quite as autonomous of other spheres as we would like it to be? The answer to these questions may hold important implications for our comprehension of what civil society is, and for the way we think of civil society as a *political project*. In effect, what I am suggesting is that our *normative expectations* from the sphere of civil society should not cloud our analysis of *actually existing civil societies*. In other words, we should learn to problematise the sphere exactly as Hegel, Marx and Gramsci had done, even though the results of our investigation may not prove to be entirely satisfactory for our political concerns. But, on the other hand, we cannot allow our political passions and normative concerns to obfuscate our understanding of this sphere.

However, it is undeniable that the analytical concept of civil society has been overcome by normative expectations to a very large extent. Consider the various arguments that normatively design civil society as not only a third but also an autonomous sphere of human interaction. Charles Taylor (1991: 117), for instance, argues that civil society is 'those dimensions of social life which cannot be confounded with, or swallowed up in, the state'. Axel Honneth (1993: 19–22) conceptualises civil society as 'all civil institutions and organisations which are prior to the state'. And Issac (1993: 356–61) speaks of civil society as 'those human networks that exist independently of, if not anterior to, the political state'.

Above all, in a well-known definition, Cohen and Arato (1992: 18) refer to a 'third realm' differentiated from the economy and the state as civil society. Civil society as the realm of associational life is contaminated neither by the logic of politics nor that of economics, for in the eyes of theorists both have been found wanting, mired as they are in conflict on the one hand and competition on the other. Civil society in the hands of these two authors becomes

> ... a normative model of a societal realm different from the state and the economy and having the following components: (*i*) plurality: families, informal groups, and voluntary associations whose plurality and autonomy allow for a variety of forms of life; (*ii*) publicity: institutions of culture and communication; (*iii*) privacy: a domain of individual self-development and moral choice; and (*iv*) legality:

structures of general laws and basic rights needed to demarcate plurality, privacy, and publicity from at least the State and, tendentially, the economy (ibid.: 346).

Admittedly, the idea of civil society as an autonomous third sphere, with its attending imagery of solidarity and self-organisation, is immensely attractive. For only if we accept this as our basic premise can we proceed to assume that it is here that atomised and impersonal societies can be emancipated from the alienation that besets them, and warm, personalised relationships among people be restored. Indeed, the concept of civil society seems peculiarly apt when it comes to realising the Habermasian project of rescuing and regenerating the life world. What makes it attractive, according to Adam Seligman, is

> ... its assumed synthesis of private and public good and of individual and social desiderata. The idea of civil society thus embodies for many an ethical ideal of the social order, one that, if not overcomes, at least harmonizes the conflicting demands of individual interest and social good (Seligman 1992: 8).

As can be seen, the shadow of Adam Smith and his *Theory of Moral Sentiments* looms large over these conceptualisations.

But, however attractive and seductive the idea of civil society as a third sphere of human interaction may be, however much it may seem to provide an answer to our pressing and intractable problems, the idea itself seems to me to be deeply problematic. For it brings up not only the problem of boundary maintenance between spheres, it also throws up the additional problem of how boundaries contain separate and discrete logics. In the subsequent section, I argue that this kind of separation between spheres of individual and collective life is both misplaced and confusing. In effect, it can blur our understanding of civil society to a large extent.

IV

The Constitution of Civil Society

The question that we need to ask at this stage of the argument is simply this: can we think of *any* sphere of human activity as either autonomous or as marked by a different logic? The assumption behind the 'third sphere' argument presumably is that when people, once they are out of the household, enter into transactions with other members in civil society, these interactions will be marked by neither conflict, mediation or compromise that is the stuff of politics; nor will they be characterised by competition over scarce resources, which is the stuff of economics. This kind of bounding off of civil society leads to some confusion, for we will have to assume that each and every sphere of human action is marked by a different sectoral and organisational logic. But it is precisely this that is reiterated by Cohen and Arato when they say that 'economic activities in the substantive sense are (at least in part) included in civil society, but economy as a formal process is outside of it' (Cohen and Arato 1992: 75).

They go on to suggest that while the borders between the economy and civil society are not sealed off, the economy can be differentiated from civil society. This really means that at some point and at some site, civil society may be engaged in economic transactions; but this is not a *general* feature of civil society, though it may be an *occasional* one. What is important is that the *ethos* of the market does not constitute civil society. Further confusion is added when they suggest that we separate political, i.e., non-state society from civil society. Not only is civil society not political, the domain of politics does not affect it. Besides, we now have another site of human association added to the three spheres—the public sphere, i.e., the non-state sphere of politics. In this fourfold classification of collective life, civil society as the realm of warm, sociable and personalised associational life is markedly differently from the economy, the public sphere and the state, though on occasion members of civil society may execute activities that spill over into the other domains.

Other conceptualisations of civil society fill up the 'third sector' with voluntary groups and refer to it as the 'voluntary sector' or the 'non-profit sector'. Here, professional NGOs, foundations and philanthropies shoulder welfare and community rebuilding activities, provide education, health and community development in a mode that is different from the state. But once again this sphere is supposed to function in isolation from or even counter to the logic of the market and the state (Van Til 1988; Salmon 1994). Indeed, multilateral funding agencies have tried to build up this sphere as an alternative to the state by funding non-governmental agencies and by passing the state in the process. Some groups do not seek to bypass the market since the rolling back of the state from both civil society and the market forms an integral part of this agenda. Other avatars of civil society vigorously promote the activities of NGOs as providers of services and upholders of democracy, as an alternative to the market. In any case, civil society is definitely delinked from the state and, in some cases, from the market.

In sum, whatever we fill civil society with—associations, voluntary agencies or social movements—it continues to be thought of as a third sphere, which is neither related to the state and market nor constituted by them. In other words, it emerges in formulations that are uncontaminated by the impulses that characterise other domains of human interaction. Here, people can sort out their problems at the level of the neighbourhood, community and workplace with some prospect of reconciliation, for, unlike the other spheres, civil society is neither conflictual nor marked with power relations.

By the logic of this argument, collective life, that is life where individuals come into contact with each other outside the household, can be separated into different arenas of activity. Each sphere possesses its own logic and momentum and no arena either includes the other or constitutes it. Collective life can thus be conceptualised as hh (household) + cs (civil society) + e (the economy) + p (politics that includes the public sphere as well as the state). The perspective on collective life is, to put it mildly, additive.

But an additive notion of collective life is beset with its own problems. Copernicus once wrote about the astronomers of his day thus:

> With them it is as though an artist were to gather the hands, feet, head, and other members for his images from diverse models, each part excellently drawn but not related to a single body, and since they in no way match each other, the result would be a monster rather than man (Kuh 1962: 83).

I think this illustrates to a nicety the problems that arise when we first subdivide collective life into plural and mutually exclusive categories in thought, and then add all the parts we ourselves have created in order to construct a whole. Something of the same kind seems to beset additive social scientists. They first break down human activities into mutually indifferent and exclusive categories, invest each with its own logic and range of problems and methods, and then add them up to give us a picture of collective life. In this picture, no one category influences, let alone constitutes, the other; no category is central to human life and no category determines how we approach other categories of activity. But—and this is the question—do categories of collective existence not constitute each other?

Certainly, we can accept such separation as a heuristic device. We can in effect think of various spheres of human interaction in terms of the *different* ways in which human beings make their own history, howsoever badly they may make it. So we can, in purely theoretical terms, refer to different sets of interaction in the household, the economy, in civil society and in politics. However, what is problematic is the implication that these sectors of human activity do not constitute each other, or that they are marked by an exclusive and discrete logic that differs from site to site of such inter-action. Therefore, whereas we can with some legitimacy conceptualise civil society as a site where people associate in ways that are distinct from the way they associate in the economic or in the political sphere, we can hardly assume that civil society is free from the ethos or the logic that permeates the other spheres. This is so for several reasons.

1. At an obvious level, civil society needs a framework that institutionalises the normative prerequisites of rights, free-dom and the rule of law. But this framework is provided by none other than the state. Ironically, therefore, the very state that civil society supposedly positions itself against, *enables* the former in the sense that it provides the legal and political setting for the sphere to exist and maintain itself. Shades of Hegel, who had suggested that the state is a precondition for the existence of civil society, prove especially strong here. The autonomy of civil society from the state emerges as an optic illusion.

If we accept this point, we cannot help but concede that it gives the state additional power to define which kinds of civil society organisations are permissible under the law. Expectedly, while the state can accept organisations of indus-trialists, such as the Federation of Indian Chambers of Com-merce and Industry (FICCI), Confederation of Indian Industry (CII) and even university teachers unions that struggle for higher salaries, it has a definite problem when it comes to groups that challenge the legitimacy of the system. For in-stance, the Indian state has been notoriously coercive when it comes to, for example, organisations of landless peasants seeking redistributive justice. But it is a different matter when representatives of land owning and dominant sections of peasantry seek higher procurement prices or cancellation of loans. Towards them, the state is soft.

This makes sense only when we recollect that states have their own notions of what is politically, culturally and socially permissible. And while these notions will *enable some sec-tions* of civil society, they will necessarily *disable others*. State action, therefore, poses momentous consequences for civil society inasmuch as it can lay down the boundaries of what is politically permissible. It thus shapes the structure of civil society organisations to a formidable extent.

2. Of course, actors in civil society have the right under the law to challenge state-given notions of what is politically permissible provided they do so in ways that cohere to the legal limits of political action. They can use the permissible means of opposition—moving courts, public action, dharnas and marches. What they cannot do is to challenge the state in ways that it does not allow—militancy, for instance, however justified it may be in the face of the brute exercise of state power. Thus, both discourses and political action in civil society have to function within certain parameters or pay a high penalty for transgressing these boundaries.

We can therefore conclude with some justification that the much vaunted autonomy of civil society is constrained from the word go. Within the frontiers of what is politically permissible, of course, actors in civil society can exercise vigilance against arbitrary exercise of power, check and monitor violations of human rights, demand accountability, demand that the state delivers what it promises and battle unjust policies. Thay can do all this as long as they respect the frontiers of political action.

3. However, we also need to accept that the relationship between the state and civil society is not just one of opposition, since actors in civil society need the state for various purposes; or that the relationship between the two can with perfect reason be collaborative and cooperative. This is understandable, for a women's group can hardly demand new rights for, say, gender justice without demanding that the state take action to ensure it. At some point the demand for a uniform civil code by women's groups in civil society will need to be institutionalised in the form of law. Civil organisations can scarcely carry out developmental work without the state providing them with resources, personnel and management. Alternatively, civil society groups fighting, say, casteism, will

need the state to enact laws for the purpose. Various groups engaged in providing literacy to the people would of necessity look to the state for both funding as well as institutionalising their efforts in the form of the right to primary and adult education.

In effect, what I am trying to argue is that civil society actors will draw upon the state both to reform state institutions (to redress violations of human rights, for instance) as well civil society itself (for example, through enacting laws restricting sexual harassment at the workplace). This means—and this is a point that is not generally grasped by many advocates of civil society—that the state frames the limits of, as well as the social initiatives in, civil society.

4. One of the uncomfortable realities of political life is that states not only lay down agendas, they also employ a variety of means to garner acceptance for these agendas. This is clear when we consider the way in which the current government has aroused nationalism and raised it to a high pitch of hysteria through the exploitation of the first nuclear explosion at Pokhran and then the war against Pakistan in Kargil. Civil societies, we will have to accept with some amount of discomfort, can be manipulated in ways that are not healthy for the ethos of civil society itself. For popular support for state-sponsored action in civil society breeds somewhat unfortunate consequences for all those groups who oppose the state. It is not surprising, then, that groups who questioned the nuclearisation or the Kargilisation of India, have been typed by other groups in civil society as anti-national and unpatriotic. Theorisations of civil society as an autonomous sphere simply neglect to see how the sphere can be colonised by the legitimising strategies of the state.

5. Further, that associational life is always the source of democratic activism that we can counterpoise to the arbitrary state is an idea riddled with ambiguity. Should we assume that organisations in civil society are not permeated with politics and power, which curtail democratic activity in definite ways? Think of patriarchy that consolidates itself in the sphere of

civil society and in the household, or the practices of caste
that mould interpersonal relationships, or class equations that
are almost always weighted against democratic groups. Or
should we assume that politics and power in associational life
are not as stultifying? But as any astute observer will tell us,
society itself is riddled with power equations of all kinds—
those of patriarchy, class, caste and religion. Society, as Foucault has argued, is saturated with power, for power stalks
every avenue of human interaction. Directing our attention
away from visible and formalised codes of power, Foucault
said that power is ubiquitous and immanent, and that it has
neither a beginning nor an end.

> The individual is not to be conceived as a sort of elementary nucleus,
> a primitive atom, a multiple and inert material on which power
> comes to fasten or against which it happens to strike.... In fact, it is
> already one of the prime effects of power that certain bodies, certain
> gestures, certain discourses, certain desires, come to be identified
> and constituted as individuals (Foucault 1980: 98).

This individual is not the vis-à-vis of power; he is one of its
prime effects. The individual whose equality, justice and freedom civil society is supposed to uphold, is already in himself
the effect of a subjugation that is much more profound than
himself. If this argument makes sense, then civil society as
the associational aspect of society cannot be conceptualised
as free of power.

6. There is a more profound issue at stake here. We will not
be able to understand the complexities of civil society unless
we understand what the state is. And the state, as Marx told
us a long time ago, is not suspended in mid-air from society,
so that other spheres of society can function independently
of it. It is neither disembodied nor disembedded from the
power structures of society, for *the state both condenses and
codifies the power of the social formation.* If this is so, we need
to note that *the power codified at the level of the state is
gathered up and condensed from society.* In other words, state
power rests on a constellation of power in society.

Certainly, the state cannot be reduced to power structures in society, for it plays a key role in producing, codifying and constructing power. The specificity of the state lies in the fact that it codifies a dominant set of power relations in society, gives them fixity and thereby gives society a sense of stability. For instance, in a society marked by proprietors of property, the state will endeavour to secure property rights against those groups who challenge these rights in the form of, say, laws, or the judicial process that privileges the right to property. The state thus possesses the power to select, categorise, crystallise and arrange social power in formal codes and institutions. This gives to the state its status specificity and its own distinctive brand of power. In contrast to society, where power balances are precarious and unstable since they are prone to challenges from subordinated groups, the state grants a certain kind of coherence, however minimal, to the power relations of society. As both a concentrate and codifier of power, the state materialises as a discrete form of power. In effect, since the state through a set of specifically political practices confers fixity on otherwise unstable social blocs in society, society is constituted through the state and exists within the parameters laid down by it.

However, this power is always drawn from society, from the nodal points of power relations that define a social order. Any perspective that disregards this is bound to suffer from myopia, for it detaches social and economic from political power. If this is so, then the state as the codified power of the social formation is not detached from civil society where power is expressed and contested: it is the apex organisation of power. It follows, then, that civil society cannot be abstracted from the state and defined as a separate sphere since the two are organically connected through structures of power.

7. Therefore, theories that tell us that associational life is the answer to state power because associations are democratic per se are not only misplaced, they give us an erroneous picture of civil society. Consider Robert Putnam's celebrated analysis of social capital (Putnam 1993, 1995: 65–78). Putnam

conceives of civil society—in the sense of dense networks of associations—as generating what he calls social capital, which he defines as any feature of social relations that contributes to the ability of society to work together and accomplish certain goals. He therefore suggests a correlation between the density of social associations that manage to bridge social cleavages, the creation of civic culture and strong democracy. High levels of civic engagement, argues Putnam, contribute to the sustaining and fostering of democracy.

This is not a new idea. Civic republican thinkers had suggested long ago that the vibrancy of any democracy rests on the cultivation of moral virtue, moral commitment and the fostering of public spiritedness among citizens. But this is not the thrust of Putnam's argument, for he relies solely on the density of associational life as an indicator of high levels of citizen participation in democratic life. According to him, 'associationalism' produces habits of cooperation, trust, social networks and norms, i.e., social capital—which is an indispensable prerequisite of democracy.

The concept of social capital as originally outlined by James Coleman (1988) had suggested that it is a feature not of individuals but of social relations. Coleman had in effect argued that social capital is context-dependent. Therefore, when, say, international bankers interact professionally, their transactions are marked by norms of reciprocity and trust. The presence of reciprocal norms and trust within a particular set of transactions constitutes a resource, since it facilitates financial transactions in society. This resource can be termed social capital. However, since social capital is context-specific, the banker need not carry trust with him to other social contexts, for instance, to land transactions with a property dealer of whom he may be properly suspicious and sceptical, whereas on the other hand he trusts other bankers. Outside a specific context, norms and values may not translate themselves into social capital since they inhere in particular sets of social relationships. Or, to put it another way, each form of capital depends on a specific context to realise itself. People need not necessarily internalise these values; it is enough that in a given setting they behave according to these values or behave as they are expected to behave. But, as Coleman warned, it is important to note that this capital is unevenly distributed in society and not everyone has equal access to it.

More importantly, according to Coleman, not all forms of social capital are equally valuable as resources to facilitate individual or collective action. Social capital, as employed by Coleman, is a morally neutral category. It can facilitate transactions among a group of fascist organisations as much as it can be used by a group of human rights activists to the same effect. Further, access to various forms of capital is shaped substantially by inequalities of social location such as race, gender, class and geography. We cannot aggregate social capital to produce some measure of the resources available in and to a society. Putnam, on the other hand, by attaching a normative weight to the concept of social capital, abstracts it from social contexts and attributes it to individuals. Not only does he reduce the concept to associational life per se, he concentrates on only that form of life that permits civil engagement. In other words, he limits his focus to the kind of social capital that produces the civic spirit. He thus moves away from Coleman's formulation that emphasises socially embedded and context-specific resources.

For Putnam, associations produce habits of cooperation and trust, and social networks and norms that, in certain kinds of groups, ultimately issue in social trust and civic engagement. His theory of social capital assumes that the more we *connect* with other people, the more we trust them and vice versa. Generalised social trust in each other, trust in public officials, and the tolerance that trust requires as a precondition are integral components of social capital that has, in turn, a beneficial effect on citizen participation. Social capital is thus a source of healthy democratic activity that breeds participation.

However, Putnam's thesis is open to question on several counts. For one, how do people build trust and reciprocity in associational life independent of wider contexts? For instance, the state can launch political repression or propel shifts in the pattern of cultural hegemony, while the economy can plunge the state into economic disaster. All this can radically alter the balance between groups in civil society, even as social conflict over resources can bedevil relations of reciprocity and trust or what Putnam calls social capital. Consider how in India the politics of both Mandalisation and Mandirisation during the 1990s have furthered the fault lines and cleaved social associational life in the country. Both these trends were propelled and propagated by agents and actors outside the ambit of democratic associational life. Both had disastrous consequences for civil society as people were torn apart by the politics of caste and religion. We can hardly accept Putnam's assumption that social associations function independently of the state to further civic engagement, just as we cannot agree with theorists who claim that civil society as a third sphere is comfortably bounded off from politics and the state.

Second, confining our attention to social associations that are beneficial to civic engagement is not only morally irresponsible, but it also leads to a distorted understanding of civil society. For if civil society consists of associational life per se, then we have to accept that associations of every stripe and hue exist in this space. Patriarchal forces exist alongside feminist groups, religious fascists exist along with movements against communalism, class oppression exists alongside groups fighting for redistributive justice, and pro-state associations that further and strengthen the dominant project of society exist alongside groups that challenge the legitimacy of the state. Some further civic engagement, others inhibit it; some expand the domain of civil society by bringing in formerly disadvantaged groups, others debar these groups from civic life. The enemies of democratic life exist in civil society itself, as groups well organised to make demands are perhaps in a position to have these demands satisfied.

Third, if, as Putnam suggests, we were to characterise healthy associational life only on the basis of the thickness of bonds within associations, we would realise to our discomfort that the most communal of organisations such as the Vishwa Hindu Parishad (VHP) and other minority fundamentalist organisations are characterised by strong bonds of social solidarity. We can also include in this category the Ku Klux Klan or the Mafia, as any reader of Mario Puzo's remarkable novel *The Godfather* will tell us.

If we take this as our referent point—that social organisations are the reason for civil society to exist, then we have to accept that the sphere contains every kind of group. We can hardly expel, say, the various Chambers of Commerce—the FICCI or the CII from civil society. They are as much part of civil society as working class groups fighting for a better living. We can scarcely expel groups of agro-industrialists who will benefit from the Narmada dam and admit the Narmada Bachao Andolan. But this will mean that civil society, far from being a realm of solidarity and warm, personalised interaction, is itself a fragmented, divided and hierarchically structured realm. Here we will find organisations of the dominant classes existing alongside organisations of the dominated battling for survival; patriarchal structures existing alongside women's groups struggling for a place in the sun; and caste-based groups along with Dalit movements fighting for dignity.

In this perspective, civil society emerges not as the *site of sociability* per se, though this may well be a consequence of associational life, but as a *site for struggle* between the forces that uphold the status quo and those that battle it in an attempt to further the democratic project. It is important to realise here that dominant groups in civil society, far from constituting a sphere that is oppositional to the state, actually defend and extend its power into the domain of civil society. In this connection we need to remember Gramsci, who had cautioned us that civil society is the domain where dominant class forces establish hegemony through precisely the same social networks that are supposed in liberally theory to battle the state by establishing a radically different ethos.

V

If this argument is at all persuasive, we may need to alter our understanding of civil society in the following ways:

1. Civil society as associational life cannot be identified with democracy per se. However, I suggest that it is a precondition of democracy inasmuch as it constitutes both the site as well as the cluster of values and institutions that are intrinsic to democracy. In other words, democracy requires as a precondition a space where various groups can express their ideas about how society and politics should be organised, where they can articulate both the content and the boundaries of what is desirable in a good society.

The absence of this site would mean the absence of democracy, for people would not possess either access to a space or the freedom that is necessary for democratic interaction. Imagine a society that calls itself democratic and yet denies its people the opportunities to associate freely in order to carry out discussions or contestations on what should constitute the good life. That is why in authoritarian states the struggle for civil society primarily demands the consolidation of a space where people in association with others can debate and contest their own versions of the political. It is this dimension of the struggle that the phrase 'civil society against the state' indicates.

This achievement is by no measure a mean one. People demand that regimes recognise the competence of the political public to chart out a discourse on the content and limits of what is politically permissible. Civil society in this instance stakes a claim to autonomy from the state: that people have the right to associate with each other, that this right should be recognised by the state, and that the state should institutionalise this natural right in the form of the legal freedom to associate. Correspondingly, civil societies have demanded the institutionalisation of this right in the shape of the rule of law, rights and justiciability. However, in the post-victory scenario, this demand may be necessary but not sufficient for democracy.

Formal democracy, as critical theorists have pointed out, can prove to be an illusion. Freedom and rights can mean the freedom of the propertied classes to carry out their projects of exploitation. The rule of law can be employed by amoral leaderships to debar substantial numbers of people from the right to citizenship. And the market, as any critical theorist knows, is totally insensitive to those who cannot buy or sell. All this can render civil society supremely uncivil and rotten.

Taking this as our reference point, we can understand why once civil society had been resurrected single-handedly in this part of the world, and once it proved victorious over Stalinist states and Djilas' 'new class'—people in Eastern Europe somewhat ironically found that they really did not want it. It proved to be uncomfortably cold, barren and friendless. The dismantling of existing state institutions and the opening out of the market inevitably led to uncompromising austerity, massive unemployment, discrimination against ethnic minorities and resultant ethnic explosions. The rolling back of the state from any kind of responsibility for the people left those who could not fend for themselves at the mercy of those who were in a position to do so. East Europeans had exchanged the tyrannies of socialism and party apparatuses for the tyrannies of capitalism, political elites, corporate bureaucracies and ethnic majorities determined to stamp out any kind of plural life.

In other parts of the world—Latin America, for instance— the fall of military regimes after civil societies had united in waves of protest against them, brought immense disappointment as political parties that had engineered the protests split the anti-military movements throughout the region. Post-military regimes led to bitter frustration, for they failed to respond to the democratic aspirations that had been evoked by the civil society argument (Schneider 1995). Something has gone wrong somewhere.

2. This does not mean that we can dispense with the argument; it merely means that formal democracy, which the concept is associated with, is supremely insensitive to power equations in civil society. Some groups possess overlapping political, material and social power; others possess nothing, not even access to the means of subsistence. Civil society, therefore, cannot look only to the state; it needs to look inwards, at the power centres within its own domain, which may be complicit with the state, and battle them.

Therefore, what civil society does afford is the provision of both a site as well as values that can help us to battle with the inequities of the sphere itself. For instance, if the project of Hindutva has been hegemonised in civil society, anti-communal groups struggle against this particular formulation in this very sphere. Women's groups, the Dalit movement, the environmental movement—have all employed the concepts of formal democracy to battle their enemies.

3. There have been two rather profound transformations in the notion of politics in such and related processes. Politics is not about what the state does or does not do. In other words, politics is not about the legitimate power of the state to do what it wills with its people. Rather, it is about how ordinary men and women think about, conceptualise, debate and contest how people belonging to different persuasions, classes and interests could live together in society in conditions of justice and civility.

Let me expand upon this. Politics in one obvious and rather simplistic sense is about competition over state power. It is about the decision-making process in the state, about the content of these decisions and about the ways in which the holders of state power decide the fate of entire societies. This notion restricts power to the formal and the visible domain of the state. But at a deeper level, politics is about the experiences of everyday life, about how people translate their experiences in the expressive, about how the dominant groups seek to retain their power, and about the struggle of the dominated people to live in dignity. Therefore, civil society and its attendant norms of publicity, accountability, rights and the rule of law become a staging ground for a struggle between democratic and anti-democratic forces. We can ignore this aspect of civil society only at the risk of distorting our understanding of the sphere.

Conclusion

I have suggested in this essay that the idea that civil society constitutes an independent sphere of existence may distort our understanding of the sphere. For though we tend to divide spheres of human interaction into segments and accept that human beings act in different ways in different segments, we need to register that these spheres are mutually constitutive of each other. It is for this reason that I have argued that civil society is only ambiguously the source of democratic activism, for we are likely to discover in this sphere structures of power that tie up with the state. Civil society therefore emerges as a deeply fractured and hierarchically structured domain of social associations.

However, there is some value in the idea of civil society because it provides the preconditions of formal democracy. And though formal democracy is not sufficient for our purposes, it is an essential component of social and political structures. It provides the space for democratic elements to both challenge power equations in the sphere as well as transform the sphere itself. But for this, we have to accept that it is not enough that there *be* a civil society, or even a civil society that is independent of the state. Civil society is not an institution; it is, rather, a process whereby the inhabitants of the sphere constantly monitor both the state and the monopoly of power within itself. Democratic movements have to constantly widen the spaces where undemocratic practices can be criticised, and for this they have to exercise both vigilance and criticality. They have to be Janus-faced, looking to the state and the market as well as inwards. Civil society thus has to constantly reinvent itself, discover new projects, discern new enemies and make new friends. It is not something that, once constructed, can be left to fend for itself because it is a process. And this is important, for civil society is an essential precondition for democracy.

2

The Civil Society–Governance Interface

An Indian Perspective

Rajesh Tandon

The turn of the millennium is characterised by several new symbols of hope and progress, which tend to be systematically used to advance different priorities. Once such symbol is 'civil society', which is presented in its myriad manifestations as the 'voice of the people'. From 'green' protestors to self-help groups, the message of civil society has become equivalent to hope, well-being and reform in many regions of the world.

The development discourse has also thrown up a new symbol in 'governance'. Fifty years ago, when post-colonial regimes were strengthening their national governments, 'government' comprised three elements: the legislative, the executive and the judicial. The growing disenchantment with post-colonial governments for their failure to rapidly deliver socio-economic development to the people led to the emergence of the concept of 'governance', which is seen as the joint responsibility of governments, private business and civil society.

In such a formulation, civil society and governance are two symbols of the journey towards the hopeful new millennium.

While both these concepts have re-emerged in the context of global discourse, it is important to analyse their historical roots and contemporary implications in the Indian context. This chapter attempts to trace the history of the two concepts and develops a framework for analysing their interrelationships, in the Indian context in particular.

Approaches to Civil Society

The emergence of a discourse on civil society in contemporary social development has three primary roots. The first is derived from a rebellion against the dictatorial and centralised authoritarian state. The fall of the Berlin Wall in 1989 and the subsequent overthrow of centralised communist regimes in Eastern-Central Europe and the former Soviet Union heralded a new era of civil society. Hundreds and thousands of citizens, their associations, organisations, trade unions, cooperatives, media groups and small business associations joined in the efforts to overthrow dictatorial, authoritarian and centralised states.

> All of this coalesced around a new identity which was searched for and then forged. The way was prepared by the debate over the theme of civil society. At some points the subject population of most of these countries defined itself as different from, and opposed to, the established political class: the *nomenklatura*. The act of defiance was a critical step in the process of emancipation from totalitarian rule. Such defiance was symbolised by a name: the name of civil society (Perez-Diaz 1993).

Another example of the same trend came from the overthrow of military dictatorships in the Philippines in 1986, Argentina and Chile in the late 1980s and the anti-Apartheid movement in South Africa in the early 1990s. These efforts were further extended to those countries where a single-party hegemonic regime had been in existence, particularly in Africa. After gaining independence from colonial rule, many nationalist leaders set up and consolidated single-party regimes (in

Tanzania and Zambia, for example). Thus, military dictator-ships, centralised communist and single-party regimes were replaced by a democratic system of electing governments based on universal adult franchise, periodic elections and a multi-party system. In this context, the popular uprisings that led to their overthrow were characterised as phenomena of 'civil society'.

The second stream of intellectual discourse that has influ-enced the emergence of the notion of civil society in the contemporary context is the Tocquevillean concept of asso-ciations. While commenting upon the system of democratic government in America, Tocqueville examined the inherent limitations of a representative form of democracy. These inherent constraints distanced the elected representatives from the day-to-day concerns of ordinary people. They also, there-fore, placed ordinary people at the receiving end of state authority, even when exercised through democratically elected representatives. This analysis (carried out over a century ago) seemed to indicate that there was a need for strong associa-tions that could mediate between the family on the one hand, and the government on the other. The Tocquevillean view was that associations at the intermediary level help to ensure the accountability of representatives who have been 'democrati-cally authorised to govern':

> An association unites the efforts of minds which have a tendency to diverge in one single channel, and urges them vigorously towards one single end which it points out.... Feelings and opinions are recruited, the heart is enlarged, and the human mind is developed by no other means than by the reciprocal influence of men upon each other (Tocqueville 1990).

The third source of influence on civil society discourse is based on the theory of the free market and modernisation. In this approach, free market is seen as the vehicle for economic development where entrepreneurship, creativity and talent are rewarded. The political ideology of the free market includes the notion of modernisation, which has been proclaimed as an advance over traditional societies. The European experience of industrialisation, capitalism and intellectual advancement was seen as the modernisation of societies in that region. As countries of the South began to gain political freedom from colonial rule, they were expected to follow the route taken by their 'modern seniors' (colonial masters) by overcoming traditional ties, institutions, values and structures. Modernisation theory thus supported the notion of building new forms of associations based on the economic, social, cultural and political activities of individuals. Unlike traditional associations, which were based on kinship, ethnicity, caste, family, locality and neighbourhood, the modern concept of associations is rooted in secondary relationships based on occupation, profession and education:

> From Hobbes and Locke through the Scottish moral philosophers (Hume, Smith, Millar), the French Enlightenment philosophers (Helvetius, d'Holbach), and classical political economy to Hegel, there emerged a theory of civil society that explained the bourgeois system of civil law, the basic liberties of the citizen, and the capitalist economic process as an order that guaranteed freedom and maximised welfare (Milner 2001).

Freedom of association is an individual choice and a fundamental human right. Liberty, freedom and human rights are all individual-based concepts and derived from the spirit of individualism sustained in the free market ideology and theory of modernisation:

> What is emerging victorious, in other words, is not so much liberal practices, as the liberal idea. That is to say, for a very large part of the world, there is now no identity with pretensions to universality that is in a position to challenge liberal democracy, and no universal principle of legitimacy other than the sovereignty of the people (Fukuyama 1992).

These three approaches to the study of civil society bring in slightly different perspectives on its definition and purpose. The first approach tends to project civil society as a basis for *challenging the hegemony of a centralised state.* It tends to position civil society in an *adversarial* role vis-à-vis the state. It is this approach that subsequently relates to the conflicts and competitions between civil society organisations, non-governmental organisations (NGOs), development NGOs and human rights groups on the one hand, and government institutions, parliaments, public bureaucracies, etc., on the other. The concept of NGOs is largely defined from this approach, as those entities which are not governmental and may in fact be in opposition to the government.

The second approach tends to define civil society primarily through *associations* that are intermediary actors between the family and the state. Here, the thrust of civil society is to provide protection from the totalitarian tendencies of a democratic state and to act as a mechanism for funnelling the voices and concerns of citizens to legitimate political actors in democratic institutions. In this sense, civil society is seen as a *bridge* between individual citizens and their families and the state institutions and actors.

The third approach takes a much broader view of who does or does not fall under the definition of civil society. It views all non-state actors as part of civil society. This approach also *legitimises free market enterprise* and private sector capitalism, viewing economic entrepreneurial initiatives as an integral part of civil society. The concept of non-profit organisations as manifestations of civil society is largely derived from this approach.

As we will see later in this chapter, each of these three approaches has some valuable contribution to make towards the understanding of the relationship between civil society and governance.

Meaning

What, then, *is* civil society? Any definition of civil society is fraught with difficulties. What I intend to elaborate here is an operating definition that allows a perspective rooted in the realities on the ground: *Civil society is a collection of individual and collective initiatives for the 'common public good'.* In this definition, civil society is seen as linked to a public arena where the promotion of broadly defined 'public good' is the purpose of civil society action. This 'public good' could include promotion of education, health care or sanitation; it could include prevention of pollution and deforestation; it could include protection of human rights or maintenance of peace and harmony; it could also include expression of dissent.

Civil society is also conceptualised as a set of initiatives that is taken either individually or collectively. Individual action for the common public good is widely prevalent in many societies—an individual running a school or health clinic, a youth counselling centre, a drug addiction facility; an individual working to share information with tribals about their rights; and individuals writing in the media to raise questions about the policies of the government as they affect the poor.

Collective initiatives, too, can take various forms—they can be informal or they can be formally and legally incorporated. They can be either temporary or of long duration. They can be collectives of individuals, or they can be collectives or combinations of individuals, organisations and other associations.

Form

In this sense, it is the private, self-motivated and somewhat autonomous initiatives of individuals and collectives that constitute the collage of civil society. This broad definition allows us to look at civil society in three different ways. First, *civil society is a space* that is free, open and accessible. Therefore, it is a space for ideas, for action, for discussion and debate, and for contestation. In this view, civil society is the base arena where values, perspectives and norms are developed, debated, accepted and contested. Civil society also represents the space where subaltern, hitherto inaudible and unarticulated views can be expressed. The social reform movements during the early nineteenth century in India, protest poets like Kabir and Nanak, and tribal leaders like Birsa Munda are illustrations of such subaltern voices in recent Indian history.

> Society (is) characterised by a systematic opening of a room for the most diverse self-structuring, and for the broadest possible participation in public life.... It allows people to develop all facets of their personality, most especially that part that makes human beings social animals with a desire to participate in the life of the community (Havel 1997).

Civil society can also be seen as a *movement* for advancing various causes. In recent decades, causes like women's rights, human rights, children's rights, tribal rights, peace and the environment, have all been advanced through a variety of social movements. There are also movements for protest—protest against the policies and actions of powerful national and international institutions that go against the ordinary people's definition of public good; against dams, factories, mines, dislocation and displacement; against formalisation of individual property rights vis-à-vis land, water and forest without reference to collective access by forest-dwellers and tribals. Civil society as a movement enables organised efforts at raising the voices of those who are typically not heard—the voices of Dalits, minorities and women. In this respect, civil society constitutes a range of initiatives drawn from different actors, sometimes working together and sometimes alone, to espouse various causes.

Civil society is also a *set of organisations*. These are primarily self-help, mutual help and mutual support groups. Through them, families and citizens get together and look after their common public good. Neighbourhood associations, village councils, local sports and culture groups, pond maintenance committees and forest protection groups are all examples of such civil society organisations. Civil society also includes

strong membership organisations, such as trade unions, cooperatives and social clubs.

In addition, there are intermediary organisations that enhance the capacities, voices and articulations of other citizens.
Voluntary development organisations fall in this category.
Advocacy, campaigning, information dissemination, research
and development also serve as arenas for action by them. In
this context, it may be worthwhile to examine the *intellectual,
material and institutional bases* of these organisations (Tandon
1991). Given the diversity of perspectives on what constitutes
the common public good, civil society organisations are inspired by a wide range of *intellectual*, ideological and spiritual
persuasions. Ability to analyse, articulate and maintain a
perspective of common public good is an important capacity
of civil society organisations. The material base of civil society organisations comprises of resources, infrastructure,
human and technical aspects which enable them to achieve
their missions. Material base includes local resources, public
funding, international resources, resources contributed through
philanthropic efforts, etc. The institutional base provides a
framework of organising formally and legally the manner of
functioning of civil society organisations. A wide range of
options in institutional mechanisms exist in India—Society,
Trust, Trade Unions, Co-operatives, etc. (PRIA 1993). Thus
civil society as an operational construct could be viewed as
public space, a social movement or an organisation. Various
attempts have been made to develop typologies of civil society (Tandon 2000). However, what is important is to visualise
the complexity of civil society in the contemporary Indian
context.

Governance

Let us now turn to the question of governance. What exactly
is governance? It does not merely denote 'government'; rather,

it is a process of looking after public resources for the common public good. 'Governance is the manner in which power is exercised in the management of a country's economic and social resources for development' (World Bank 1992).

Governance thus requires definition, prioritisation and agreement on what constitutes public good. It also requires mechanisms, processes and institutions that will acquire and subsequently apply public resources to fulfil priority areas of 'public good'. Self-governance is one example of this. Historically in India, the management of natural resources, such as forests, water and land, was done through a collective and self-governing process, particularly in tribal and indigenous contexts. In the contemporary context, workers' organisations and cooperatives as economic entities and local bodies (panchayats and municipalities) are examples of self-governing institutions.

Governance also includes the functioning of all state enterprises; it entails the functioning of the legislature at different levels, of the judiciary, of the law and order machinery, as well as that of the public bureaucracy. Given the increasingly international character of the contemporary world, governance includes institutions at the supra-national level as well. Intergovernmental bodies like the United Nations (UN), international treaties and other institutions like the World Bank, the International Monetary Fund (IMF) and the World Trade Organisation (WTO) are also acquiring public resources to govern public good.

The definition of governance, therefore, entails not merely the performance of government bodies or the so-called 'public' institutions; it also entails the performance of various institutions in society, which address public good by using public resources. These include academic institutions, media institutions, political parties, development organisations and NGOs. Such institutions address the public agenda and influence the understanding and supply of public good. They therefore use resources that are publicly acquired and sanctioned. In some respects, the governance agenda also includes the performance of the private sector, which has begun to increasingly use public resources. These resources may include capital that, in a country like India, is largely given by public institutions (banks, financial institutions), as well as public resources like land, water and forests, which are generally controlled by public agencies.

The concept of governance that we have enumerated assumes a democratic framework. Democratic systems, procedures and processes are the basic building blocks for a discussion of governance in general, and the interface between civil society and governance in particular.

Interface

Keeping in view the manner in which various streams of thought on civil society have evolved and the more inclusive, broad-based definition of governance provided in the previous section, this section deals with the linkage between civil society initiatives and governance. This interface can be analysed in different ways at different levels.

Self-governance

Civil society plays a meaningful role in assuring self-governance of public institutions that use public resources. Civil society voices can assure us that community-based organisations, cooperatives, trade unions, sports associations, art councils, professional bodies and development NGOs establish standards and norms of self-governance that are consistent with democratic principles and practices. In this sense, self-governance requires high standards of transparency, accountability, clarity of vision and purpose, and consistency in the pursuit of public good.

In some respects, the experience of countries like India has been rather frustrating on these counts. Standards and practices of self-governing organisations have left much to be desired. The capacity for self-governance has not been adequately strengthened to enable such organisations to perform their public functions in a democratic and accountable manner. This is where associations of professionals, trade associations, NGOs and trade union federations can play a useful role. However, the capacity of such associations and federations is also rather limited in countries like India.

Another area where self-governance of public resources can be strengthened is in the context of externally induced local bodies, i.e., forest protection committees, village education committees or water user associations. Such bodies are particularly designed to enable potential beneficiaries to look after public resources for the broader public good. However, these bodies suffer from their incapacity in self-governing, in establishing norms and practices which could be measured against high standards of democratic functioning.

The experience of strengthening local self-governing bodies in rural and urban areas also seems to indicate a particular role that civil society actors play. In India's experience of Panchayati Raj institutions, the involvement of women's groups, youth groups, local voluntary organisatons, other individuals interested in panchayats, the Nehru Yuvak Kendra, etc., has been particularly valuable in assuring that panchayats and their elected leadership function as democratic, self-governing institutions (Manoj Rai et al. 2001). This is especially relevant in the case of Gram Sabhas and Gram Panchayats. Likewise, in urban municipalities, the involvement of a variety of civil society organisations (traders associations, Lions Clubs, students' groups, academia, media, etc.) is essential to make municipalities function more effectively as bodies of local self-governance. Thus a major contribution as well as an arena for future intervention is civil society's role in self-governing institutions.

Defining Public Good

The second arena where civil society contributes towards improved governance is in influencing the definition and prioritisation of public good. This is particularly relevant in a democratic polity. There are different types of interest groups that influence the public process of defining what constitutes the common public good and determining which elements of this 'good' need to be given high priority. The priority, of course, would vary, depending on location and time.

In specific ways, civil society provides an arena for articulating the voices of hitherto voiceless. In the Indian context, this has been done particularly to help Dalits, tribals, women, children and other cultural and religious minorities put forward their perspectives. However, in a society as diverse as ours, it is not possible to have a definition of public good that is uniformly applicable. It is here that civil society makes a major contribution, not only by crystallising in a public arena the voices of excluded or hitherto unheard sections of society, but also by helping in defining and prioritising 'public good'.

Another way in which civil society initiatives influence the definition of public good is through challenging and contesting dominant priorities. For example, in the Indian context, the prioritisation of rapid industrial development resulted in large-scale displacement of people and erosion of the natural resource base. Civil society organisations have taken up both these issues by contesting the very framework of the dominant development paradigm and questioning the long-term sustainability of such strategies. These challenges and contestations present an alternative formulation of public good and thereby educate society on the advantages and disadvantages of pursuing different approaches and priorities in public good.

Influencing Public Negotiations

The third role of civil society is to influence public negotiations for public good. Take, for example, policy-making.

Policy-making on issues of public good (like health, education, drinking water, sanitation, shelter, transport, communication and agriculture) is essentially a process of public negotiation carried out through the voices of different organised and unorganised interest groups. It is therefore based on the perspectives and preferences of a wide array of players interested in a particular public policy. Civil society organisations participate in this public negotiation of policy formulation in a variety of ways: by presenting perspectives and experiences based on their own work in a micro setting, by monitoring the impact of previous and related policies and raising questions about the larger public good, and by enabling the hitherto voiceless and relatively unorganised communities and interests to be represented in a forceful manner. This is where they interact with those sections of government—legislatures, ministries and departments, or the ministers themselves—that are responsible for policy-making.

Another area of public negotiation that civil society participates in is programme management. Resource allocation for various programmes based on an agreed policy can either enhance the impact of that policy or undermine it. Therefore, public negotiation of resources and the manner in which they are to be spent is another, very significant role for civil society organisations. In India, this role has been played quite effectively vis-à-vis issues related to women's empowerment, micro finance, wasteland development, social forestry and Panchayati Raj. In some respects, public negotiations on programme management also entail the experience of civil society groups in managing and implementing similar programmes on a micro scale.

Ensuring State Accountability

Civil society organisations also interact with the different arms and constituents of the state to ensure that they function with accountability. Accountability here means functioning according to the spirit and letter of the law, the constitution and customs associated with that particular constituent of the state.

The first task is to ensure the accountability of legislatures, parliaments, provincial legislatures, local bodies, elected representatives, etc. Each of these have constitutionally mandated roles, responsibilities, norms and procedures laid out for their functioning. Elected representatives who constitute the legislature are expected to formulate policies and monitor their implementation. In India, however, this process is distorted in several ways. For example, Members of Parliament (MPs) and Members of the Legislative Assembly (MLAs) have been receiving huge amounts of discretionary funds for implementing development programmes in their constituencies. This is clearly not the function of legislatures. Monitoring the use of such resources, influencing the manner in which legislative functioning takes place and holding the elected representatives accountable, both individually and collectively, are thus important functions of civil society.

Likewise, from the local level to the Supreme Court, the judiciary is expected to function in a particular manner. Monitoring the functioning the judiciary and the behavioural standards of judicial officers, lawyers and others, reviewing procedures that undermine the provision of justice for ordinary people and guarding against interpretations of the law that favour the interests of a few are some tasks that civil society performs to ensure the accountability of the judiciary.

In countries like India, civil society has another critical function: that of holding the law and order machinery accountable. The police, and in some parts of the country, the military (for instance, in the North-East, the Punjab and Jammu and Kashmir) are responsible for assuring the highest standards of human rights as constitutionally mandated and globally accepted by national governments. Yet, violation of human rights through harassment, arrest, detention, duress and intimidation by the police is a common occurrence (particularly in the case of the poor and the weak). Being vigilant against such violations is not only the responsibility of human rights organisations but also of a wide variety of citizen groups.

Another area where accountability needs to be ensured is that of development agencies and programmes. Huge amounts of resources are available to these bodies through national budgets and international cooperation. In countries like India, development agencies and their programmes have a significant impact on the lives of a large number of people, particularly the poor. Monitoring the performance of these development agencies, examining the linkage between their objectives and practice, providing them with ongoing feedback, negotiating with them and enabling beneficiaries to influence development programmes, are various ways in which civil society organisations can pressure the state's development agencies and programmes to remain accountable.

An important way in which ordinary citizens interface with the state is through public bureaucracy via the day-to-day provision of services like sanitation, water, electricity, telephony, transport, the registration of births, deaths and marriages, transfer of land and housing, health services and educational institutions. In countries like India, these public bureaucracies are inefficient, corrupt and self-serving. Ordinary citizens are harassed, intimidated, humiliated and denied services that are rightfully due to them. It therefore falls upon civil society to ensure bureaucratic accountability. Consumer associations, public interest litigations, petitions, campaigns, dharnas, media write-ups, etc., are some ways by which civil society can achieve this.

Again, in countries like India, where the democratic polity is still to strengthen its roots, political parties and the electoral process form yet another area where accountability needs to be ensured. Voter education, monitoring political parties and their candidates to make sure that they follow the code of conduct established by the Election Commission and assuring that free and fair elections are held, are some challenges that civil societies face in new democracies.

Cutting across a lot of these issues relating to state accountability are questions pertaining to the right to information. In countries where the Official Secrets Act predominates, where there is a culture and mindset of secrecy and withholding public information from the ordinary people, ensuring the right to information in law as well as in practice is a major challenge for civil society. Another broad issue relates to the gap between public commitments and pronouncements by the state and their actual implementation. Governments, after they are elected, rarely follow the political manifestos they issue at the time of elections. This is therefore one more area that requires intervention by civil society.

Another complex issue is that of the various regional and international treaties that the state enters into—on environment, population, gender justice, child labour, nuclear safety, human rights, etc. The number of such treaties and commitments has increased in recent years. National governments agree to them and sign them without necessarily translating them into policies and programmes at either national or provincial level. Campaigning to assure their implementation and monitoring them is a huge challenge for civil society organisations in the contemporary context.

Assuring Market Accountability

The role of the market, private enterprise and the for-profit sector is being increasingly legitimised and accentuated in most countries of the world, including India. Private sector associations do attempt to represent the interests of their members and participate in the public arena, and civil society actors, including associations of the private sector, have a responsibility to assure the accountability of such institutions as well. Consumer movements and organisations, for example, protect the rights of the consumer vis-à-vis the products and services provided by the private sector.

Further, the degree to which the private sector follows the laws of the land in establishing high standards of governance, in utilising public resources and the influence it exerts on public policies, is an additional area of concern for civil society organisations. Current capacities, interests and activities within civil society to assure the accountability of the private sector are relatively weak in many countries, including India.

Conclusion

The foregoing framework of civil society's interface with governance implies a comprehensive view of the issue. Different forms of civil society contribute to different aspects of the governance agenda. Thus, as a *space*, civil society provides an opportunity for *voicing* issues related to the priorities and practices of governance, while as a *movement* it typically creates collective pressure for *governance reform*. And civil society *organisations* contribute to the practical tasks associated with self-governance. These interfaces use the different opportunities available within the democratic polity to contribute towards the strengthening of governance in India.

The adversarial assertions of civil society are key to ensuring the practice of democracy in societal governance.

> After all, who needs a document to guarantee rights that people already presume they have? Ask the people who tore down fences and jumped walls. Ask the people who were cut off from their families and deprived of their jobs. Ask my fellow workers at the Gdansk Shipyard. Freedom may be the soul of humanity, but sometimes you have to struggle to prove it (Waleza 1990).

Likewise, the cooperative engagement by civil society uses available social capital to build the base for sustainable development.

> The social capital embodied in norms and networks of civic engagement seems to be a pre-condition for economic development as well

as for effective government. Development economists take note: Civics matters (Putnam 1999).

The neo-liberal ideology of less state and more private initiative is also refuted by the emerging data on citizens' perspectives. Both a strong state and a strong civil society are needed to ensure good governance for the well-being of *all* citizens, not just a few.

> At the core of this new consensus are both a *strong state* and a *strong civil* society. Citizens want and expect efficient and effective performance from their governments. They want public institutions to provide, or provide for, the essential services that assure the economic, social and physical security of all the citizens, not just some of them (Citizens and Governance 1999).

It is in this context that the complexity of this interface and mutual interaction between civil society and governance can be understood. This is indeed an intellectual and practical challenge of our times.

3

The Crisis of Governance[1]

Jayaprakash Narayan

Limits to State Power

Human society has created the unique institution of the organised state in order to maintain public order, defend frontiers and ensure harmony among individuals and groups. After centuries of struggle, only in the modern era has it generally come to be accepted that the state cannot be controlled by divine right or brute power. Neither hereditary succession nor authoritarianism is acceptable as an arbiter of political power in any civilised society. It should be noted, however, that state[2] and civil society, the clear separation between the two as well as the interaction between the two, are essentially modern notions linked to the rise of the nation-state system. In India, though the state existed for centuries, the idea of the nation-state and the recognition of limits to state power are of recent origin. Despite this, the relative autonomy of social institutions from the state's influence is a remarkable feature of our history throughout the ages. Even during the era of monarchy or authoritarianism, or other forms of personalised despotism, the limits to state power were clearly recognised in Indian society. For instance, the role of caste panchayats, village panchayats and traders' guilds has been well recognised and documented throughout ancient and medieval history. While the absolute power of despotic monarchy was accepted in the ancient and medieval state, the relative autonomy of individuals and groups from state power was also recognised and respected in large spheres of human endeavour. It is this strength and vitality of institutions other than the state that helped to nurture and sustain Indian society over centuries of turbulence and seeming anarchy. The hundreds and thousands of villages were largely untouched by state power. Consequently, the internecine wars of conquest or succession, the palace intrigues, the frequent coups and bloodshed made no serious impact on the lives of most people. Matters relating to religion and dharma have always been beyond the realm of the state. Even justice, as understood in ancient and medieval India, was to a large extent left to various social groups beyond the pale of the state.

Stagnation of Society

The relative autonomy of society from state influence resulted in two developments. On the one hand, society was remarkably stable, unaffected by the vicissitudes of political fortunes and state power. A high degree of harmony and predictability in human relations was thus ensured. As long as the king's authority was accepted in principle and taxes were paid regularly, the people were untouched by the vagaries of politics. While this was largely true during the ancient era, the situation did not undergo any dramatic change even after the advent of the Delhi Sultanate and the Mughal Empire. Many historians have forcefully brought out this autonomy of society even during the Delhi Sultanate period when the state was overtly Islamic, or the Mughal period when Islam continued to significantly influence the Indian state.

On the other hand, the insularity of society from the state ensured that the vertical fragmentation of society continued and institutions remained static and frozen. New ideas were not easily absorbed: in Tagore's memorable words in *Gitanjali*, 'the clear stream of reason has ... lost its way into the dreary desert sand of dead habit'.[3] Hierarchies and divisions of caste lines continued unaffected. Even about 10 centuries ago, insightful scholars and historians like Alberuni had commented on the stagnation of Indian society. In his *Tahqiq-I-Hind*, Alberuni pointed out:

> ... The Indians believe that there is no country like theirs, no nation like theirs, no king like theirs, no religion like theirs, no science like theirs.... They are by nature niggardly in communicating what they know, and they take the greatest possible care to withhold it from men of another caste from among their own people, still more of course from any foreigner.
>
> They are in a state of utter confusion, devoid of any logical order, and in the last instance always mixed up with silly notions of the crowd. I can only compare their mathematical and astronomical knowledge to a mixture of pearls and sour dates, or of pearls and dung, or of costly crystals and common pebbles. Both kinds of things are equal in their eyes, since they cannot raise themselves to the methods of strictly scientific deduction... (Thapar 1990: 239).

In addition to social stagnation, the limitation of the state's influence meant that no empire could really unify India and bring all the people together. The state could not submerge the many group identities and differences for the preservation and glory of the nation. Thus, while the Indian state, even in its most absolutist form, was never fascist, Indian society, even at the height of its glory, did not allow the fresh breeze of new ideas and institutions to blow in.

In the modern era, under the British, the state underwent a significant transformation. The period 1820–57 was remarkable for the activism and energy of the state. The spread of the idea of education as a secular activity—often sponsored and supported by the state, the establishment and of colleges and universities, the introduction of uniform administration and civil services, the codification of civil and criminal laws and procedures, the transformation of the land revenue system, the standardisation of taxes and the introduction of telegraph made rapid inroads into society. The breathtaking adventure of social reform through legislation, along with the ruthless suppression of anti-state and anarchic elements like Thugs and Pindaris, significantly altered the relationship between state and society. In many ways, the idea of the modern state as the arbiter of relations between individuals and groups, in addition to its traditional role of maintaining public order and defending the frontiers, came to be accepted during this period.

It is possible to argue that one of the powerful impulses behind the Revolt of 1857 was the atavistic reaction to the reformist zeal of an alien state. Eventually, after 1857, the British rulers came to believe that excessive state intervention was detrimental to the survival of the empire itself. As a consequence, for almost three decades after 1857, the Indian state was largely focused on preserving the status quo and the dividing line between state and society was rarely breached.

Subsequently, the controversy and resentment following the Ilbert Bill, the formation of the Indian National Congress, the introduction of local self-governance during Lord Ripon's period, the partition of Bengal and its subsequent reunification, the Rowlatt Act and the Khilafat Movement transformed the relationship between state and society into an adversarial struggle for freedom. It eventually became a national struggle with two contending parties—the alien state and the indigenous nationalist movement—contesting each other's legitimacy. Inevitably, people's yearning for freedom could not be contained for long and power was transferred to the Indian elite after the Second World War.

Expansion of the 'Welfare State'

With the transfer of power in 1947, the Indian state consciously and deliberately began to intervene in areas that had been hitherto left to civil society. The Constitution, which declared justice—social, economic and political—equality of status and of opportunity, and the promotion of fraternity assuring the dignity of the individual as the objectives of the Indian state, provided the necessary legitimacy to this deliberate intrusion. The Directive Principles of State Policy, which attempted to give expression to these noble constitutional values, gave the state the mandate, though somewhat diffuse, to legislate in many areas. Despite the turbulence and bloodshed that accompanied partition in 1947, great excitement and expectation were generated by the freedom struggle and independence. Obviously, there was enormous pressure on the state to fulfil these expectations in significant measure. The constitution-makers attempted to balance individual liberty and the state's interventionist role. Thus the Fundamental Rights guaranteed various liberties to citizens, including equality before the law, non-discrimination on grounds of religion, race, caste, sex or place of birth, equality of opportunity in matters of public employment, abolition of untouchability, abolition of hereditary titles, freedom of speech, assembly, association, movement and residence, protection of life and personal liberty, freedom of conscience and the free profession, practice and propagation of religion, and protection of the interests of the minorities. All these ensured that the state could not adversely affect the liberty and autonomy of individuals and groups. Only reasonable restrictions could be imposed on them in the interests of the integrity of India and security of the state, friendly relations with foreign states, public order, decency or morality, or in relation to contempt of court, defamation or incitement to an offence.

At the same time, the Directive Principles attempted to give expression to the aspirations of the people and to the ideals of the freedom struggle to control, regulate and reform Indian society. While these Directive Principles were not enforceable by any court, the Constitution explicitly stated that the principles laid down therein were nevertheless fundamental in the governance of the country and that it was the duty of the state to apply these principles in making laws. That promotion of people's welfare by securing and protecting a social order in which justice—social, economic and political—would inform all institutions of national life was accepted as the guiding principle of state policy. In particular, the constitution-makers enjoined upon the state the duty to strive to minimise the inequalities in status, facilities and opportunities, not only amongst individuals but also amongst groups of people residing in different areas or engaged in different vocations.

In the furtherance of these objectives, several principles were enunciated to guide state policy, including the right to an adequate means of livelihood, distribution of ownership and control of material resources to subserve the common good, prevention of the concentration of wealth and means of production to the common detriment, equal pay for equal work for both men and women, protection of workers and children, opportunities and facilities for children to develop in a healthy manner in conditions of freedom and dignity, organisation of village panchayats as units of self-government, effective provision for securing the right to work, to education and to public assistance in cases of unemployment, old age, sickness, disablement and in other cases of undeserved want, and suitable legislation to ensure a decent standard of life and full enjoyment of leisure and social and cultural opportunities to all workers. A Uniform Civil Code for citizens, provision of free and compulsory education for children, promotion of the educational and economic interests of Scheduled Castes and Tribes and other weaker sections, separation of the judiciary from the executive, protection of monuments and objects in places of national importance and promotion of international peace and security, have all been listed under the Directive Principles of State Policy.

The mood prevailing at the time of transfer of power and the enunciation of the Directive Principles enjoined upon the state the duty to actively legislate, supervise, monitor, regulate and control several areas of activity that were earlier regarded as legitimate spheres of civil society. Much of it was necessary and long overdue. In many ways, during the decades before the Revolt of 1857, the British had attempted to reform Indian society and this process, which was halted by the 1857 Revolt, was restarted after freedom. The abolition of untouchability, the guarantee of religious freedom and equality before the law, legislations to protect workers, children, women and minorities and positive discrimination in favour of the long-oppressed and disadvantaged sections of society, were both necessary and welcome, given the enormous hold of tradition, superstitions, ignorance and prejudice over much of our society. However, the frenetic activism of the Indian state had several far-reaching consequences, whose impact is still being felt today.

Hyperactive State and Governance Crisis

The ubiquitous role of the hyperactive Indian state has made deep inroads into most people's lives. As the state started affecting the lives of a very large number of people, influence peddling and mediation through power brokers became all too common. The citizens' dependence on the state for livelihood increased, as the state became the biggest employer of organised workers. Even today, about 19 million persons out of a total of organised, wage-earning workforce of about 27 million, are employed by the Indian state (Union and State governments and public sector undertakings). Such a large and overwhelming role of the government as the principal employer in the organised sector is unique and exists only in South Asia. The citizens' dependence on the state for livelihood, inputs in agriculture, permits, licences and quotas; the monopolies of the public sector; the VIP quota culture for everything ranging from a railway ticket to a cricket match; needless restrictions on trade and marketing of agricultural products; the state's monopoly in almost all public goods and amenities; its control and ownership of all public utilities—means that civil society has become vulnerable to the depredations of state machinery as never before.

This has spawned a centralised and anaemic culture and most state institutions have become hotbeds of corruption, crime, intrigue and nepotism. Power has become an end in itself and is no longer a means to public good. Unbridled and irresponsible populism, knee-jerk opposition to those in power, the unbridgeable chasm between rhetoric and action, endless opportunism and shameless plunder of the state's resources have become the hallmarks of our governance system. All that matters is a hand in the till of the state and an opportunity to indulge in legal plunder and constitutional brigandage. Once in power, principles, ideology or public opinion are of little consequence. Appointment of public servants to key offices, transfer of inconvenient employees, licensing, distribution of patronage in the form of subsidies and benefits to the poor, the public distribution system, government contracts and tenders, mining licences, permission to exploit forest produce, maintenance of law and order, crime control, investigation and prosecution, execution of public works and toll gates have all become playthings of state functionaries. Most players in the power game are not enthused by any idealism but have become mercenaries who rig polls and resort to violence at the behest of 'leaders'. In return, they expect to partake in the plunder and share the booty. The resultant corruption and parasitism have made politics the most attractive and least risky commercial proposition. In fact, the word 'politics' itself has acquired a very pejorative connotation. The high degree of economic power wielded by the state and the deliberate efforts to prevent legitimate accumulation of individual wealth in the name of socialism have meant that no civil society group is able to command the resources or influence to combat abuse of state power.

This intrusive and interventionist role of the state has not only undermined individual initiative, it has also hampered social harmony and economic growth. As the state has focused most of its energy in the economic sphere of the licence-permit-quota-raj, the legitimate and vital sphere of state activity has been ignored—to the detriment of the public. Public order has been a casualty, with increasing lawlessness and near-anarchy prevailing in many pockets of the country. Dispensing justice, which is a sovereign and critical function of the state in any civilised society, suffered grievously on account of its preoccupation with the regulation and control of the economy and public ownership of the means of production. More than 30 million cases are pending in various courts of law in India and most people have lost faith in the capacity of the justice system to resolve disputes in time or to punish culprits. As the sanctity of contracts could not be upheld and contractual obligations could not be enforced through the courts of law, entrepreneurship suffered and economic activity stagnated. People were forced to depend on brute muscle power for rough and ready justice. With politics occupying centrestage in society and abuse of power unchecked, criminals soon made inroads into politics. The Election Commission estimates that more than 700 legislators (out of the total 4,072) in the states have a criminal record.

Tools of Power

Power is essentially the ability to influence events, resources and human behaviour for the larger public good. In a democratic society, people elect their representatives to exercise such positive power. Control of the state exchequer, supervision of the state employees and the power to make laws are the three fundamental tools available to a government in the discharge of its functions. Every single day the Indian state—all governments put together—spends about Rs 1,500 crore (15 billion). This astronomical sum of over a crore of rupees every single minute—day and night—should provide us goods and services of quality. This amount is roughly equivalent to Rs 5,000 per head per annum, or about Rs 125,000 per family of five during a five-year term of an elected legislature! In fact, if this money is used properly, we could easily provide basic amenities to most people, create the infrastructure required for universal school education of reasonable quality, and ensure that primary health care is accessible to all. It is estimated that about 8 crore (80 million) children between the ages of 5 and 14 are not in school. If money alone is the issue, all it takes is an expenditure of about Rs 16,000 crore (160 billion) to build 16 lakh (1.6 million) classrooms as capital investment and a further annual recurrent expenditure of Rs 8,000 crore (80 billion) to employ 16 lakh (1.6 million) teachers. Arithmetically, this is equivalent to about 11 days of national and six days of state expenditure respectively. And yet the Indian state cannot provide universal access to school education even after 53 years of democratic experiment.

Similarly, if we take the issue of sanitation, some 70 per cent of Indians have no access to safe, hygienic toilets and are forced to defecate in public. Apart from health problems on account of lack of hygiene and sanitation, public defecation is aesthetically unpleasant, terribly inconvenient and, most of all, offensive to human dignity. Again, if money is the issue, to build a safe toilet in every one of the 14 crore (140 million) households that are in need, would cost no more than Rs 35,000 crore (350 billion) at Rs 2,500 per toilet. Many organisations like Sulabh International have demonstrated that Rs 2,500 is adequate for a safe, modern hygienic toilet without any frills. And yet most Indians have no access to basic public services and amenities that are taken for granted in any civilised society. It is by now universally acknowledged that very little of this huge quantity of public money spent every day translates into services and public goods. Which is why basic infrastructure in power, road and rail transport and ports is in a state of disrepair, retarding economic growth. This situation can only be described as constitutional brigandage and legal plunder. And the state, instead of serving the citizens, is actually partaking in the plunder.

The other facet of our dysfunctional state is its vast and labyrinthine bureaucracy, which is self-perpetuating. Of the nearly 1 billion Indian population, the organised wage-earning sector accounts for only about 27 million workers, who in turn constitute only about 8 per cent of the workforce. Of these, as many as 19 million are employees of the government. While the size of the government as a proportion of the population or its expenditure as a proportion of the Gross Domestic Product (GDP) is by no means unusual when compared to other countries, in most government employees in India do not provide any services of real value to the public. First, government employment is highly skewed in relation to the needs of the people. For instance, in Andhra Pradesh, out of the nearly 9,00,000 State employees (excluding those working in public sector undertakings), as many as 2,80,000 are clerks, who by definition are merely support staff helping in decision-making. A further 18,000 employees are attendants, peons and drivers who only serve their political and bureaucratic masters. Over 50 per cent employees are thus in the non-productive sector. There is a huge shortage of teachers and health workers in the government. Many schools function with only two teachers. And those who are employed by the government often do not provide quality service. More than 95 per cent of the teachers engaged in government schools do not send their own children to the schools where they teach. Most primary health centres exist only in name and provide little quality service to the public. There is an increasing disjunction between the needs of the public and those of the government employees. As a result, stake-holding and power-wielding are completely divorced from each other.

In a country with rigid social hierarchies and vast poverty and illiteracy, any person with the advantages of education and a regular, wage-earning job automatically wields considerable power. When the job is in government, with all its colonial hangovers, the roles of public servant and citizen are easily reversed. The public servant is transformed into the master and the citizen becomes the subject. The extraordinary degree of lifetime security given to a bureaucrat at every level, with virtually no chance of being brought to book, makes it impossible for any government to enforce accountability. Added to this, the political compulsions to indulge in populism and direct subsidies, converting the citizen into a recipient and the government functionary into a giver, promotes corruption and helps in reversing the roles between master and servant. Consequently, most government employees are horrified to learn that they are intended to serve the public as they are paid by the public exchequer!

We have thousands of laws in our statute books. Most of them are archaic and obscure. Many are on paper and never implemented. Even when the state desires to enforce a law, institutional mechanisms have become so weakened that it is no longer possible to ensure the compliance of citizens. The intellectual and moral resources available to the political and bureaucratic class are so limited that creative legislation to resolve national dilemmas is becoming increasingly difficult. Needless political contention on otherwise fundamentally sound proposals makes the framing of new and effective legislation almost impossible. As the justice system has all but collapsed, a whole new industry of administering rough and ready justice using strong-arm tactics has been set up local hoodlums in most of India. The clout and money these hoodlums acquire makes sure that they are the ones who later enter political parties and eventually acquire state power.

Follies of Omission and Commission

The failure of the governance process and the misuse and disuse of the tools of money, employees and legislative power have resulted in a grave crisis. Most citizens have given up hope of the state acting effectively and in time to protect their legitimate interests. In fact, the state has increasingly become an obstacle in people's march towards progress. The anonymous tyranny experienced by almost every citizen who encounters government machinery at any level and the legal plunder of state resources have impoverished our society and the bulk of our people.

School education and primary health care, which are symbols of civilisation in a modern society and without which sustained economic growth is not possible, have been woefully neglected as the state has neither the resources nor the political will and attention span to provide these basic services to the public. Key physical infrastructure, entirely controlled by the state for over four decades, has languished for want of resources and managerial ability on account of state monopoly. There is an endemic shortage of power, ports, roads and railroad services. Only in the telecommunications sector has there been significant improvement in the last decade, largely due to vigorous attempts to break state monopoly and the relative ease of transplanting communications technology even in relatively backward areas. But given the predatory nature of the Indian state, even in this otherwise sensible initiative there has been considerable plunder and bungling.

While the state has failed to perform its essential tasks, it has shown remarkable eagerness to needlessly regulate other facets of civil society. Complete monopoly of the electronic media until the advent of satellite television, prevention of the spread of television for long, sporadic, if largely unsuccessful, attempts to muzzle the free press by censorship and draconian laws, and other preventive detention laws applied with mindless rigour in an arbitrary manner during the notorious Emergency period between 1975 and 1977, are some striking examples of the state's attempts to curtail individual liberty. The extra-legal executions in the name of encounters, the abuse of police machinery by almost all parties in government, the habitual torture and illegal detention despite clear legal and constitutional provisions to the contrary are sad examples of state tyranny in an otherwise soft, ineffective governance structure.

In addition, cooperatives that were given a legal status at the turn of the century during the British Raj were controlled rigorously after independence, stifling individual and group initiative in contravention of the freedom of association guaranteed under the Constitution. Even formation of societies and their regulation became more restrictive in many pockets of India, unlike during the colonial era when a very liberal and humane societies law was enacted and enforced with clarity and fairness. Higher education was completely controlled by the state with very poor results in terms of promoting creativity, knowledge, skills and leadership in society. Clearly, the state has failed in discharging its obligations to the citizens and has acted as a stumbling block in the fulfilment of individual potential and group initiatives.

Negative Influence of Society

Through the follies of omission and commission, inaction and excessive action and criminal neglect and draconian arbitrariness, the functioning of the state has adversely affected civil society. As William E. Gladstone observed, the proper function of government is to make it easy for the people to do good and difficult to do evil.[4] In this respect the failure of the Indian state is glaring and debilitating for society. The positive authority of government to curb evil and promote good has become increasingly restricted, whereas the negative power of abuse for pelf, privilege, patronage, petty tyranny and nuisance value has been largely unhindered. As a consequence, the state has become ineffectual in the public eye and even legitimate reform efforts have come to naught. Most social legislation, for instance, is generally on paper and has had no impact on regulating or moderating human behaviour. Abolition of untouchability and dowry are two instances of the state's failure, despite pious intentions and sometimes genuine efforts.

This sorry state of affairs is unacceptable in any civilised society, much less in a democratic society. The citizen is the focal point of any democracy. We elect a government to serve our collective needs, to make and enforce laws to regulate human behaviour, to promote the greatest public good possible and to provide us common services ranging from public order to education and health care. The citizen is the true and ultimate sovereign and the measure of a government's functioning is citizen's satisfaction. A government accountable to the citizens, who are its true master, and public servants responsive to the needs of the taxpayers, who are their paymasters, are essential elements of a democracy. The derailment of our democracy and the failure of the Indian state, which stunts our potential as a society and as a nation, have caused untold misery to millions.

It is the relative strength of civil society, nurtured over centuries, and the stability of social institutions like the family and community, which have largely withstood the vagaries of time, that are sustaining a modicum of order, peace and harmony in society and allowing some modest growth and economic prosperity. In the face of the state's failure to perform creditably, the citizens have to assert their own sovereignty and transform the nature of governance. The tools available to achieve this are elections, political parties and citizen activism. Let us examine the extent to which people can deploy these tools to bring about the desired change.

Electoral Politics: Rules of the Game vs Change of Players

The behaviour of the electorate is becoming increasingly plebiscitary in nature. However, the Westminster model adopted by us recognises only power that is gained by acquiring legislative majority—by fair means or foul—without reference to public opinion or people's mandate. As people's mandate and power are easily divorced, the rulers are increasingly obsessed with survival at any cost. As a result, it is now axiomatic that integrity in public life and survival in public office are no longer compatible. In this milieu, the vote, instead of being a unifying, cleansing and energising tool, has become a divisive force, or at best a means for the expression of anger and frustration. Electoral behaviour in most parts of the country over the past 25 years clearly shows that the dominant mood of the electorate is to reject the party in power. Often this rejection is despite the perception of the elite that the government has performed creditably and that the alternative chosen by the people is even less attractive on analysis. Obviously, voters perceive the issue differently. As far as they are concerned, the government of the day failed to fulfil their expectations. Even populist governments, which successfully transferred assets and resources to the people through direct subsidies and welfare schemes, incurred the wrath of the electorate, as much as those that had long-term perspectives. This only shows that people are disgusted with the political process itself and that there is deep-seated resentment and unrest about the imbalance between the exercise of positive and negative power and their own marginalisation and disempowerment.

In the judgement of the people, no arm of the state escapes blame—whether it be the political class, the bureaucracy or judiciary. The politicians are most reviled because in their case the imbalance in the exercise of power as well as the incompatibility between honesty and survival are far more clearly evident. In this demonology, the bureaucracy comes next because in its case there is lifetime security irrespective of performance and therefore it is possible to be dishonest and yet survive. The judiciary is last in vilification, since it is largely immune from the vagaries of politics and there is minimal interface with the general public on a day-to-day basis. However, the judiciary is no less culpable, to the extent that there is gross inefficiency, delay and inaccessibility, in many cases almost amounting to miscarriage of justice. As the old adage goes, the loser in a civil suit laments publicly in court and the winner sheds tears privately at home!

This rejection of the governing class by the voter can be construed to be both positive and negative. The positive significance is the demonstration of the voter's yearning for comprehensive reform and rejection of the status quo. The negative factor is the increasing instability and fear of the ruling classes to face the electorate. All these maladies constitute a first class recipe for corruption, greed and shortsightedness on the part of those in authority. Corruption has become endemic and is widely perceived to be a ubiquitous feature of our governance. No class of public servant is exempt from it. People who are victims of this daily corruption do not have effective institutional mechanisms for resisting it. Those who have the will to resist do not dare do so for fear of greater personal loss than the potential gain resulting from resistance. As a result, it is more convenient and less cumbersome to become a part of the process than to fight against it. Every individual in this vicious cycle therefore prefers the status quo either to maximise personal gain or minimise personal pain, even as society at large loses more than individual gain and is increasingly debilitated. To explain this phenomenon, Robert Wade coined the expression 'dangerously stable equilibrium' (Wade 1985).

Electoral Verdicts: Macro vs Micro

The election verdicts at various levels in the country have an important lesson to offer us. At the macro level, the verdict broadly reflects public opinion. We have already seen that, more often than not, this verdict is a reflection of people's anger and frustration and is manifested in the rejection vote. But when we come to the constituency level, the picture is far more disturbing. At the local level, caste or subcaste, crime, money and muscle-power have become the determinants of political power. In order to have a realistic chance of success, all parties are compelled to put up candidates who can muster these resources in abundance. The net result is that irrespective of which party wins, the nature and quality of political leadership remain largely the same and the people end up being the losers. This is followed by another rejection vote in the next election, and the vicious cycle keeps repeating. Where the candidate cannot muster money or muscle-power, he stands little chance of getting elected, irrespective of his party's electoral fortunes. Increasingly, in several pockets of the country, people are spared the bother of even having to go to the polling station! Organised booth capturing and rigging ensure victory without people's involvement.

There is much that is wrong with our elections. Flawed electoral rolls have become a menace. About 40 per cent errors are noticed in electoral rolls in many urban areas and bogus voting in town exceeds 20 per cent, making a mockery of elections. Purchase of votes through money and liquor, preventing poorer sections from voting, large-scale impersonation and bogus voting, purchase of the opponents' agents and forcing agents and polling personnel to allow false voting, booth capturing and large-scale rigging, bribing the polling staff and police personnel to get favours and to harass opponents, use of violence and criminal gangs, stealing ballot boxes or tampering with the ballot papers, inducing or forcing voters to reveal their voting preferences through various techniques, including 'cycling', illegally entering the polling stations and controlling the polling process—all these are an integral part of our electoral landscape.

Many scholars wonder how, despite such massive irregularities, electoral verdicts still seem to largely reflect public opinion, and how parties in power often lose elections. The answers are simple. Happily for us, though parties in power are prone to abusing authority for electoral gain, there has never been any serious state-sponsored rigging in most of India. Irregularities are largely limited to the polling process alone. Most of pre-polling activity, including the printing and distribution of ballot papers, and post-polling activity, including transport and storage of ballot boxes and the counting of ballots, are free from political interference or organised manipulation. Which is why parties in power have no decisive advantage in manipulating the polls, and electoral verdicts broadly reflect shifts in public opinion. However, the massive irregularities in the polling process make sure that the candidates who deploy abnormal money and muscle-power have a distinct advantage. Sensing this, most major parties have begun nominating 'winnable' candidates without reference to their ability or integrity. Thus, almost all parties sanction the use of money and muscle-power, and often they tend to neutralise each other. The net result is that candidates who do not indulge in any irregularity have very little chance of being elected. Election expenditure—mostly for illegitimate vote buying, hiring of hoodlums and bribing officials—is often 10 or 20 times the ceiling permitted by law. Criminals have a decisive or dominant influence on the outcome of elections in many parts of India and have often become party candidates and won on a large scale.

Election Expenditure and Corruption

The vast, unaccounted expenditure in elections has a direct bearing on the governance process and the ubiquitous corruption in our administration. To take the example of one state,[5] it is estimated that major political parties spent about Rs 600 crore (6 billion) during the recent elections. Most of this expenditure was both illegal and illegitimate and was spent on money and liquor to woo voters, bribe officials involved in the polling process to connive in rigging and other malpractices, and to hire hoodlums to distort the elections through impersonation, rigging and booth capturing. The political process feeds on corruption and, in turn, promotes it. The appetite of parties and candidates for ill-gotten, unaccounted funds is legendary. Correspondingly, there is a great urge to replenish the expenditure incurred on elections with a decent return on investment and insurance to cover the risk of failure in a winner-takes-all election and as provision for future elections.

Combined with these requirements is the Indian perception that public office is for private gain. The politician who spends an average of 10 years as a political worker waiting to be nominated as a candidate of a major party and who forsakes gainful employment in the pursuit of politics, expects that he and his family will be provided for for an entire lifetime and sometimes for several generations. This makes the system exceedingly corrupt. On an investment of Rs 600 crore (6 billion), a return of at least Rs 3,000 (30 billion) crore is required to sustain it. However, most of this money is routed through the vast bureaucracy in the form of rent seeking or an illegitimate fee for every conceivable public service ranging from a birth certificate to the registration of a sale deed. Given the vast size of the bureaucracy, it is inevitable that about 90 per cent of corruption proceeds are retained by it even as the per capita receipts are much smaller than those of politicians. In effect, this means that for every rupee spent by politicians during elections, they expect a return of Rs 5, which in turn translates into corruption of the order of about Rs 50 at the grassroots level. However, the citizen will not willingly pay a bribe for routine public services unless he or she is compelled to do so. Most corruption in India is extortionary. The delay, inefficiency, humiliation, indignity, inconvenience and often lost opportunity may cost 10 time or more if palms are not greased. As a result, most citizens submit to corruption, as they know from past experience that the alternative is much worse.

Why do Citizen Vote Badly?

We still have to answer one important question relating to expenditure and corruption—why do citizens often vote badly in the first place? There are umpteen instances of really worthy candidates being defeated at the hustings even as known criminals and corrupt persons are elected to public office. After decades of experience, most citizens have come to the sad conclusion that no matter who is elected, the only ones who end up as losers are the people themselves. Even if every person elected loses the next election and his nearest rival is elected to public office, there will be no appreciable change in the quality of governance. This remarkable inertia and seeming intractability of the governance process have convinced citizens that there is no real long-term stake involved in electoral politics. Therefore, many poor citizens are forced to take a rational decision to maximise their short-term gains. As a result, the vote has become a commodity that can be purchased with money or liquor. Often, it is an assertion of the primordial loyalties of caste, religion, group, ethnicity, region or language. Very often, even in the absence of any material inducement or emotional outburst based on prejudice, sheer anger against the dysfunctional governance process makes most voters reject the status quo. Frequently, this rejection is indiscriminate, with no rational evaluation of the alternatives. In short, even the illiterate, ordinary voters are making the assumption that the vote has no serious long-term consequences and the choice is between Tweedledum and Tweedledee.

New Entrants into Politics

Given the profile of the new entrants into politics over the past three or four decades, it is evident that hardly anyone with intellect, integrity, commitment to public service and passion for improvement can enter the political arena and survive. Almost every new entrant has chosen politics for the wrong reasons. A careful analysis shows that political inheritance is the most common reason for entry. This is closely followed by those who have large inherited or acquired wealth and have decided that investment in politics is good business. In recent years, many local musclemen, whose services were earlier sought for extortion or gathering votes, are now directly entering the fray and gaining political legitimacy. A few persons have entered politics out of personal loyalty to, and close contacts with, those in high public office. Film stars, whose faces are widely known and admired, have predictably starting converting their popularity and image into elective office. If we exclude inheritance, money and muscle-power, personal contacts, stardom and accidents of fate, we find hardly a handful of people in this vast country of ours who have entered politics with a passion for public good and survived for any length of time. There is no activity more vital or noble than governance. In the true sense, politics is about promotion of happiness and public good. But if the best men and women that society can boast of are prevented, repelled or rendered incapable of surviving in the political arena, then governance is bound to be in shambles.

Failure of Political Parties

The question, then, is, how do we resolve this crisis speedily and peacefully? For such a resolution is critical for good governance, human happiness, economic prosperity and social harmony. In a rational polity, the problems of governance have to be addressed through participation in the political process. It is the duty as well as the right of citizens to join political parties, acquire positions of leadership and influence in them, articulate an alternative vision for society and polity, seek elective public office, obtain people's mandate and bring about necessary changes. However, this political process is utterly perverted in India and does not provide opportunities for enlightened and public-spirited citizens to participate in it. Political parties have become incestuous under the control of oligarchic coteries. Once someone ascends to a position of leadership in a party, often for reasons other than public support or a broad vision for the future, that person controls citizens' access to membership, expels members at will whenever his position is threatened, does not allow democratic electoral processes within parties to change leadership, and in general exercises absolute and arbitrary control over the party. In short, political parties have become instruments of self-aggrandisement and personal power. They enrich themselves with illegal, unaccounted funding and use it to further tighten their control over the members and the electoral process. The choice of candidates nominated by parties for elective public office is entirely at the discretion of the often self-appointed authoritarian leadership. As a result, political parties have ceased to be institutions of political socialisation and agents of change.

In addition to the failure of parties as instruments of change, the increasing role of money and muscle-power and the distortion of the electoral process, which lends itself to enormous manipulation through rigging, booth capturing and bogus voting, make it impossible for an honest citizen to successfully seek elective public office through fair and legal means. This complex scenario makes the Indian governance crisis seem intractable. On the one hand, in a democracy, the only answer to a crisis in governance is more and better democracy engineered through political processes. On the other hand, the political process has become inaccessible to the best men and women in society unless they are willing to compromise to such an extent that they become a part of the problem rather than the solution. In India, the greatest challenge facing civil society today is to somehow break this vicious cycle and reverse the decline in governance.

At the same time, it is unrealistic to expect people to be able to make a significant impact in the electoral arena without a party label. Throughout the world political parties are the arbiters of politics and the nation's fate. They exercise enormous influence on public discourse, literally drowning all other voices by the noise levels they generate and the endless newspaper space and radio and television time they appropriate. They have a direct impact on public policy affecting millions of lives and are the only effective instruments to acquire power, control the state apparatus and govern. Against this backdrop, it is virtually impossible for honest and well-meaning citizens to make a significant political contribution from outside the party system. The fact that the role of independents in legislatures is at best marginal and is consistently declining only illustrates the importance of parties in democratic governance.

It is unimaginable to think of a liberal democratic society without influential political parties. There is no genuine democracy in which parties do not play a dominant and decisive role in both elections and governance. The well-meaning but somewhat naïve attempts by idealists to promote partyless democracy have floundered in all countries, including India. The heroic efforts and advocacy of partyless democracy by Lok Nayak Jayaprakash Narayan are a telling illustration of such an idealistic vision of a democratic society based on the free will of individual citizens without intermediation by political parties. However, this unalloyed idealism could not withstand the power of organised political parties and ultimately failed to take off. Many scholars believe that apart from competitive elections, the existence of a whole series of intermediate institutions in society espousing particular political values is critical for the survival of a liberal democracy. In practice, it is well recognised that electoral political action outside political parties is almost always doomed to failure. This applies equally to countries like the United Kingdom with strong and well-organised political parties and to nations like the United States with very loosely organised political parties and an enormous accent on individual liberty. Even in the US, an occasional independent like Ross Perot may significantly influence public attitudes on certain crucial issues for a time, but cannot realistically hope to capture the levers of power.

First-Past-the-Post System

Thus, the only realistic option available to citizens who wish to be involved in political action is joining political parties.

Unfortunately, given the nature of our political parties and the distortions in our electoral process, it is increasingly difficult, if not impossible, for decent citizens to acquire influence in parties and get elected to public office. Honesty and survival in politics is becoming increasingly incompatible. As parties function in an autocratic and unaccountable manner, more as private fiefdoms than as instruments of political socialisation, the best citizens in society are repelled by political activity. A party represents the aspirations, dreams and beliefs of millions of people and is a product of decades of history, emotion and tradition. It is therefore not easy for individuals to try and form new political parties overnight. In particular, the first-past-the-post (FPTP) system makes it virtually impossible for new political groups to make an impact. In our present electoral system, wherein an individual wins by obtaining the largest number of votes, there is a tendency on the part of parties to move heaven and earth to win a particular constituency. Highly respected and credible individuals stand very little chance despite considerable public support unless they resort to the same ugly practices that have become the hallmark of politics in our country. As a result, politics remains elusive for citizens who could, in a saner polity, provide great leadership.

In fact, politics is almost always described in pejorative terms. As a consequence of this, civil society is largely alienated from the political process. One possible way out is a system of proportional representation (PR), in which a party can have a presence in the legislature on the basis of its overall popular support, irrespective of whether or not the party can win constituencies in the basis of the largest number of votes obtained. There is a realistic possibility of parties shifting their emphasis to increase their vote share if the PR system is introduced. There is evidence to suggest that illegitimate efforts to win a few constituencies may actually run counter to the larger objective of enhancing the voting share in a whole State or nation. At present, because of the dominance of local factors in constituency elections, the party's overall vote share does not seem to be important. Winning every constituency at any cost is the aim of most mainstream parties in the FPTP system. However, in the PR system, once the overall vote share and the image of the political party become critical for success in the elections, the nature of campaigning and electoral process will undergo a radical, positive transformation. Even more significantly, influential groups that have some base but no realistic chance of winning elections would, in the PR system, have the opportunity to grow and become serious players in the political landscape, thereby forcing reform.

Illiteracy—Cause or Consequence?

Another issue that needs to be dispassionately examined is the impact of illiteracy and ignorance on the electoral and political system. Informed citizenry, active citizenship and collective assertion are critical civil society functions in a mature democracy. However, the reality is that the very low levels of literacy prevalent even today, despite decades of rhetoric, have made ordinary citizens very weak in the face of the might of the state. Many people secretly believe that universal adult franchise in a largely illiterate society is not desirable. Ironically, the verdict of the poor and illiterate is roughly the same as that of the literate and informed population in society. Human beings are endowed with the same amount of dignity and they have the same democratic right and freedom of choice irrespective of their origins, level of literacy, wealth, talent and accomplishments. In fact, it can be argued that illiteracy is not a cause of misgovernance but is actually perpetuated by the failure of governance. The literacy levels of many countries that had comparable human development indices about 50 years ago have dramatically improved after the Second World War. If anything, illiteracy is perpetuated by incompetent administration and dysfunctional political processes. To argue that illiteracy is the cause of failure of governance is a clever inversion of logic, wholly devoid of merit.

Apart form examples like South East Asia, Sri Lanka and the State of Kerala, the experience of Tamil Nadu in recent years clearly demonstrates that strategic interventions by the state can make a spectacular difference to literacy in a relative short span of time. Some time in the early 1980s, the M.G. Ramachandran government in Tamil Nadu introduced the mid-day meal scheme in schools. The motive was probably to attract the votes of the poor, enhance the image of the ruling party and its leader, and a genuine concern for the plight of the poor coupled with a desire to promote literacy. Unlike other government promises and programmes, the mid-day meal scheme in Tamil Nadu was actually well implemented and was the focus of a lot of political attention. As a result, the poor sent their children to school. A well-conceived, well-implemented programme thus altered people's behaviour. Since the schools had become the centre of political attention, the quality of schooling also improved significantly. Simultaneously, higher investments were made in school education, as a result of which literacy levels went up and, in particular, female literacy made rapid strides. Today, among the major States, Tamil Nadu has the second highest literacy level in India. In the past few years, this high level of literacy has translated itself into low levels of population growth. Tamil Nadu is now very close to reaching a stable population level. All this transformation has taken place in less than two decades and has resulted in higher skill levels, increased investment, more employment and rapid economic growth.

Compare this with Andhra Pradesh, where populist programmes of a different kind were implemented with equal sincerity and vigour. In 1983, the N.T. Rama Rao government introduced a subsidised rice programme, making rice available at Rs 2 per kg. The scheme was well implemented and the motives were perhaps similar to those in Tamil Nadu. However, it did not alter people's behaviour in any positive way. As a consequence, the poor largely remained poor and their skill levels did not go up. In fact, it is possible to argue that the savings made by the poor because of the scheme went into alcohol consumption and other such unproductive and sometimes harmful activities. Among all the Indian States, Andhra Pradesh today ranks the third lowest in the literacy ladder. It is clear, therefore, that literacy level cannot be a precondition for democracy and universal adult franchise. In fact, it is good governance and sensible strategic initiatives that are the preconditions for higher literacy and the positive benefits that flow from it.

Is Economic Liberalisation Enough?

It is widely believed that the economic liberalisation process initiated in 1991 will somehow find answers to our governance crisis. It is also widely recognised that economic reform is long overdue. However, while necessary, economic reform is by no means sufficient to resolve our national dilemmas. Even if the role of the state is redefined to give it a sharper role in a narrower area, an efficient and just state in a free society is a vital precondition for both economic growth and human happiness. Even in a liberalised economic environment, the state still has the duty to discharge vital responsibilities. Public order, crime investigation, speedy justice, good quality school education that is accessible to all children, universal primary health care, maintenance of minimal standards of sanitation and civic amenities, providing vital infrastructure like roads and facilitating economic growth through other infrastructure development like power and ports—are all legitimate functions of the state irrespective of the economic system we choose. It is the state's failure to provide good governance and to enforce the rule of law that explains in large measure the limited success of economic reforms. In the absence of good governance, economic reform by itself will at best lead to modest growth for some time and its fruits will be transient and self-limiting. Inadequate human development and the failure of our delivery systems have led to appallingly low levels of literacy and skills, poor health coverage and hopelessly inadequate infrastructure. The vast majority of Indians are thus left outside the pale of the nation's productive process.

The situation is further complicated as abuse of power is now finding expression in the critical sovereign areas of state function, as opposed to the earlier days when economic patronage of the state was abused for personal gain. As long as the licence-quota-permit-raj was in vogue, most players of the power game were content with distorting competition and extending patronage on a selective basis for a consideration. The political class and bureaucracy thus lined their pockets at the cost of fair competition, creating monopolies and distorting market forces and hurting the hapless citizens in the process. However, since 1991, the role of the Indian state in licensing and other related economic activities has been on the decline. But in the absence of effective institutional checks against the abuse of authority, the state continues to have a wide latitude in areas of sovereign functioning, such as public order, administration of justice, crime control, investigation and related matters. No matter how much we limit the role of the state, there are vital areas that will always remain within its ambit. When conditions for good governance are not fulfilled, abuse of power becomes the norm. When economic decision-making power is denied to the state, such abuse of power will find expression in sovereign areas. Over the past several years there has been mounting evidence of such a phenomenon resulting in the increased criminalisation of politics, greater politicisation of crime investigation, and an even stronger nexus between the political class, state agencies and organised criminal gangs and operators. In effect, abuse of power in the critical areas of state functioning leads to complete lawlessness and undermines the foundations of our society and civilisation. In any case, even with economic liberalisation, the state will have to continue to play an important role in ensuring fair competition. A rogue state, whose legitimacy is in question, whose appetite for ill-gotten funds is uncontrollable, and whose accountability to the people is suspect, will continue to use the limited economic decision-making power under its control for personal gain at the cost of public good and economic growth.

Obstacles to Active Citizenship

There are millions of Indians who are deeply concerned about the future of the country and the democratic system. A frequent topic of conversation among us is the decline of our democratic institutions and the condition of the Indian state. However, this concern is not translated into any meaningful and sustained action because of three formidable obstacles. First, most people do not have adequate exposure to institutions of governance to appreciate the larger malaise affecting the Indian state. In the absence of a holistic perspective, people tend to view the crisis through a tunnel, leading to a highly skewed and partial understanding, very akin to a blind man describing an elephant. These partial perceptions do not enable us to unravel the intricate and vital linkages among various institutions. And without such an understanding it is not possible to begin any meaningful reform to resolve the crisis facing our governance.

Second, India defies easy description or analysis. The huge population, the vertical fragmentation of our society, the relative immobility of the population, the enormous poverty and drudgery, and the complex cultural baggage leading to an uneasy co-existence of several layers of our society—from the medieval period to the modern era—all these constitute a mind-boggling and often frightening reality that paralyses all participants and observers into inaction.

Third, in the modern, technological world, with increasing opportunities for rapid economic growth, most well-informed and perceptive Indians are consumed by day-to-day individual and family concerns. The history of the freedom struggle led us to believe that legitimate personal concerns for survival and growth are incompatible with the quest for national good. During the freedom struggle, our nationalism was largely based on anger against racial bigotry, cultural atavism as a defence mechanism to shore up self-esteem and an idolatrous sense of patriotism with the deification of Mother India serving as an emotional anchor. Colonial economic exploitation was certainly a factor in shaping Indian nationalism, but its role was relatively subdued in giving expression to nationalistic fervour. Against this backdrop of emotionalism and patriotic fervour, individual concerns seemed to be irrelevant and incompatible with the national goal. However, in a modern, democratic nation-state, it is very difficult to generate and sustain such heightened patriotic fervour. Neglecting personal goals in a rapidly changing world, even for a few years, can have very painful economic and emotional consequences for most people. Therefore, the fear of insecurity and uncertainty at the prospect of having to sacrifice personal life for the national cause deters most thinking Indians.

Governance Reforms

What, then, is the answer to this grave crisis? The nature and magnitude of the problem is undoubtedly daunting and we are witnessing the collapse of the Indian republic. However, the crisis is by no means intractable or immutable. Its resolution lies in the recognition that what we need is not merely a change of players but a fundamental transformation of the rules of the game. Such a reform process would need to encompass several spheres of governance, ranging from political parties to the administration of justice. Democratisation of political parties to enable the best men and women to participate in the political process; far-reaching electoral reforms to ensure free and fair elections, enabling the best leadership to emerge;

democratic decentralisation and empowerment of citizens to the extent that the relationship between the vote and welfare of citizens and between taxes and public services provided is clearly established; public service reform to make the bureaucracy an effective instrument of good governance; greater separation of the executive from the legislature to make honesty compatible with survival in elective public office; a speedy, efficient and accessible justice system; and institutional self-correcting mechanisms and safeguards against the abuse of public office—all these should be integral components of governance reform. Isolated efforts, no matter how well meaning and necessary, are bound to be frustrated when unaccompanied by other necessary reforms.

The question, then, is: what should be the role of civil society in reforming the Indian state and making it an instrument for promoting human happiness and public good? The state has largely failed to achieve its own stated constitutional objectives and has become dysfunctional. The political process, which ought to provide solutions to these crises, has become a major problem in itself and has added to the woes of the people. Economic liberalisation, which is desirable and long overdue, cannot by itself bring about the desired change and may, in fact, be halted by an unaccountable rogue state. If such a crisis is allowed unhindered, there are obviously grave dangers to civil society.

Dangers to Civil Society

First, there is increasing lawlessness and anarchy in most parts of the country. As all governance structures fail, the citizen is no longer sure that the state can meet its obligations in any sphere. The all-pervasive corruption, harassment, delays, inability of the courts to render justice in time, the complexity of our administrative system that makes it wholly unintelligible to hapless citizens, the frequent breakdown of public order and increasing insecurity—are all manifestations of this anarchy. Already, there are several pockets in the country where life is no longer predictable. Justice, human rights, freedom and public services of high quality are all remote concepts that have no relevance to the day-to-day life of ordinary citizens.

The second danger ahead of us is the possibility of despotism by invitation. As the propertied and educated middle and upper classes, which have a great stake in peace and order, become increasingly disenchanted with the governance process, they are coming to the dangerous conclusion that freedom and democracy are synonymous with chaos and anarchy. Most of the urban middle classes have already become votaries of some form of authoritarianism that can bring order and peace, at whatever cost, so that they can pursue economic growth unhindered. In this milieu, the threat of dictatorship does not lie in a possible coup d'etat but may creep into the system with the acquiescence of the middle and upper classes—the political class, the bureaucracy, the armed forces, the police, the professionals and the business class. In their desperate quest for order, they have little understanding of the nature of dictatorship or its limitations, and the lessons of history are all too readily forgotten. Setting aside the fact that freedom and democracy are the inalienable birthright of every citizen, there is no possibility of a centralised, despotic regime succeeding any better than a dysfunctional democracy. If, by some modern electronic marvel, the centralised regime does find the means of governing our vast and complicated polity, there is no reason why ordinary people, who have no real stake in order for its own sake, should give up freedom and adult franchise, which are the only elements that lend dignity to their impoverished lives. The rejection of despotism by the poor and the deprived is bound to result in massive upheaval and bloodshed, leaving society vulnerable to even greater chaos and disorder. As a wise man said, while the capacity of man for justice makes democracy possible, the propensity of man for injustice makes democracy necessary. Morally or pragmatically, there is no substitute for democracy.

Any effort to the contrary is not only doomed to failure, but will also drive the nation to disaster.

The third grave danger threatening the nation is the spectre of Balkanisation. As authority and order break down, and as the governance apparatus fails to serve its main purpose of maintaining public order and ensuring cohesion and harmony in society, disintegration becomes inevitable. As the centralised and inert polity proves incapable of reform, many thinking persons, daunted by the vastness of the nation, its incredible plurality and the complexity of problems, may be compelled to conclude that only way to bring about reform that would strengthen democracy and fulfil people's aspirations is to break up the country. In addition, the economic liberalisation process itself may exacerbate this latent tendency towards Balkanisation. As some regions and States respond more positively to growth impulses, and have a better social and economic base to enlist mass participation in the production process, they will be far ahead of the rest of the country. The disparity between, say, 12 per cent annual growth rate in one region and 2 per cent growth rate in another, may not at first appear to be dramatic, but within a decade it will be very great. If both regions start at the same level of GDP per capita, the faster-growing region will have two-and-a-half times the GDP per capita at stable population. If the faster-growing region already has double the GDP per capita, then the disparity will be five times. Such disparities among regions are unsustainable in a democratic society. The resultant mass migration from the poorer regions to the more prosperous areas in an already overpopulated country will wreak untold havoc and suffering. The ensuing social strife will inevitably led to the erosion of barriers against entry and eventually to Balkanisation.

People's Sovereignty and Collective Assertion

The answer to this enveloping governance crisis has to lie with civil society itself. In any democracy, it is the universally accepted norm that people are the ultimate sovereigns and the government is elected, with officials appointed as public servants to provide governance on behalf of the people, who are their true masters. Every government functionary, whether elected or appointed, from the president of the republic to the lowest-paid employee in the neighbourhood is paid by the state exchequer and therefore accountable to the public. The Constitution itself is a creature of the collective will of the people. When the state becomes dysfunctional with grievous consequences, the people always reserve the right to take action. In fact, it is the duty of all citizens to exercise constant vigil over the functioning of their servants and institute mechanisms to ensure more effective and harmonious functioning of the state's institutions. Collective and informed assertion on a day-to-day basis in matters relating to all public services at the local and community levels is the most elementary duty of the citizen. Even mandatory services, such as getting a residential certificate, enrolling the name of a citizen as a voter, obtaining a driving licence or getting a land sale registered, involve delay, corruption, inefficiency, hostility, apathy and harassment, causing humiliation and indignity to most citizens on a daily basis. The frequent changes of government have made no real difference over the years. However, at the local level, collective and informed assertion by citizens will significantly improve the quality of public services even within the existing rules. Individuals are too weak and isolated to fight effectively and can be victimised and harassed by rogue functionaries of the state. But assertion without precise knowledge of the way public services are supposed to be delivered will have little positive outcome. Mendicancy and parasitism will only convert citizens into subjects seeking alms from the almighty state. Assertion of public will in a peaceful and democratic way is therefore necessary.

Everywhere we have innocent citizens who are afraid of police constables, people who cannot gain access to a government office without a bribe, parents who cannot get a decent education for their children in government schools, consumers who cannot get provisions in ration shops, citizens who cannot vote freely, children who have no access to immunisation even in health centres, farmers who cannot sell their products at fair market prices, commuters who cannot reach their destination on time, public utilities that overprice services, and litigants who cannot get justice for years. In such a milieu, democracy becomes a meaningless concept and governance becomes constitutional brigandage. Arrogant governments and inefficient public servants imperil our freedom and self-governance becomes a mockery if citizens remain passive spectators of the misdeeds and inefficiency of those who are paid to serve them. Empowerment of citizens and stakeholders is key to improving the quality of our public services. Public servants should be constantly aware that the real power vests in the people and that they are merely functionaries who serve them. When citizens are marginalised and kept in the dark, unfettered discretion, arbitrariness, favouritism and partisanship become the norm. Only alert and active citizens can establish the rule of law. An informed citizenry is the basis of a successful democracy. It is only through constant assertion by alert citizens that we can improve the nature of our government and the quality of public services. A citizen seeking a public service to which he is entitled is not a supplicant begging for alms; he is the master asserting his right and making the servant accountable.

Instruments of Accountability and Participation

However, in the absence of effective instruments to promote transparency and accountability, mere informed public assertion at the local level is not enough. Information on matters of governance, citizens' charters codifying standards of performance in public services and establishing systems of accountability, empowerment of local governments in order to establish a clear, intelligible and well-defined relationship between the vote and welfare of citizens and between taxes and public services, and measures for achieving speedy justice at the local level, are all instruments that can be put in place within the existing constitutional framework at the State and local level. While governments have paid occasional lip service to these measures, there has been no serious effort to build enduring institutions to serve the public cause and make governance accountable. Citizens' initiatives and people's movements ought to focus on all these specific, practical, measurable and broadly acceptable institutional mechanisms and force elected governments to respond to their demands, both at the local and State level. Unless such well-defined and universally acceptable measures are identified and public opinion mobilised, no government is likely to initiate tangible or enduring action to empower citizens and make itself accountable to them.

But until opportunities to effectively participate in the political process are provided, all these instruments will remain inadequate. Political parties, which now function as closed oligarchies and personal fiefdoms, should be comprehensively reformed. Free, open and non-arbitrary membership; regular, free and fair elections within the party; complete transparency and accountability with strict disclosure norms on all matters relating to funding and its utilisation and swift penalties for their violation; and democratic choice of party candidates for elective public office through secret ballot are necessary preconditions for effective political participation by citizens. Democratisation of the political parties should be accompanied by comprehensive electoral reforms to make elections genuinely free and fair, and to enable public opinion to be translated into legislative presence. Simple procedural reforms will ensure that electoral rolls are accurate and up-to-date. For instance, if citizen-friendly institutions like post offices become nodal agencies for making available electoral rolls and for filing applications for inclusion or deletion of names, there will be significant improvement in the electoral process. Given the serious flaws in electoral rolls and the absence of voter identity cards, large-scale impersonation, rigging and booth capturing have become the norm in many pockets of India. Muscle-power and criminal elements have begun to increasingly dominate political activity. Simultaneous efforts to curb persons with a criminal record from contesting are therefore vital to ensure a healthy interface between politics and civil society. Reforms to ensure accountable and transparent use money in elections are equally critical for improving the health of our polity.

Citizen activism is necessary to closely monitor the election process and exercise vigil over the functioning of political parties and the conduct of elections. Such an Election Watch movement is essential for two reasons. First, the distortion and perversion of political parties and the electoral process have become the biggest stumbling block to governance reforms in India. Second, during elections, people's minds are sharply focused on issues related to governance and it will be relatively easy to spread public awareness about the failure of the existing governance structure and the specific reforms needed. For instance, electoral rolls are notoriously flawed all over the country and the names of eligible voters are often missing; on the other hand, names of those who are ineligible or not residing in the locality, or even dead or fictitious persons, find a place in the voters' lists. Voter identity cards have not been made available to the citizens despite an expenditure of Rs 1,000 crore (10 billion), and such identity cards have not yet been made mandatory in the exercise of franchise. As a result, massive rigging by impersonation, booth capturing and various other malpractices have become common, making a mockery of democracy. Notorious criminals and rapaciously corrupt persons are nominated as candidates for public office with impunity. Voters thus have no real choice in elections, and no matter which party wins, people always end up as losers. Public discourse is distorted at all times and during election campaigns there is hardly any worthwhile debate on issues affecting citizens' lives. Strong, non-partisan and credible people's movements can play a vital role in mobilising public support for cleaner and fairer elections and in forcing parties and candidates to respond to people's demands.

Perhaps the most vital requirement for active citizenship is a high level of literacy and access to basic amenities like sanitation to uphold the dignity of citizens. The example of Tamil Nadu shows how sensible, strategic initiatives can make a significant impact on literacy. Similarly, we need a great people's initiative like the sanitation movement of the 1840s in Britain, backed by strong government support and commitment of resources. Illiterate people, who are denied the basic dignity of privacy of sanitation, cannot be expected to understand fundamental duties or assert their fundamental rights.

Undermining Democracy

One question still remains to be answered. If the state is but one, though vital, institution in society, is it not unrealistic to expect it to resolve our many social dilemmas? Doesn't such an unbalanced view of state-society relations end up placing disproportionate emphasis on state-driven changes? While the governance process should fulfil the minimum preconditions for civic participation, many of the obstacles are social and not necessarily political. From the 1830s to the 1940s, social reform movements were engineered by several liberal intellectuals and crusaders. In fact, many of our great national leaders effortlessly integrated the national struggle for independence with social reform effort. Narayana Guru, Jyotiba Phule, Vidyasagar, Rammohan Roy, Dayanand Saraswati, Veeresanlingam Pantulu, Mahatma Gandhi, Babasaheb Amedkar and several other stalwarts regarded social reform as the end and political power as merely one of the means to achieve it. Sadly, with the advent of freedom, there has been no serious or concerted effort to change social attitudes and promote a democratic culture in society.

There is much that is good in our culture and tradition. The strength of the family as an enduring social institution, the communitarian spirit that still pervades most of our rural society, the sense of right and wrong that informs most human conduct, the natural assimilation, eclecticism and syncretism dominant in our ethos, and the remarkable capacity for adjustment, coexistence and contentment are some of our strengths as a society. However, there are several societal flaws that undermine our democracy. In the words of an Indophile, Dr Carolyn Elliot, they can be summed up as an absence of a sense of equality, trust and common fate.[6] Most Indians instinctively accept and perpetuate distinctions on account of birth, caste, wealth, power and occupation. That all human beings are entitled to equal dignity and that all productive work to fulfil society's needs have the same value are not part of our belief system and worldview. This can only be corrected by movements within civil society; political institutions and laws can at best be useful adjuncts. In Myron Weiner's words, the 'psychology of caste' still dominates the thinking of most Indians (Weiner 1991).

Second, the educated and better-off sections of society instinctively reject the notion that all citizens have the capacity for self-governance. Even elected politicians and paid public servants harbour great mistrust about the ordinary citizens' capacity to decide what is best for them. There is an unspoken assumption that people need to be told what to do and that they cannot be trusted with power. The resistance to genuine local self-governance and people's empowerment is the most visible manifestation of this mistrust. The edifice of a sound democracy can be built only on the strong foundation of trust and faith in the unalienable right to self-governance and the intrinsic capacity of the common people to achieve uncommon goals.

Finally, the sense of a common fate, which is so vital to bind people together in an orderly society, is missing in us. As former President Narayanan aptly said during his Republic Day address to the nation:[7]

We ignore the social dimension of our actions and practices. The late Dr Adiseshaiah, one of our prominent economists and academicians, wrote about his mother that she was a highborn lady who kept her house spotlessly clean. Every morning she used to sweep and clean the household herself and then dump the rubbish in the neighbour's garden. Self-regarding purity and righteousness ignoring others has been the bane of our culture. It has created a gulf in our society between people even with regard to basic needs and fundamental rights.

A civilised society can be sustained only if citizens recognise that rights and duties coexist and that in fact, one's rights translate as the duties of others and vice versa. Individual behaviour in our society is often detrimental to collective happiness. The impunity with which people jump queues, the frightening violation of traffic rules, and the habitual spitting on the streets and littering are but a few random examples of such socially debilitating behaviour. This ugly social trait, combined with governmental apathy, ensures that unfulfilled potential and avoidable suffering continue to persist.

The social attitudes of the governing classes and their unceasing efforts to perpetuate the rigid social hierarchies are abundantly in evidence in our daily life. One of the chief concerns of the average, urban, middle-class housewife is her child's admission to a prestigious, private, English-medium school, or her inability to get cheap domestic help, preferably a child worker. R.K. Laxman illustrated this mindset superbly in a cartoon that shows two boys, one healthy and dressed in a school uniform standing erect, and the other weak and ill-clad groaning under the weight of a load of books. The mother of the school-going child tells her friend: 'It's really cruel burdening the kids like this! I had to hire that boy to help my son!' Instead of empowering the poor and improving their skills through quality school education, our democratic process has instead perpetuated social hierarchies by allowing the elites to retain control, divorcing the stakeholders from power.

A related social malaise is the excessive obsession with the immediate family and progeny, with little care or concern for public good. Great democracies are built as much with individual efforts to build social capital as through enduring and wise institutions of the state. The sanitation movement in Britain in the nineteenth century, the great universities, public libraries, museums and parks built through the support of far-sighted individuals and foundations in the United States are examples of civil society initiatives to promote public good. The great North American universities of Harvard, Yale, Carnegie Mellon, Johns Hopkins, Cornell, Vanderbilt, Stanford, McGill, Duke, the Illinois Institute of Technology and Vassar College were built through private charities. Great institutions like the Smithsonian Museum and Brooklyn's Institute were funded entirely privately. Several private foundations assiduously promote public causes, those commemorating Ford, Kellogg, Rockefeller, Mellon, Carnegie and Kresge being among the better known. Many hospitals, public parks and other public goods have also been privately funded. Recently, Bill Gates' effort to help eradicate preventable disease from the globe is a good illustration of the ease with which private wealth is utilised for public gain. The privileged classes in India have not yet recognised that they owe much of their wealth and success to society.

All these social attitudes can only be altered and improved through civil society measures. The state can at best play a supportive role by creating a system of high reward and low risk for desirable behaviour and high risk and no reward for unacceptable behaviour. Sadly, over the past five decades, civil society's initiative in this regard has been stifled by the all-pervasive state. Society as a whole needs to come to terms with this serious deficiency and counter it through the propagation of socially desirable behaviour and the promotion of people's initiatives for creating social good.

It must be understood, however, that society and state are in constant flux. Both interact with and alter each other in a fundamental way. That civil society shapes the nature of the state as profoundly as constitutions and laws is undeniable and widely accepted. But what is not clearly recognised is that the nature of the state has a profound and often lasting impact on society. The loosening of caste hierarchies and the widespread, if inadequate, notion of equality in society is largely a product of the political process and the state structure that guarantees universal adult franchise, equality before the law and fundamental rights irrespective of birth and status. The liberal-democratic state created by the American founding fathers did not at first recognise women and blacks as equal citizens. However, the ideals of the American state inevitably came into conflict with unjust institutions and ugly practices over a period of time. This led to a civil war in the 1860s, resulting in massive bloodshed. About 10 per cent of the American population died in the effort to liberate the blacks and give them a vote. Similarly, the democratic ideals and institutions could not for long accept denial of voting rights to women, and in the 1920s the struggle of women suffragettes bore fruit. The 1960s civil rights movement led by Martin Luther King was largely a result of the ideals of the state and legal structures coming into conflict with the social rigidities of the southern States. Ultimately, society had to yield and things were never the same again.

In other words, a modern, liberal, state based on the doctrines of human rights and universal franchise, people's sovereignty and the rule of law is bound to come into conflict with traditional social rigidities, undemocratic practices, irrational prejudices and shameful hierarchies. But for such conflict to arise and lead to social transformation, the fundamental requirements of a democratic state need to be fulfilled. For instance, if the state does not create conditions for the free and fair exercise of universal franchise through proper voter registration and identity cards, it will end up promoting polling irregularities and promoting feudal power. Similarly, if there is no transparency in governance and no instruments of accountability at the citizens' disposal, democracy will become ineffective in checking the abuse of authority and will end up perpetuating the hold of traditional power brokers on state and society. If the process of power is highly centralised, then people will never understand the link between their vote and public good: democracy will be hijacked by moneybags and musclemen, again perpetuating the dominance of the rich and powerful.

While the republic of India, founded in 1950, has been informed by modern, liberal and humane values, the institutions and practices have often been illiberal and inherently undemocratic. Without the reform of these institutions and practices, and the correction of the many aberrations that have crept in, democracy has been reduced to winning a plurality of vote in a flawed election process and the exercise of unaccountable and arbitrary authority over the lives of citizens. A state that cannot enforce the rule of law leads to an unjust and anarchic society. In effect, a flawed democratic process tends to accentuate social rigidities instead of modernising society. As a result, the modern, liberal, democratic state, which ought to be a significant part of the solution to society's maladies, has itself become a part of the problem. That is why the influence of the state has been emphasised in this chapter. There has to be concerted effort to make the state an effective and just instrument of social transformation, even as society has to be made more conducive and fertile for the flowering of a genuine democracy. The modern state has a great role in shaping society, just as civil society has a seminal role in democratising the state. In order to achieve both these goals, we need active citizenship and social movements for reform. In a democracy, citizens cannot be delinked from society or vice versa. Collective and informed citizen assertion is the key to the transformation of both the state and society.

Concern to Concerted Action

No one can seriously dispute the need for citizen assertion, but sceptics may wonder whether such a national effort for governance reforms is possible. However, there is deep distrust and resentment at the failure and paralysis of governance in the country. Millions of Indians, from Kashmir to Kanyakumari, and from Guwahati to Ganganagar, are yearning for fundamental reforms heralding better governance. Sadly, this concern is dissipated as no concerted attempt is made to capture and channel it into a creative national endeavour. Recent history in Eastern Europe has shown us that when there is widespread and deep dissatisfaction with a governing process, its cumulative impact will eventually trigger cataclysmic changes. If institutions, people's initiatives and ideas are in place to seize the moment, then a relatively peaceful and painless transformation for better governance is possible, as evidenced in Germany. If, however, no concerted and timely effort is made to constructively channel people's anger and yearning, then the results could be devastating, as the plight of the erstwhile Soviet Union amply testifies. In many ways, Indians are ready for the rejuvenation of their republic and the transformation of its governance structure.

Is Stability the Answer?

Those who believe that political stability is the answer to this crisis are forgetting the lessons of the past 50 years. For about 46 years after the transfer of power, we had a stable, single-party rule in India with only five prime ministers. Of these, three were from a single family and they presided over our destiny for nearly 40 years. Such extraordinary stability did not help us realise our potential as a nation, nor did it promote human dignity and happiness any more than the remaining period of instability. Undoubtedly, stability of governments and smooth and predictable policy changes are necessary for good governance. However, mere stability is no substitute for good governance and accountability, or for people's empowerment. In fact, long periods of instability in a democracy may actually lead to major reforms, as evidenced by the collapse

of the Fourth Republic in France in 1958. The Indian experience shows that major policy shifts and reforms are often
engineered more by compulsion than by conviction. The failure to dismantle even the most obnoxious and counterproduc-
tive elements of licence-permit raj until the nation was in
danger of default and perilous economic ruin is an example
of such criminal inertia. Similarly, there is no evidence to
suggest that the governing classes will herald political and
governance reform in periods of stability. Major reform is
more likely to be initiated when the status quo is unsustainable. If the average politician has a stable tenure to recover
in multiples the 'investment' made during elections, he has no
real incentive to change the rules of the game.

Window of Opportunity

Many people wonder whether the leviathan of the Indian governance structure can ever be transformed to promote human
happiness to the fullest measure. It is undeniable that our society
and state suffer from great inertia and seeming resistance to
enduring change. However, great societies often undergo dramatic changes through the compulsion of circumstances. The
increasing fiscal imbalance in governments at all levels, with the
combined fiscal deficit of the Union and the States exceeding
10 per cent of GDP, is no longer sustainable. At the same time,
the situation can only be improved through wise, far-sighted and
resolute action. Miracles do not happen of their own accord;
they must be made to happen. Our highly centralised, unaccountable governance structure and the political culture that
militates against integrity in public life have made the status quo
unsustainable. Only when citizens become the centre of the
democratic universe can this crisis be adequately addressed. In
a way, the fiscal crisis provides the nation a priceless opportunity
to reform the polity and governance and enhance the capacity
of civil society to assert its sovereignty.

The persistent political instability, the impending fiscal collapse of governments at all levels, the unsatisfactory economic growth on account of infrastructure bottlenecks and governance failure, the expectations raised by irresponsible rhetoric and competitive populism, satellite television, the breakdown of the rule of law and public order, rising political and social conflicts because of the rapid and uneven growth of population, and the death of ideology and conversion of political parties into cynical instruments of the power game—all presage fundamental changes in civil society. If this challenge is accepted by civil society and the crisis is converted into an opportunity, then fundamental governance reform is within our grasp.

There is nothing intractable or immutable about our governance crisis. As mentioned earlier, there are enough strengths in our society to see us through these difficult times. The institution of the family, the spirit of tolerance and accommodation most Indians instinctively embrace, the sense of dharma that informs various actions of countless people, and the strong influence of society on individual behaviour are all positive forces that can be creatively applied to mobilise civil society. The governance system should provide civil society the space to act by creating an enabling environment. Meaningful political and electoral reforms to facilitate active citizen participation and intervention, strategic interventions to facilitate universal literacy, speedy programmes to provide everyone access to sanitation, effective and genuine devolution of powers to local governments and stakeholders, and the creation of instruments of accountability such as the right to information and the citizens' charter are some of the minimum preconditions for active citizenship and assertion of popular sovereignty. The need of the hour is to rediscover the true meaning of Swaraj as explained by Mahatma Gandhi in his simple yet remarkable and inimitable style:[8]

I will give you talisman. Whenever you are in doubt or when the self becomes too much with you, apply the following test:

Recall the face of the poorest and weakest man whom you may have seen and ask yourself if the step you contemplate is going to be of any use to him. Will he gain anything by it? Will it restore him to a control over his own life and destiny? In other words, will it lead to Swaraj for the hungry and spiritually starving millions?

Then you will find your doubts and your self melting away.

The task is difficult but vital. The struggle is hard but necessary. The risks are high but cannot be avoided. The effort will demand all our courage, resourcefulness and endurance. As someone said with great prescience, there is nothing more powerful than an idea whose time has come. This is the time for holistic reform of our governance structure and for building a strong, democratic, self-governing India, all of whose citizens enjoy peace, freedom and harmony. *History beckons us.*

Notes

1. This paper draws heavily from the author's paper accepted for publication in the compilation 'The Citizen and the State' as part of the study of political reforms by the Centre for Policy Research.
2. The word 'state' is used here in its juridical sense, and 'State' denotes a province of the Indian Union.
3. Available on http://www.sacred-texts.com/hin/tagore.htm
4. See http://www.madwed.com
5. As the estimates are tentative, the name of the state has not been provided.
6. Dr Carolyn Elliot, Former Director, Indo-American Centre for International Studies (IACIS), Hyderabad (1997–99). The statement was made in a personal conversation.
7. Address to the nation by K.R. Narayanan, the former President of India on the eve of the Republic Day—2000 available on http://presidentofindia.nic.in/S/html/krn/speeches/republic/jan25_2000.htm
8. See http://www.mkgandhi-sarvodaya.org/gandhi's_talisman.htm

4

Civil Society and the Goal of Good Governance

T.K. Oommen

Civil society is a concept that enjoys wide currency in our times and yet there is no consensus even among theorists about its meaning. In its first incarnation, civil society only alluded to civilised societies. Thus the anthropologist Richard Puttenham contrasted civil society in Europe with savage societies in the recently discovered New World in 1589, where in men were dispersed like wild beasts, lawless and naked. Seventy-five years later, in 1664, Hobbes published *Leviathan*, which may be considered the political counterpart to Puttenham's anthropological discourse. A hundred years after the publication of *Leviathan*, in 1766 Adam Ferguson, qualified by some as the father of modern sociology, wrote *An Essay on the History of Civil Society*, in which he argued that Europe had already attained civility, the most exalted position in the assumed hierarchy of societies. That is, in all these discourses, civil society as a totality occupied the highest position among the variety of societies.

In the second incarnation of civil society one can identify two intellectual genealogies: the works of Hegel, Karl Marx and Antonio Gramsci on the one hand and the Franco-Scottish school on the other, with Tocqueville as the central figure. However, while there is no uniformity of conceptualisations *within* these genealogies, the similarities between them are considerable. Juxtaposing the universal altruism of the state with the universal egoism of civil society, Hegel wanted civil society to be subordinated to the state. In contrast, Marx wanted the state, which can turn tyrannical, to be subordinated to civil society. But civil society can also be a site for crass materialism and Marx did not absolve it of this blemish. Part of the problem with the Marxian conceptualisation lies with the unwarranted hope that the state will wither away and its tendency to equate civil society with the capitalist mode of production (Cohen 1982).

Gramsci's conceptualisation of civil society goes beyond the economic context. Further, he locates civil society not in the structural but in the superstructural sphere. However, the precision Gramsci achieved in the definition of civil society is lost in his all-embracing definition of the state. The incorporation of civil society into the state robs the state of its legal specificity and autonomy, and civil society of its real purpose, namely, functioning as a countervailing power to the state if and when required. Alexis de Tocqueville (1956), too, juxtaposes the state with civil society, the latter being the theatre of private interest and economic activity. Further, what are designated as civil society, both by Marx (the site of crass materialism) and Tocqueville (the theatre of private interest and economic activity) are actually market forces. Thus the specificity of the two genealogies is lost. And herein lies the advantage of viewing what Tocqueville labels 'political society' as civil society.

Civil society, according to Tocqueville, is the protector of individuals from the tyrannical state. That is, if the state is democratic, we don't need civil society. For Gramsci, civil society is the protector of the state. This means that in a 'good society', the two merge. If, in Tocqueville's view, civil society is anti-state, in Gramsci's view it is pro-state. According to both, civil society has a democratic role. However, there is some confusion here between a space and its quality. I suggest that civil society ought to be viewed as a space between the state and the market; the quality of that space is another matter. Just like a state can be authoritarian or democratic, civil society, too, may have such differing orientations or may have such segments within it. Such a view may be considered as the third incarnation of civil society (Oommen 1996: 191–202).

Conventionally, the leviathan of the state was juxtaposed with civil society, which encapsulated the market. But latterly, the market has emerged as a behemoth, often challenging the authority of the state. As is well known, one indicator of modernisation is structural differentiation. Today, the three most important players are state, civil society and the market, and each of them is fiercely asserting its respective autonomy. In fact, 'good society' is now being viewed as one in which these spheres are progressively and increasingly becoming more and more autonomous. So much so that Cohen and Arato refer to civil society as a 'third realm', differentiated from the economy and the state. According to them, civil society consists of:

1. Plurality: families, informal groups and voluntary associations whose plurality and autonomy allow for a variety of forms of life;
2. Publicity: institutions of culture and communication;
·3. Privacy: a domain of individual self-development and moral choice;
4. Legality: structures of general laws and basic rights needed to demarcate plurality, privacy and publicity from at the least the state and, tendentially, the economy (1992: 346).

A few points need to be noted here. First, the autonomy of the three sectors—state, market and civil society—does not invest them with autarchy. Second, autonomy does not necessarily erode reciprocity. Third, the boundary demarcation between these spheres does not mean that they do not overlap or interpenetrate. Fourth, there is a division of labour between these spheres. And finally, it is a balance between the three spheres that makes for a 'good society'.

Let me turn to the notion of good governance. This has become a buzzword in the contemporary political lexicon; indeed, it is a ruling idea. Its intellectual origins lie in liberal theory, which views conservative governments and organised business interests in unison. Here, there is a collaboration between state and market interests. The idea is propelled and propagated by the Bretton Woods institutions—the World Bank, the IMF and the WTO. However, this is not a reason to reject the idea. The notion of good governance is a logical extension of the Structural Adjustment Programme (SAP). Its aim is to complement SAP by political reforms to achieve greater accountability, transparency and efficiency in public service along with the protection of civil and human rights, and to ensure the rule of law through an independent judiciary. As Rosenau says:

> ... governance is not synonymous with government. Both refer to purposive behavior, to goal oriented activities, to systems of rule; but government suggests activities that are backed by formal authority, by police powers to ensure the implementation of duly constituted policies, whereas governance refers to activities backed by shared goals that may not derive from legal and formally prescribed responsibilities and not necessarily rely on police powers to overcome defiance and attain compliance. Governance, in other words, is a more encompassing phenomenon than government. It embraces governmental institutions, but it also subsumes informal, non-governmental mechanisms whereby those persons and organizations within its purview move ahead, satisfy their needs and fulfill their wants (1992: 4).

That is, governance encapsulates government but it also goes beyond and encompasses non-governmental mechanisms to meet the needs, wants and aspirations of citizens. Which is to say that the state and civil society are co-responsible for citizen welfare. This view recasts the civil society–state relationship from its earlier confrontational orientation into a cooperative engagement. Further, good governance as an idea should be rescued from being monopolised by the collaboration between the state and market and used for their exclusive advantage.

Generally speaking, the state is intended to focus on citizens; the market is primarily concerned with customers and civil society's engagement is with communitarians—members of a community who come together to solve problems. I suggest that good governance should be viewed as a conjoined effort of the citizen, the market and civil society. Its aim should be to transcend state-centrism, moderate the rapacity of the market and exorcise extremist orientations from civil society.

I

Against the backdrop of these conceptual clarifications, we can now turn to the four prerequisites of good governance with special reference to India. These are: (*a*) informing the process of recruiting the ruling elite with legitimacy; (*b*) facilitating proportionate representation for all segments of population in governance; (*c*) ensuring respect for the dominated by the dominant; and (*d*) instituting a reward–punishment mechanism.

While direct democracy may be desirable, it can only be practised in the context of local self-governments, that is, in city corporations, town municipalities and village panchayats. But even at this level, it is confronted with two limitations. The first is the limited availability of expertise and knowledge in regard to certain sectors within the locality. The second is practical difficulties in involving all adults in the decision-making process on a regular basis. Which is to say, both representative democracy and delegation of decision-making authority will come to obtain even at the level of local self-governments. Herein lies the importance of endowing the governing elite with adequate legitimacy.

From its inception, the Indian national state has acknowledged the importance of universal adult franchise. It has also instituted appropriate and adequate machinery that is endowed with constitutional authority and autonomy to conduct periodic elections—the Election Commission. While it cannot be claimed that elections have always been 'free and fair' in independent India, it may be asserted without fear of contradiction that they have become increasingly so over a period of time. The press and the electronic media have played an active role in rendering the election process in India a relatively 'free' enterprise.

The weak spot in Indian elections has been their funding. Contesting candidates are not funded by the state; and the tradition of active involvement by citizens in generating election funds is not sufficiently strong. Consequently, Indian elections are funded by mainly private corporations—the institutions of the market—not as altruistic acts to sustain a clean democracy but as investment from which ample pay-offs are expected, particularly from the winning candidates and party once they form the government. This, in turn, means that candidates' entry into and sustenance in politics is substantially influenced by their ability to fund elections. And since, as has just been pointed out, the source of funding is more often than not the market institutions, it necessitates an alliance between the government (party/parties in power) and the market forces. This is the seedbed of much of the corruption in India and civil society can play a crucial role in minimising, if not eliminating, the corruption emanating from this source.

As state funding of elections is not the norm, the relevant institutions of civil society should be actively engaged in the mobilisation of such funds. Further, voluntary donations of corporate houses to political parties should be made transparent so that the possible linkages between them are known to all concerned. In India, as of now, the visibility of election funds is extremely low. If the recruitment process of the ruling elite, particularly the lawmakers, is not transparent, corruption is bound to seep in. A vigilant civil society should act as a watchdog in this context, thereby contributing to good governance.

In a democracy, those who govern should be drawn more or less proportionately from different segments of the population. This does not happen in India. In our four-tier government structure—panchayats, *zilla parishads*, state assemblies, parliaments—women are 'adequately' represented only at the first two levels and that, too, because of the 73rd Constitutional Amendment. One-third representation by women is considered 'adequate', even though they constitute half of India's population. At the parliamentary level, all attempts to pass a legislation providing women with even 33 per cent representation have remained unsuccessful to this day. To complicate matters, most political parties, in spite of their promises, have not fielded the requisite number of women candidates. Although a section of civil society is largely supportive of this measure towards gender justice, the idea has not yet gained wide acceptance.

The problem of representation in legislatures is largely met in regard to Scheduled Castes (SCs) and Scheduled Tribes (STs) through the policy of reservation. As for Other Backward Classes (OBCs), their numerical superiority, reckoned at 50 to 60 per cent of the population, ensures their representation in legislative bodies thanks to universal adult franchise, although it took a few decades for even this to happen. While the OBCs are gaining a decisive dominance in numerical terms, in most State Assemblies and in Parliament, those who occupy top political positions (ministers, governors, etc.) are disproportionately drawn from the twice-born caste groups—Brahmins, Kshatriyas and Vaishyas. The most powerless and under-represented category in legislatures is the religious minorities, which are either numerically negligible (e.g.,

Buddhists, Bahais, Jains, Jews and Zoroastrians) or socio-culturally stigmatised (the Christians and Muslims). The fact that although the vast majority of the latter two categories are converts from SCs or OBCs, their being deprived of the benefit of protective discrimination renders their representation grossly inadequate in terms of their numerical strength. To conclude, women and religious minorities are not adequately represented in our legislative bodies, which is serious lacuna in initiating good governance.

This under-representation is not simply a democratic deficit but also an experiential deficit. The legislative process requires taking into account all the relevant experiences of the diverse social categories in a society. The representation in the executive wing of the state, too, is very skewed in terms of the social bases of the Indian population. Once again, while those who are eligible for protective discrimination (SCs and STs) have a notable presence and those who are traditionally privileged (upper caste men) are over-represented, others are grossly under-represented. For example, women, who comprise about 50 per cent of the population, constitute only 7 per cent; Muslims, who comprise 12 per cent, constitute only 2.1 per cent; and the OBCs, with almost 60 per cent share of the population, comprise only 2 per cent of the Indian Administrative Service (IAS). In contrast, Brahmins, who constitute only 5 to 7 per cent of the population, are grossly over-represented in the IAS with 37.7 per cent (Goyal 1992: 125–30). Once cannot speak of good governance when the distribution of those who are responsible for implementing the laws of the land and the rules of government is so skewed across social categories.

A similar situation obtains with regard to the judiciary. Given the absence of protective discrimination, the higher echelons of the judiciary in India are monopolised by the traditionally privileged upper caste males. Women, SCs, STs, OBCs and religious minorities are all under-represented. That the judiciary, too, reflects the same skewed representation of social categories does not augur well for good governance and is vehemently frowned upon by many. Civil society thus has a critical role to play in educating all concerned about the imperative need for the legislature, executive and judiciary to be fairly representative.

It is also necessary to remind ourselves of the importance of the representative character of knowledge producers and communicators. While knowledge can be creatively used to ameliorate or improve the human condition, it can also be deployed to maintain the status quo. To a certain extent, the differing uses of knowledge depend upon those who produce and communicate it. Feminists have often noted the negative role of patriarchy in producing knowledge and perpetuating attitudes and value orientations favourable to male dominance. This also applies to racial dominance.

In the case of India, the traditional hierarchical society had evolved an elaborate division of labour, which assigned production and diffusion of knowledge as the exclusive prerogative of Brahmins. This had enduring consequences as manifested by upper caste monopoly in most of the prestigious professions that required long pre-entry training usually imparted through family elders. With the institutionalisation and opening-up of modern education about a century ago, the situation is gradually changing. And yet, deep prejudices persist in regard to the unsuitability of women, lower castes and certain religious minorities to pursue certain occupations. The participation of individuals drawn from all segments of Indian society in the production and dissemination of knowledge is a prerequisite for an alert civil society and for institutionalising good governance (Oommen 1999).

The third prerequisite for good governance is respect for the dominated by the dominant. This is a requirement in all societies but particularly in those where the ethos of Social Darwinism persists in the name of merit. The cut-throat competition, which the maxim 'the survival of the fittest' fosters, is not conducive to developing a compassionate attitude towards the dominated when the majority of the population is adjudged to be congenitally inferior. This was the case in traditional

Indian hierarchical society, vestiges of which continue to persist with a vengeance. Systematic efforts are therefore needed to inculcate respect towards the dominated right from childhood. For this to happen, the curriculum in educational institutions, particularly in schools, will have to be suitably restructured.

No systematic effort has been made to foster respect for the dominated in India, although there is an attempt to accommodate some sections of them in different sectors of society. The policy of reservation initially introduced for SCs and STs, and later extended to the OBCs and women (at the Panchayati Raj level), is a step in this direction. But the introduction of this measure without creating the required value orientation has resulted in an attitudinal lag expressed through pejorative and contemptuous phrases such as 'Sarkari Brahmins', and 'Mandalisation'. These allude to persons (and processes) who presumably come to occupy positions without possessing the requisite merit. This is exactly the opposite of 'respect for the dominated'. Consequently, those who come to occupy positions through reservations end up being demoralised. Remedies for social injustice become intimations of intimidation. This creates enormous tension in civil society—often covert but occasionally overt. The manifestations of this tension also surface in the context of governance when persons with handicapped social backgrounds form their own specific associations, such as the Muslim Intellectual Forum, the Scheduled Caste Employees' Association or the Women's Guild.

The fourth imperative for good governance is instituting a reward–punishment mechanism. No society can function efficiently without ensuring rewards for conformity and achievement and punishment for deviance and failure. While material incentives invariably constitute an important item of reward, symbolic rewards can often substitute and reinforce them. In many societies, the occupations and professions that command high respect are not necessarily the highest paid and vice versa. Human beings yearn for recognition but there are different ways in which they seek to achieve this.

The corollary of rewards for conformity is punishment for deviance. Therefore, the system cannot ignore or be indifferent to those who do not conform to prescribed norms. Punishment to the deviant also works as a deterrent to potential deviants. But it may not be very productive to condemn deviants instantly; it is necessary to provide them with opportunities to reform. If some of them do change, it will have a demonstration effect on other deviants. Thus the reward–punishment mechanism should be viewed as an enabling device in the construction of civil society and in institutionalising good governance.

It is necessary here to make a distinction between two types of deviance: one is deviance from the existing normative pattern resulting in social problems; the other manifests as protest which challenges the status quo and results in innovation. The latter type of deviance is also often resisted, condemned or even punished in the beginning but gradually, when its beneficial effects become known, the 'innovator-deviant' is applauded and rewarded. Similarly, conformity to some of the obsolescent norms (e.g., such practices as sati and dowry) invites punishment when abolished by law or through reform. Which is to say that the normative structure itself is an evolving one and good governance requires that the direction of change be channelled in favour of the deprived and towards social justice. Civil society can and should play a very vital role in facilitating social transformation in the desired direction. Thus, the link between good governance (read governance that brings about social justice) and civil society (which should facilitate the process) is organic.

It could be argued by some that the four prerequisites for good governance are not mutually consistent; in fact they are contradictory. For example, both proportionate representation in the legislature, executive and judiciary and respect for the dominated could be seen as undermining merit. But in a society where inequality has been legitimised and institutionalised for centuries, to insist on merit is to promote a perverse elitism legitimising traditional privileges. Therefore to provide for protective discrimination in societies such as India is but to correct this traditional imbalance. At the same time, the process of protective discrimination is bound to produce an elite category from the traditionally underprivileged. Those who fall into this category shouldn't be allowed to perpetuate a new elitism that would undermine opportunities for the less privileged in the category. Fostering vested interest, be it of the traditional or the new elite, is antithetical to developing a civil society that can contribute to good governance. Good governance therefore requires that while the rights of the dominated and minority groups are recognised, they be not allowed to degenerate into vested interests. Once again, civil society can and should articulate this perspective without taking a partisan view. But this does not often happen because most interlocutors are afraid of the unpopularity that taking such a stand would almost certainly bring.

II

In order to ensure that good governance transcends good government, we need to create a balance between the state, market and civil society. The foundational flaw of the socialist state was the imbalance between these three actors. Civil society was abridged, if not abrogated, and the state became its inspirer. The market was encapsulated in the state through the command economy. In fact, the state became the sole effective actor in society. The welfare state attempted to balance the three entities but with the demise of the socialist state, the welfare state, too, has practically abandoned its social responsibility. The market has become not simply vibrant but rapacious. Civil society in increasingly articulate and audible, but both the state and market remain largely impervious to the sound and fury it produces.

Whether or not civil society in India contributes to good governance can only be discerned in terms of the goals to be achieved through good governance itself. These comprise reducing disparity, minimising discrimination and eliminating collective alienation.

The idea that the *degree of disparity* does not matter to the extent that the basic needs of the poorest are met, has been in vogue for quite some time (Aron 1970). During the Cold War era it was fashionable to compare the economic disparity that existed within the first and second world countries, putting those with less disparity on a higher moral pedestal. Thus Scandinavian countries, which attained considerable equality among their citizens, were viewed as morally superior as compared with other countries in the first world. The wage difference between the state employees in China was much less than between those in the Soviet Union, rendering the Chinese system more equalitarian hence morally superior than that of the Soviet Union. But reduction of disparity within polities is not pursued as a serious goal any more.

The notion of meritocracy legitimises the wide disparity between individuals and indirectly between groups. According to this perspective, if one is rich and well off, one deserves to be so. This view assumes that equality is only an instrument that provides individuals the opportunity to become unequal, the currently favoured phrase for which is 'level playing ground'. But a society that abandons the principle of distributive justice and latches onto meritocracy without taking into account the prevailing inequality in opportunity between groups cannot ever claim to have good governance. This is because good governance should produce a society that eschews discrimination of co-citizens based on age, gender, race, class, caste, religion and region. Good governance should evolve a society in which there is no extreme form of disparity; if disparity does exist, it should be well within the limits of tolerance.

Under extreme conditions of disparity, discrimination is likely to get institutionalised. And under conditions of institutionalised discrimination, the discriminated will feel alienated from the system. Thus disparity, discrimination and collective alienation feed on each other. The alienated will not have the urge to participate in the system because they will not have any stake in maintaining the system. The end product of good governance, then, ought to be a society from which the sources of discrimination and collective alienation have disappeared.

The three challenges—disparity, discrimination and collective alienation—constitute a hierarchy, the first being the most widespread and perhaps the least problematic, the third the most problematic and found only in a few societies, with the second, discrimination, falling in between. That is, disparity is almost ubiquitous. Even in 'successful' capitalist democracies (e.g., the USA) it is staggering. Its root cause is the lopsided emphasis given to political democracy while ignoring social and economic democracy. B.R. Ambedkar warned Indians of this monumental flaw in 1949: 'In politics we will be recognising the principle of one man one vote. In our social and economic life, we shall, by reason of our social and economic structure, continue to deny the principle of one man one value' (1969: 186–87). The reference to social structure refers to social discrimination and economic structure refers to economic disparity.

In India, disparity exists in a wide variety of contexts. Prominent among these are class, gender, rural-urban (Bharat versus India) and regional (BIMARU states versus the rest). The Indian rich have become richer and the disparity between the emerging middle class, the soul of new India, and the poor has widened in the past 50 years, even as the poor improved economically. While we have made tremendous progress in food production, millions go hungry even today. And even as we are proud of our achievements in science and technology, the shacks that pass for schools in urban slums and most of rural India can hardly provide the compulsory universal education promised in the Constitution. In 1993 there were 4,000 primary schools in rural India without teachers, and 26,000 primary schools without even one room each. Unless we urgently address this widening disparity, both discrimination and collective alienation will accelerate.

If disparity is widespread, discrimination is confined to specific contexts—gender, language, tribe and caste. Discrimination against women starts even before their birth as manifested in selective foetal abortion. When they are born, girl children are accorded grudging acceptance and then subjected to discrimination based on nutrition, clothing, education and freedom when they grow up. This amounts to discrimination against about 50 per cent of the Indian citizenry.

Discrimination against linguistic groups is more politico-economic than socio-cultural. It often manifests in domiciliary prescriptions introduced by the states and moblisations against outsiders—those who do not belong to the region—by the local population. The well-known cases of mobilisations against outsiders in the 1960s and 1970s were confined to some of the major cities and piloted by the Shiv Sena in Mumbai, the Kannada Chaluvaligar in Bangalore and the Lachchit Sena in Kolkata. However, latterly, the sons-of-the-soil mobilisations have become more regional, enveloping entire linguistic regions. But the entitlements that accompany single citizenship and the compulsions of the emerging free market are gradually containing the anti-outsider impulse. It needs to be underlined here that this is a potential source of disorder in several regions if local economic conditions deteriorate and the proportion of migrants exceed the acceptance level of the local population.

While anti-outsider sentiments manifest essentially as competition for economic opportunities, when they are combined with cultural and political rights, their potential for mobilisation becomes acute. Manifestations of this are particularly visible in the tribal belts of the North East. The typical reaction to these mobilisations of most people—be they bureaucrats, politicians, academics or journalists—is that they are 'secessionist' movements and hence inimical to the ongoing process of 'nation-building'. But if nation-building at the minimal level is to be understood as an effort to keep India as one entity, we need to have a more empathic understanding of these identity assertions. More often than not, what these 'secessionist' movements are demanding is nothing but the preservation of their cultural identity along with economic equality. Failure to recognise the texture of their aspiration is to nurture, however unwittingly, collective alienation.

There is yet another level of identity assertion manifesting in 'separatist' movements. The demands for Chhattisgarh, Jharkhand and Uttaranchal as separate states afford examples of this. These movements are accorded greater legitimacy as compared with 'secessionist' movements because they are only demands for autonomy within the Indian Union. But it is often forgotten that (*a*) the difference between the secessionist and separatist movements is only a matter of degree, and that (*b*) the difference in the movements' goals is often dictated by their respective geo-political location. The plausibility of encysted tribal communities of central India pursuing secessionism is indeed very low as compared with communities that live on interstate borders. In both cases, the discrimination experienced by these collectives has great potential for collective alienation (Oommen 1990).

If discrimination against women, linguistic communities and Adivasis is based on one or another dimension, discrimination against Dalits is multidimensional—economic, social, political and cultural. Domination over them is cumulative. The most visible sites of domination and discrimination against them are found in Bharat or rural India; and within Bharat, the BIMARU states, and among the latter, in Bihar. It is instructive to make a brief excursus into the recent violence against Dalits in Bihar, an extreme manifestation of discrimination against them.

The atrocities against the cumulatively deprived rural Dalits in Bihar are perpetrated by caste *senas*. In the last two decades (1979–99) there have been at least 10 *senas* operating in nine districts of Bihar. These are constituted mainly by OBCs (Kurmi, Yadav) or the upper castes (Rajput, Bhumihar). One of the *senas*, namely, the Ranvir Sena, led by Bhumihars has been involved in 20 massacres in the past five years resulting in some 300 murders. This chilling statistic is perhaps only the tip of the iceberg and indicates the rapacity of the violence that prevails in rural Bihar. Perhaps it is more pertinent to note that these massacres had nothing to do with rural transformation, but were simply intercaste revanchist eruptions. While by all accounts Bihar represents the worst case, violence in the rest of Bharat, particularly in the other BIMARU states, is not absent. This is an eloquent pointer to the pathology that prevails in India's civil society.

An important point to be noted here is that good governance is meaningless for these hapless victims of caste violence unless they are assured of the requisite physical and social security. The majority of Dalits cannot but feel totally alienated from society. On the other hand, drawing support from extremist political outfits that operate as vigilante organisations, Dalits have started wreaking vengeance against their upper and intermediate caste oppressors. The erstwhile *coercive equilibrium* that prevailed in rural India is being displaced by anomie and anarchy. The state, which should operate as an impartial and final arbiter, is totally invisible. In Bharat, even the hope of good governance remains in suspended animation.

There is wide disparity across states with regards to human development. The Human Development Index (HDI) combines expectation of life at birth, educational attainment and state domestic product per capita in a single index. On a 0 to 100 scale, the HDI for 1995 varied from 63 in Kerala to 34 in Bihar, the value for India being 45. Other BIMARU states have the following scores in the scale: Uttar Pradesh 36, Madhya Pradesh 37 and Rajasthan 38. The only other state with a score of less than 40 is Orissa.

The considerable disparity between the states that the HDI for 1995 discloses is discomforting. If an entity is to have a harmonious and healthy existence, its constituting units should be more or less equal. If the disparity between the units is very large, the less developed units are likely to feel alienated. Paradoxically, it is the political hegemon—the Hindi belt—that is developmentally backward in India. This is an uneasy situation.

So far, I have tried to indicate that both disparity and discrimination inevitably lead to alienation. But there is another source of alienation that operates independently of these sources. Although Dalits are subjected to cumulative domination, they are viewed as insiders in Indian society. However, a section of Hindu nationalists, particularly those who belong to the Rashtriya Swayam Sevak Sangh, the Vishwa Hindu Parishad, the Shiv Sena and the Bajrang Dal, consider some 150 million Indian citizens, who follow faiths of alien origin as not denizens, but outsiders to Indian society. These are Muslims, Christians, Baha'is, Zoroastrians and Jews. It is true that a small section of individuals from these communities are economically well off and this section is not always subjected to social discrimination. But the *externalisation* of those who follow non-Indic religious faiths eats into the very vitals of the hoped-for Indian 'nation'; it represents the sociocultural AIDS of the Indian polity. This exclusionary orientation is the very antithesis of good governance. And yet it is inspired by certain elements in India's civil society.

The strain of thought I am referring to is nothing new. In 1939, M.S. Gowalkar declared: 'In this country, Hindus alone are national, and Muslims and others, if not actually antinational, are at least outside the body of the nation' (1939: 56). This pronouncement relates to the Indian subcontinent and the carving out of two predominantly Muslim countries from the territory of the subcontinent has only strengthened this attitude. It has been argued by many that this orientation is (*a*) old and withering away, (*b*) exclusive to Muslims, and (*c*) the vast majority of Hindus are tolerant. It is necessary to briefly examine these points.

There is no evidence to suggest that this attitude is actually withering away as is evident from the numerous articulations and actions of those who belong to the Sangh Parivar and the Shiv Sena. Even those who do not belong to these extremist groups share this view. For example, in an interview published in *The Times of India* dated 12 February 1999, Swami Nikhilananda, an 'enlightened' monk of the Chinmaya

Mission, said about those who convert to non-Indic religions: 'With a change of religion, a person tends to shift his loyalty to other countries. The converted person will be more inclined towards the nation and culture associated with his new faith.' That the Swami is utterly wrong in ineluctably associating nation, country and religion is no solace for the victims of his pronouncement.

Until recently, the principal 'other' in India since 1947 has been the Muslims. Several rationalisations have been proffered to 'explain' this. One, the Muslims conquered India. Two, they are responsible for the division of Mother India. Three, India has two Muslim majority neighbours, of whom at least one is overtly hostile. Four, the Muslims comprise nearly 12 per cent of India's population, amounting to 120 million, acting as a vote bank and posing a grave threat to India's security. Five, Muslims are multiplying with a vengeance to take over India. And finally, Muslims exhibit extra-territorial loyalty, whether in the Kashmir dispute or Indo-Pak cricket. Not one of these rationalisations can stand empirical or logical scrutiny. But they propel the *demonisation* of one out of every eight Indian citizens.

None of the 'rationalisations' just outlined can be advanced in the case of Christians, yet there was unprecedented violence against them in 1999. It is true that there were instances of anti-Christian violence in the past. But they were few and far between. In the last 50 years, there have been only 50 instances of physical violence against Christians. But in the year 1999 there were 110 cases of atrocities against them. The ostensible reason for unleashing attacks against Christians, a demographically insignificant and politically obscure minority, is that they are indulging in coercive conversion. Even if an undesirable conversion campaign invoking fraudulent means is in existence, the response to it should be through the instrumentality of the law, which provides for ample remedies. The fact is that coercive conversion is often an excuse to attack Christians. They, like Muslims, are followers of an alien religion—they are outsiders to the 'nation' as defined by the Hindu militants.

The argument that the vast majority of Hindus are tolerant is a vexatious one. In fact, the majority of people in all countries, irrespective of their religious affiliation, are invariably 'tolerant' in that they are usually indifferent to what the militant sections of civil society indulge in. If one is to go by the response of the people at the time of periodic Hindu–Muslim riots and the recent anti-Christian attacks, vast sections of our civil society are indeed indifferent. More than that, our civil society is utterly fractured and fractionated; there is no consensus even about the undesirability of the most abhorrent acts, as was illustrated in the articulation that followed the torching of the Australian missionary and his young sons. This is worrisome in that it points to the lack of a collective conscience in India. We cannot claim that good governance exists when our collective conscience is cabined, cribbed and confined or when civil society is numbed.

III

I have suggested that there are three tests of good governance: minimising disparity, eradicating discrimination and avoiding collective alienation. I have also tried to indicate that they constitute a hierarchy as they are interrelated. It is my contention that *externalisation*, i.e., treating a section of citizens as outsiders to the polity is the most formidable of the three challenges. One cannot build anything if the bricks involved are not counted for the purpose of construction. Smooth construction can proceed only when the bricks to be used are treated more or less equally, that is, without *discrimination*. Eliminating externalisation and discrimination are necessary steps to evolve a 'good society' from which extreme *disparity* can be expunged. These should be the ultimate goals of good governance and in this context, civil society has a capital role to play.

5

Corruption and the Right to Information

Harsh Mander

From time to time, corruption surfaces in our polity as a major issue engaging and agitating the ordinary citizenry. On such occasions, not only the context but also the catalyst that brings it into focus varies: it may be activism by the media, the judiciary, the civil services or, as is more frequent, by the wider civil society.

The pervasiveness of corruption in India is a well-established and often reiterated fact. This chapter goes beyond discussing the nature of corruption to propose an effective measure whereby ordinary citizens can take up the fight against public corruption. I focus here on corruption by public authorities, which I believe is an indication of the rupture of institutions of governance. I also look at corruption from the vantage point of the poor and marginalised.

Corruption is a complex and multidimensional issue with a multitude of interacting and overlapping factors that contribute to its promotion. Amongst these, lack of transparency within the bureaucracy is an important factor responsible for promoting public corruption. In view of the fact that the poor and disadvantaged sections of society bear the maximum brunt of corrupt acts that are facilitated by a lack of transparency, I argue here that the right to information is an important means to increase bureaucratic transparency and check corruption. While it is important to recognise the limits of bureaucratic transparency, especially in cases where public security is at stake, it is equally important to recognise that it is only through an enforceable right to information that the ordinary citizen can ensure that government acts and decisions promote public welfare and accountability. In this context, the Mazdoor Kisan Shakti Sangathan's (MKSS's) struggle for the right to information significantly demonstrates how vigilance and assertion by even the most disadvantaged section of society can check corruption and the arbitrary exercise of state power.

The chapter is divided into two parts. Part I looks at the phenomenon of corruption by public authorities in India, particularly by civil servants, its dynamics, impact, causes and the methods and dilemmas associated with its possible control. Part II argues that the movement for the right to information in India has demonstrated that citizen vigilance and mobilisation for demanding accountability are effective ways of checking public corruption. It is only through the creation of effective legal spaces for the exercise of people's right to information that the most powerful, sustainable and reliable barriers to corruption in public life can be created.

I

Causes and Control of Corruption in India

Definition of Corruption

In a literal sense, the word 'corruption' means to change from good to bad, to debase, to pervert. In the context of public office, the most widely accepted definition of corruption is the misuse of public office, power or authority for private gain. Corruption by public authorities may involve two (or more) parties or take the form of an individual activity. The refusal to control corruption in his/her jurisdiction, even while remaining personally honest, falls within the scope of this definition.

Although corruption in the private sector is as deep as that in the public sector, I choose to focus here on corruption by public authorities or civil servants. In the literature, a distinction is sometimes made between petty and grand corruption.[1] The distinction is a real one but there is a danger of using it for rationalising, even if by implication, petty corruption as being based on need rather than greed. Given the negative impact that both forms have on the daily lives of citizens, I shall examine and confront both forms of this malfeasance together.

There is also sometimes a spurious distinction made between 'legitimate gifts' and 'bribes'. However, gifts that do not involve the giving and taking of cash nevertheless involve the same explicit or implicit obligation of reciprocity, of the same kind as is involved in cash bribes. They therefore constitute corrupt transactions and can be regarded as the *packaged grey areas of corruption*. From the ubiquitous Diwali gift, which has evolved from boxes of *mithai* and baskets of fruit to expensive suit lengths, gold and silver, to the acceptance of favours in the form of loans of cars, travel and hotel hospitality, house rent, placement of one's relatives in multinational companies, etc., the scope and variety of such grey areas is very large in India.

In many ways, the packaged grey area corruption is more dangerous than openly giving and taking money. Not only is it more difficult to detect, it also makes it much easier for recipients to rationalise the bribe to themselves and gain social acceptability. Thus, corrupt transactions by public authorities cannot be defined in terms of scale, content (cash or kind), secrecy or the probability of being found out. Instead, any transaction that is intended to influence the misuse of public

---

Box 5.1
Dynamics of Corruption

Corruption takes diverse forms in the complex interface of public authorities and the public.

Speed money is paid to overcome delays that riddle the bureaucratic functioning of government departments.

Goodwill money is a prearranged and regular payment in cash or kind to public servants to keep them in good humour in the hope that they would be positively disposed towards the client in the event of future decisions affecting the fortunes of the client.

End money refers to money or favours that are offered specifically to influence official decisions in favour of the client.

Blackmail money is paid when the official traps the client in a situation where he/she must pay or else face adverse consequences, such as in cases of registration of false revenue, tax or police cases. Unlike the other three categories, the initiative to be corrupt in this case comes from the authority and not the client.

---

office for private benefit is a corrupt act, even if it is packaged in culturally acceptable terms, or in forms that would not invite punitive outcomes.

Impact of Corruption

Given that corruption is rampant in the public sector, an important question that arises relates to the impact of such corruption and whom it affects the most. While the negative impact of corruption is an oft-discussed topic the fact that it is the poorest and most marginalised sections of society that bear the brunt of corruption has not been adequately recognised.

An important impact of corruption is the misdirection of public investments such that decisions related to them are less influenced by considerations of public authority than by opportunities for corruption. This occurs in two ways. One is the misdirection of funds in favour of large, centralised and complex projects rather than dispersed decentralised programmes. This allows large-scale leakages as graft and commissions as against projects requiring less financial resources. Decentralised and dispersed schemes, where the mechanisms for vigilance and detection are weak, provide another avenue for such leakages, albeit at a smaller level: for example, in village-level infrastructure works undertaken by contractors. As a result, while public expenditure is seemingly made on development projects, much of it goes into the pockets of opportunist intermediaries. This is of great significance in India where, despite 50 years of investment in the welfare and development of marginalised sections, a large proportion of this population continues to remain in the clutches of poverty and is denied basic necessities.

Further, *goods and services provided by the government* in the name of development and welfare are, in fact, only *illegally available at a price*. Critical rights to land, shelter or natural resources are affirmed only if and when recorded by the state, mostly at a price. Thus, the distribution of these goods and services is severely biased against those who do not have the capacity to pay. These are precisely the people for whom these programmes are, in theory, designed to provide a social safety net.

Corruption in fiscal management and collection also militates against the poorest, because they have less power and influence to evade both direct and indirect tax burdens. It may be argued that the really poor may not be taxpayers per se, but they bear a disproportionate share of the burden of indirect taxes and of the inflationary impacts of fiscal profligacy. In many ways, *the poor actually subsidise the rich*.

There is also irony in the fact that although large industry has substantially deregulated, *small and petty producers continue to grapple with mindless controls*, very few of which have been dismantled. Deregulation has made almost no impact at the district and village levels. For instance, according to the laws in Orissa, only the leaseholder, the Tribal Development

Cooperative Corporation and its traders can process hill brooms (a type of grass). The tribals (one of the most marginalised sections of society) can collect the grass but cannot bind it into brooms, nor can they store or sell the collected grass in the open market. The poor are thus prevented both from value addition through processing and storage, as well as the right to get the best price for their produce. Similar restrictions exist in several states of the country.

The same unrealistic legal and policy structure militates against much of the informal sector in towns and cities. In most parts of India there are almost no legal means for someone who is very poor to secure access to land for shelter or livelihood. Survival and work are therefore forced into the outer fringes of illegality, which renders the urban poor constantly vulnerable to extortion by various arms of the regulatory administration.

The poor, even without corruption, are greatly disadvantaged in any interface with the state due to their economic, social and political powerlessness. However, corruption by state authorities further intensifies this inherent powerlessness.

Causes of Corruption

Corruption is a symptom of the collapse of the institutions of governance that are supposed to manage the relationship between citizens and the state. The legitimacy of the state is related to its responsibilities for ensuring the allocation of scarce resources, in accordance with principles of justice, for development, for the protection and welfare of the disadvantaged, for sustainable management of natural resources and for ensuring the rule of law, peace and security. Corruption represents the subversion of these state responsibilities for the enrichment and aggrandisement of public servants.

The opportunities to be corrupt are fostered by several systemic features of the bureaucracy. These include lack of transparency, accessibility and accountability, cumbersome and confusing procedures, proliferation of mindless controls and a lack of reward and punishment system. Not only has the state expanded to intervene in every aspect of a citizen's life, the degree of discretion available to public servants is also very large and does not require them to be accountable to the citizen. Rules and procedures are complex, poorly defined and disseminated, and prone to change at short notice, subjecting the client public to inordinate delays and exploitation by public servants and touts. These problems are further aggravated by the absence of effective professional sanctions in the civil services. The fact that systemic awards are not linked to integrity and the extremely low probability of detection or punishment makes corruption an activity *with low risk and high return.*

The social acceptability of corruption and the growth of consumerist values lend further support to bureaucratic corruption. Today, society has tacitly granted social legitimacy to corruption in every sphere. This allows the corrupt to throw restraint to the winds and flaunt their illegal wealth through lavish lifestyles and conspicuous consumption, grotesquely disproportionate to all legitimate and known sources of income. Supporting this is the burgeoning of consumerist values fostered by seductive advertising, especially on the electronic media, in a permissive environment created by the debunking of restraints imposed in the past by the stated socialist goals of official policy. There is an increasing unwillingness amongst civil servants to feel satisfied with a prestigious vocation, albeit at a salary that guarantees no more that a middle class existence. This sharp imbalance between means and aspirations fuels corruption, especially of the grey and packaged kind.

Systemic Efforts to Control Corruption

The Indian state has evolved certain systemic responses to contain corruption. The existence of anti-corruption laws is

---

Box 5.2
Legal Provisions for Controlling Corruption

The IPC makes the following offences by public servants punishable:

- Public servant taking gratification other than legal remuneration in respect of official act (Section 161).
- Taking gratification by corrupt or illegal means, to influence public servant (Section 162).
- Taking gratification for exercise of personal influence with public servant (Section 163).
- Abetment by public servant of offences (Section 164).
- Public servant obtaining valuable things without consideration from persons concerned in proceedings or business transacted by such public servant (Section 165).

The PCA 1998 contains many features that strengthen the capacity of the stare to prosecute offenders for corruption. These include a wider definition of public servants, provisions to establish special courts and stringent punishment and investigation of offences related to corruption at senior levels. An important provision is that the burden of proof is shifted to the person of holding assets disproportionate to income.

---

an instance. There are a number of strong legal provisions, both under the Indian Penal Code (IPC) and the Prevention of Corruption Act, 1998, or the PCA, to control public corruption.

However, most of these laws become non-cognisable in relation to public servants as only a few cases come to light, and those that are revealed are generally soft-pedalled with departmental action and treated as breaches of the conduct rules for public servants rather than as criminal liability.

In a situation where corruption is 'systemic' and pervasive, where both parties to a bribe benefit and in which most victims of corruption are politically and economically relatively powerless, detection and enforcement is poor. Weak and ambivalent detection, registration, investigation and pursuit in courts is another cause for poor deterrence. Besides, the performance of other watchdog institutions like accountants and the press is also extremely patchy in this regard. In summary, while it is possible to control the cancer of corruption by stricter enforcement of anti-corruption laws, even this would require public vigilance and pressure to create and maintain the necessary political will to ensure their enforcement.

The internal control of corruption in public system is critically dependent on the quality of its leadership. The first step in controlling corruption among one's subordinates is a firm will on the part of the supervising officer that is clearly communicated to others and is backed by the actions of the former. An officer committed to controlling corruption must have integrity, be fully accessible to the client public and take prompt action in the event of any legitimate and reliable complaint.

The social and systemic barriers that militate against the fostering of such leadership in public office have already been elaborated upon. It is important to recognise that while such qualities of leadership are indispensable for the success of any campaign for probity instituted by public authorities, it is also true that such leadership is more likely to be fostered in an environment of social mobilisation.

Pro-poor administrative reforms initiated by civil servants, such as demystification of rules and procedures, dissemination of such information, dismantling of mindless controls and other means to promote transparency, are other important measures that have intermittently helped to counter corruption. Efforts to demystify rules and disseminate information have generally been sporadic, temporary and based on individual initiatives that are not sustained once the initiating officer is transferred. Despite government rhetoric, measures to decentralise remain confined to the urban organised industry, leaving petty and small producers to deal with unnecessary government regulations. In spite of the enactment of the legislation related to local self-governance, decisions regarding the management of community resources and those related to local development continue to be at the mercy of government officials.

For sustainable impact it is therefore necessary to systematically and effectively reduce state intervention in citizens' lives. There needs to be a drastic reduction in the discretionary power of public authorities. Further, this needs to be complemented with an increase in people's participation in the planning and implementation of policies and programmes.

In summary, the fundamental weakness of the approaches outlined in the preceding paragraphs is that they do not propose a proactive role for ordinary citizens to check corruption. Rather, they are based on the premise that ordinary citizens is not only powerless against corruption, they are also solely dependent on institutional mechanisms and the goodwill of public authorities to check this malaise. They ignore the role that citizens can themselves play to control this vice. Thus, while such mechanisms help control corruption to a limited extent, given administrative and political will, the most effective barrier against the malaise lies in the effective and informed mobilisation of ordinary people. The actions of a small group of people in Devdungri village in Rajasthan, the MKSS, which is effectively fighting against construction works through a vibrant mass campaign, are an example of this.

II

Right to Information: A Grassroots Struggle in Rajasthan

Information is the currency that every citizen requires to participate in the life and governance of society. The greater the access of citizens to information, the greater would be the responsiveness of the government to community needs. Alternatively, the greater the restrictions that are placed on access, the greater would be the feelings of 'powerlessness' and 'alienation'. Without information, people cannot adequately exercise their rights and responsibilities as citizens or make informed choices. Government information is a national resource. Neither the particular government of the day nor public officials create information for their own benefit. This information is generated for purposes related to the legitimate discharge of their duties, and for the service of the public for whose benefit the institutions of government exist and who ultimately (through one kind of import or another) fund the institutions of government and the salaries of officials. It follows, therefore, that the government and its officials are merely 'trustees' of this information for the people.

The movement for the right to information is based on the premise that information is power and that executives at all levels attempt to withhold information to increase its scope for control, patronage and the arbitrary, corrupt and unaccountable exercise of power. Therefore, simplification of rules and procedures, complete transparency and proactive dissemination of relevant information amongst the public is potentially a very strong safeguard against corruption.

The most decisive grassroots movement for the right to information, which succeeded in linking the entire movement in the country to the survival of and justice to the most disadvantaged rural people, was launched by MKSS as part of the people's movement for justice in wages, livelihoods and land in Devdungri village in Rajasthan. Located in a poor and drought-prone region, the landholdings in Devdungri village are too small to be viable even if there is rain. With few alternate sources of rural livelihood, distress migration in the lean summer months is high. Government interventions mainly take the form of famine relief works, such as construction of roads and tanks, with extremely high levels of corruption and extremely poor durability. Wages, even for government relief works, are low and payment too erratic to provide any real social security.

Right from the beginning, MKSS was drawn into the local struggles of the poor, relating mainly to land and wages, but also to women's rights, prices and sectarian violence. On May Day, 1990, the organisation was formally registered under the name MKSS. Its ranks grew as MKSS built a strong cadre drawn from marginal peasants and landless workers, the majority of whom belonged to lower socio-economic groupings.

In the winter of 1994, MKSS' work entered a new phase with experiments in fighting corruption through *jan sunwais* or public hearings. This movement, despite its local character, has had statewide reverberations and has shaken the very foundations of the traditional monopoly, arbitrariness and corruption of the state bureaucracy.

In the specific context of development and public relief works with which MKSS had been deeply involved for so many years, the right to information translated itself into a demand that copies of all documents related to public works be made available for a people's audit. These included the muster roll, which lists the attendance of the workers and wages due and paid, and bills and vouchers relating to purchase and transportation of materials.

In the *jan sunwais* organised by MKSS, these are read out and explained to the people for identifying and noting discrepancies. It is not that in the past people were unaware of muster rolls being forged, records fudged, materials misappropriated and so on. But these were general fears and doubts, and in the absence of access to hard facts, they were unable to take any preventive or remedial action. The public hearings changed this dramatically. Ordinary people spoke out fearlessly and gave convincing evidence against corruption while public officials were invited to defend themselves. The process resulted in two demands. One, that all citizens should have the right to make copies of all bills, vouchers, muster rolls, etc., relating to any work undertaken by the government in their village. Two, that funds misappropriated or embezzled should be immediately recovered and spent for the purpose for which they were designated.

Initially, the government authorities opposed this move and tried to obstruct the proceedings in every possible way. For example, the local administration in the four districts where public hearings had been organised, refused to register criminal cases or institute recovery proceedings against the officials and elected representatives against whom incontrovertible evidence of corruption had been gathered during the course of the public hearings and their follow-up. Despite such opposition, the hearings evoked hope, both among the disadvantaged and the progressive elements within and outside government. In October 1995, the Lal Bahadur Shastri National Academy of Administration, Mussoorie, which is responsible for training all senior civil service recruits, took the unusual step of organising a national workshop for officials and activists to focus attention on the right to information.

Meanwhile, responding the public opinion that coalesced around the issue, on 5 April 1995, the Chief Minister of Rajasthan announced in the state legislature that his government would be the first in the country to confer on every citizen the right to obtain for a fee photocopies of all official documents related to local development works. However, even after a year later, this assurance was not followed up by any administrative order. MKSS launched a dharna in Beawar, a small town, to press for the issue of administrative orders to enforce this right. The state government responded by issuing an order on the first day of the dharna, allowing citizens the right to *inspect* such documents for a fee, but *not to obtain certified copies* or even photocopies. MKSS rejected this order as toothless and diversionary, because in the absence of a legally valid copy, a citizen who detects defalcation can undertake no action, even file a police complaint. Further, no time limits and penalties were prescribed for compliance with this order.

In order to press for a more cast-iron government circular, MKSS continued its dharna. A delegation met the Chief Minster at the village Jawaja, where he verbally conceded to the demand but refused to issue written instructions until the elections were over. The stalemate continued.

Meanwhile, each day since the launching of the dharna witnessed an unprecedented upsurge of homespun idealism in the small town of Beawar and the surrounding countryside. Donations in cash and kind poured in daily from ordinary local people, including vegetables and milk from small vendors, sacks of wheat from farmers in surrounding villages, tents, volunteers to cook and serve cold water, take photographs, etc., and monetary help from even the poorest. Even more significant was the daily assembly of over 500 people listening to speeches and joining in the slogan shouting, songs and rallies. Active support cut across all class and political barriers. From shopkeepers and professionals to daily wage labourers along the entire political spectrum of the right wing fringe to communist trade unions, all extended vocal and enthusiastic support. In Jaipur, over 70 people's organisations and several respected citizens came forward to extend support to MKSS' demand. The mainstream press was also openly sympathetic.

In the end, an official press note was issued on behalf of the Rajasthan state government, which said that the state government had taken a decision to establish a committee that would give practical shape to the assurance made by the Chief Minister. Another year passed. Despite several meetings with the Chief Minister, senior cabinet members and state officials, no order was issued and shared with the activists, although again there were repeated assurances. In the end, May 1997 saw the beginning of another epic dharna, this time in the state capital of Jaipur. After 52 days, the Deputy Chief Minister made an announcement that six months earlier the state government had notified the right to receive photocopies of documents related to panchayats. Despite the irony of the fact that an order related to transparency had been kept secret, it was welcomed as a major milestone as far as the right to information was concerned because, for the first time, it recognised the legal entitlement of ordinary citizens to obtain copies of government-held documents.

MKSS and other groups set about organising people to use this important entitlement. However, in a majority of cases, they continued to face an obstinate bureaucracy and recalcitrant local government representatives who still refused to supply copies of documents. MKSS has responded to such problems by registering complaints with authorities from the local level to the state government, highlighting the illegal withholding of information in the press, and organising and mobilising the people to peacefully and democratically pressure the authorities.

In 1999, the Rajasthan government declared that it was committed to the passage of a powerful bill for the right to information. It invited MKSS and the National Campaign for People's Right to Information to prepare a draft. The draft, which was the result of consultation with citizen groups and concerned individuals is now passed as an Act, thus giving citizens the right to claim information from the government and get it.

The struggle by MKSS remains significant because of its fundamental promise that ordinary people should not be condemned to remain dependent on fortune to provide them with an honest or courageous official or social leader to release them from the stranglehold of corruption. In fact, they should be empowered to control and fight corruption directly. For this, they require a cast-iron right to information. Another important highlight was its ability to link the issue of corruption to the struggles and concerns of the most disadvantaged sections of rural society.

Conclusion

In India, corruption amongst public authorities is both pervasive and systemic. Symptomatic of a collapse of the institutions of governance and representing serious distortions of the state mechanisms for ensuring equity, development, justice and order, it is rooted in an erosion of social values and lack of transparency and accountability in the Indian state machinery.

As a parliamentary democracy with periodic elections, a Constitution that guarantees its citizens the freedom of speech and expression (amongst other fundamental rights), annual reporting requirements, publication of information and administrative law requirements, the Indian state is designed to promote accountability to the people and transparency of functioning. However, the practice is far removed from the theory. An over-expanded state, multiplicity and complexity of rules and procedures, centralised, 'expert'-dominated and opaque policy-making and the continued existence of colonial laws, have all contributed to the creation of a culture of secrecy, distance and mystification within the bureaucracy, not fundamentally different from the colonial times. In summary, the lack of bureaucratic transparency and accountability contributes, in large measure, to the growth of public corruption. While the impact of corruption tends to be debilitating for all citizens, the major brunt of this vice is borne by the weakest and most marginalised.

It is in such an environment that civil society's movement for the right to information plays such a significant role. By seeking to give citizens an enforceable right to question, examine, audit, review and assess government acts and decisions, and to ensure that these are consistent with the principles of public interest, probity and justice, it seeks to significantly expand citizens' democratic space. By giving all citizens further opportunity to participate in the political process in a more full way, it seeks to enhance the quality of participatory political democracy. The cumulative impact of the availability of such information to citizens would be to check corruption and the arbitrary exercise of state power.

On the one hand, the Indian state provides a large space for corruption to take root. On the other, it also periodically provides the space for progressive elements within the state to institutionalise mechanisms to control corruption. These range from anti-corruption laws to pro-people administrative reforms. However, these efforts have been patchy and inadequate. In most cases ordinary citizens are relatively unaware of such measures. Where they are aware, fear of retaliation makes people unwilling to exercise their right to enforce them. In the case of the right to information, government efforts have consisted of periodically trying to modify the Official Secrets Act.[2] But the efforts have been largely cosmetic and designed to maintain the control of public authorities on public information. As a result, government measures have failed to have the desired effect on corruption.

It is in this context that the intervention by the civil society organisation MKSS gains significance. First, it challenges the non-existence of legislation on the right to information. Second, it points out and challenges inadequacies and loopholes in the legislation that has been enacted by the Rajasthan government. In the process, it also confronts and challenges direct and indirect attempts to subvert the enactment of an effective legislation by vested interests within the bureaucracy. Direct attempts include hindering *jan sunwais* and refusing to provide the information necessary to carry out such hearings. Indirect efforts include the enactment of a legislation allowing people to 'inspect' documents on local development works but not giving them the right to 'photocopy' such documents (in order to prevent initiation of recovery proceedings against corrupt officials) and preventing changes in sections of existing legislation like the Official Secrets Act that are contradictory to such a right. To fight the attempts by vested interests within the bureaucracy to obstruct the right to information MKSS has joined hands with progressive elements within society as well as in the bureaucracy.

While institutionalising such rights is important in terms of giving people the legal basis to fight corruption directly, it is not a sufficient condition to check corruption. Only through the proactive exercise of this right by the people can corruption be checked. In the final instance, civil society helps to mobilise people in order to help them exercise their right to information in an effective manner. The impact of *jan sunwais* is multidimensional. At one level, it helps to break the passivity of the ordinary citizens accustomed to being powerless victims, enabling them to directly confront corruption. By reading out in a public meeting the names of officials involved and the amounts embezzled by them through falsely reporting payment of wages, MKSS helps to make corruption a personal experience for the villagers. In turn, this provides the impetus for a collective demand for immediate redress through repayment of the misappropriated amount. As a result, misappropriation of public funds is checked and state authorities are made more accountable to the people in whose name development programmes of the state are legitimised. Public condemnation of corruption helps to reduce the social legitimacy accorded to it. Finally, MKSS is, if only in part, responsible for initiating efforts to bring in a comprehensive legislation on the right to information along with changes in the Official Secrets Act.

By enabling marginalised people to fight against corruption, the movement for the right to information seeks a momentous enlargement of their space and strength in relation to the structures of the state. In short, it proves that an active, vigilant and assertive citizenry is the most reliable and sustainable barrier to corruption.

Notes

1. Petty corruption is found where public servants who may be grossly underpaid depend on small kickbacks from the public to feed their families and pay school fees. Grand corruption involves high officials who make decisions on large public contracts.
2. The Official Secrets Act is a replica of the erstwhile British Officials Secrets Act and deals with espionage. However, it has the damaging 'catch-all' Section 5, which makes it an offence to

part with any information received in the course of officials duty to non-officials. In 1977, the working group formed by the government to look into the amendments of the Official Secrets Act recommended that no change was required in the Act as it was intended to protect national safety and not to prevent legitimate release of information to the public. In 1989, yet another committee was set up, which recommended restriction of the areas where governmental information could be hidden and opening up of all other spheres of information. In 1991, sections of the press reported recommendations of a task force on the modifications of the Act and the enactment of a freedom of Information Act, but no legislative action followed. The most recent exercise has been the constitution of a working group in 1997, which recommended some chages in the Act and a draft law. However, nothing has come of this effort.

SECTION II

SECTION III

6

Save the Chilika Movement[1]

Interrogating the State and the Market

Ranjita Mohanty

The Chilika Bachao Andolan (Save the Chilika Movement) was a movement by the people, mostly fishermen, who in the early 1990s successfully resisted the Integrated Shrimp Farm Project (ISFP). The project—a joint venture of the Tata Iron and Steel Company (TISCO) and the Government of Orissa—for intensive prawn cultivation and export, posed a direct threat to the livelihood of fishing communities living around the lake. The fishermen were supported in their struggle by non-fishermen (mostly farmers, but with some of them also engaged in fishing), students, intellectuals and human rights activists. The lake, an otherwise quiet and scenic spot, was stirred by many voices of resistance opposing the Tata business house, the government and the development idiom that gives priority to the commercial use of local resources over their use for subsistence. The movement was episodic and uneven, with different streams of thought and action among which it was not always possible to achieve synchronisation. Yet, all these separate formations together gave the resistance the form of a movement. Despite internal conflicts and contestations among the people and the leaders, the worth of the resistance lies in raising some critical governance issues pertaining to policy formulation, resource use and control and socio-economic equity, not only with regard to the specific instance but also the broader question concerning the prevalent paradigm of development. In addition, and more importantly, it pointed out how the Indian state relates to ordinary people and how ordinary people would like to transform this relationship.

The relationship between civil society and good governance rests on the assumption that a vibrant civil society enhances the quality of governance. There is no denying the fact that collective initiatives in many ways restrain and reform the state and in this sense indeed contribute towards good governance. Nonetheless, the exploration of the interface between civil society and governance reveals in more than one way the tensions that underlie this interface. Thus, while the efficacy of collective action would lead to the conclusion that people are capable of interrogating the state and conceptualising a good life and a good society, the conflicts of interest in civil society and the appropriation of benefits by the dominant and powerful sections would suggest that this emancipatory version of civil society and the uncritical faith in it need to be questioned. That is, civil society needs to look both back and forth—it needs to question the state when the state becomes overbearing and, at the same time, it needs to question the power equations within its own sphere. As Touraine says, social space is both the locus and target of contemporary movements (Touraine 1983). The agenda of good governance, therefore, not only includes the democratisation of the state but the democratisation of society as well. How effectively actors in civil society perform this dual, albeit interrelated, role and what constrains their action forms the focus of this chapter.

Context

The wider popularity, or more appropriately, the celebratory status civil society has enjoyed during the last two decades is due to the wave of democracy which swept through the erstwhile communist countries in Eastern Europe and the authoritarian regimes in Latin America and Africa. As is now well known, it began in 1989 with the fall of the Berlin Wall and the collapse of the Soviet bloc, and then moved further with the challenge posed to the military regimes in Argentina, Chile and the hegemonic apartheid and single-party rulers in Africa. The people languishing without civil rights and the rule of law under authoritarian, hegemonic regimes could come together to challenge the state and overthrow it, thus supporting through their action the notion of the efficacy of collective strength in curbing state power. Whether this triumph of civil society, which has generated so much euphoria among a wide variety of actors, really does make civil society that celebratory and emancipatory is open to debate, because this resurgence in civil society is closely tied to the march of the free market and the actors in civil society, as the experience of East European countries shows, fall victim to political bureaucracy and capitalist elites soon after the overthrow of the hegemonic state. However, few would disagree with the fact that these contemporary civil society assertions prove the strength and determination of ordinary men and women and their collectives to challenge authoritarian states. They thereby testify that people are not only capable of defining their vision of good society and polity; they can also organise themselves to demand the rights and freedom necessary to actualise this vision.

The aim here, however, is not to go into the conceptual history of civil society or the contemporary conceptualisations in the growing literature on it. Rather, it is to tease out the unique thread that makes civil society a distinct concept worth exploring, and which lends it the ability to attract a wide variety of people who critically or uncritically subscribe to it. Except, perhaps, for Gramsci, whose writings view civil society as a site for the perpetuation of state hegemony, most conceptualisations of civil society see it as an independent, non-political realm between family and state[2] or a third sphere, different from the state and the market.[3] Such conceptualisations fill the space of civil society with a variety of actors—movements, trade unions, non-government organisations (NGOs) and non-profit organisations. These collectives may counterpose themselves against the state in order to curb its power, or may collaborate with it to enhance its performance and, in the process, reform it.[4] This formulation is extremely attractive to people fighting authoritarian regimes as well as to those who believe in the efficacy of people's associations to restrain and reform the state. The latter version may well be applicable to democracies like India, where the state is not overtly authoritarian and there are constitutional rights and laws to safeguard the freedom of citizens. Thus, while in overtly authoritarian and military regimes people crave for a space where they can form associations and engage in the politics of the good life in a sphere that is not under state surveillance and pressurise the state to grant them the rights and liberties to transform their vision into reality, in democratic states people are given this space through the institutionalisation of rights, freedom and laws. They therefore, assert their collective strength when the state deviates from its role or becomes overbearing. Conceptualisations like this make civil society extremely desirable, for they reflect on the strength and responsibility of ordinary men and women to come up with their own conceptions of the good life, the kind of society they would like to live in and the kind of polity they would like to be governed by. What these conceptualisations fail to capture is that civil society is equally capable of being undemocratic, discriminatory and exclusionary. It is as much susceptible to corruption by the inequalities in society as the state. Civil society is attractive to people because it is informed by the values of egalitarianism and is emancipatory, but this should not blind us to the power struggles in this sphere or the conflicts and contestations that may mar its democratic values. As we proceed to analyse the Chilika movement, it will be clear how inequalities in society prompt collective action, but also how collective action is constrained by inequalities and divisiveness. Therefore, the process of democratisation of the polity, which takes place in civil society, is intrinsically related to the democratisation of society.

Another problem with these conceptualisations is that by locating civil society as a realm between the family and the state, or as a third realm different from the market and the state, they in effect end up delinking civil society from the state. In the zeal to emphasise the autonomy and independence of the third sphere, theorists of civil society ignore the fact that in countries like India where governance is in the hands of a constitutional, democratic state, however inadequate or formal it may be. In such countries, the state that on the one hand provides the framework in the form of rights, freedoms and laws to enable people to come together for collective action, inadvertently conditions the initiatives of civil society on the other. And if we were to capture the essence of the state and civil society on the basis of their ultimate ideals, we would have to concede that notwithstanding the deviations, they share the same vision—that of universal freedom and universal rights (Mohanty 1999). That is to say, the overlap between the boundaries of the state and civil society is as much a concern in this discussion as the differences.

Coming to governance, in contemporary times the World Bank is credited with making the term popular in development discourse (World Bank 1989, 1991, 1992 and 1994). The failure of its economic policies in the sub-Saharan African countries led the Bank to conclude that something was terribly wrong with governance in these countries, and therefore, to equate administrative inefficiency, corruption, lack of transparency, lack of accountability, violation of the rule of law, etc., with bad governance. The solution to this was sought in achieving, in the Bank's terminology, 'good governance' or enhancement in the quality and process of administration. The Bank nevertheless avoided taking a stand on the type of political regime or form of governance that would be required for good governance and focused merely on administrative reforms (Guhan 1998). The conceptual gap was filled by bilateral donors who, by making developmental aid conditional to democracy and the granting of civil rights, equated good governance with the political regime of democracy.[5]

Around the same time as governance was being thought problematic in many countries around the globe, the manner of the overthrow of authoritarian regimes in Eastern Europe, Latin America and Africa made civil society the new mantra for achieving good governance. The linkage of civil society with good governance therefore, rests on the assumption that a vibrant civil society and the collective engagement of people with governance structures will result in the ushering of a liberal-democratic political environment and make the administrative agencies efficient and responsive to people's needs. The emphasis on good governance is sought to provide congenial political and administrative conditions for the growth of the market and also to reform the state in the badly governed developing countries by making civil society the vanguard in promoting liberal-democratic ideals. Thus, the earlier sanctions imposed through making development aid conditional to the presence of democracy and civil rights have been replaced by rewards in the form of support to civil society in developing countries, in the hope that they will foster democracy, transparency, accountability and the rule of law in these countries. Historically speaking, the timing of the tying up of the terms—civil society and good governance—could not have been better.

While it is important to remember that governance, which, beginning with the World Bank, has become the buzzword of the development aid vocabulary, is intrinsically linked to the liberalisation of the economy and the opening up of space for the market, it also needs to be reiterated that irrespective the genesis and popularity of the term, 'good governance' is itself a desirable *state de affaires*. Nevertheless, the definition of governance and the linking of civil society with good governance raise some questions and concerns.

Most conceptualisations of governance are not embedded in the wider social context in which inequalities and divisiveness of various kinds affect governance structures and where the celebratory status bestowed upon civil society hides the conflicts and contestations taking place in this sphere. They do not take into account the wider social and political system in which 'political' and 'social' are not distinct but overlapping and that this reduces the autonomy and independence of the state and makes civil society vulnerable to conflicts and contestations of various kinds.

It is this simplistic understanding of governance and civil society that underlies the exceedingly optimistic assumption that, everything else remaining the same, civil society initiatives *alone* can help in promoting good governance. That dominant interests and power structures of society often vitiate governance agencies cannot be overlooked in any discussion of governance in India. This brings us to the heart of the civil society and good governance assumption that, given the legitimacy of the democratic regime, the enhancement in the quality and competency of administration would result in good governance and collective initiatives in civil society would be able to effectively pursue this end.

Arguments like this, resting on assumptions of social neutrality, do not take into consideration the entrenched inequalities and divisiveness in a country like India. The contexts of inequalities put different groups in unequal relationship with each other and vis-à-vis the state. Therefore, not only is collective action constrained in myriad ways, the instances of powerful groups allying with governance agencies may well mean that the actors in civil society cannot deal with governance agencies in complete isolation from the wider social setting in which unequally placed groups compete with each other to appropriate scarce resources and in which fulfilment of political aspirations makes the electoral politics of democracy manipulate sectarian interests. In such a situation, can bad governance imply only ineffective and incompetent administration? Can improvement in the quality and performance of administration be called good governance? And last but not least, can we assume that in the same environment in which dominant interests oppress and alienate the marginalised, civil society actors can always elicit a positive response from the state? If the relationship between the state and civil society is far from congenial, what implication does that have for civil society and its democratic agenda? I raise these questions in the context of collective action in Chilika. By doing so, I suggest that existing notions of governance need to be expanded to accommodate both the wider social and political systems. I also suggest that notwithstanding the tremendous odds against which civil society actors have to work, instances of collective action show that disadvantaged and marginalised people are not only capable of interrogating and challenging the state, they are equally capable of refashioning their relationship with the state. These notions of governance, which come from the people, should, as I have earlier pointed out, be considered as constitutive elements of good governance.

Development, Resource Use and People's Movements

Mobilisation by marginalised groups to protect their livelihood resources against commercial use is not new in India. During the colonial regime, there were tribal and peasant uprisings against state intervention in the customary practices of the people. The replacement of customary management of common property resources by state management led to conflicts of interest, which manifested in people asserting their claim, right and control over their subsistence resources. After independence, the then current development ideal prompted the state to pursue economic growth through industrialisation. Commodity production became the core of the Indian economy, and industry, mining and giant irrigation

projects took shape in quick succession to change the economic and social landscape. The development path of the
Indian democratic state was ideally designed to benefit the
disadvantaged and promote equity and social justice. Ironically, India's democratic development agenda was subverted
by dominant forces that appropriated the benefits of development to the disadvantage of the marginalised, who had
suffered social and economic vulnerability in the past and who
the development projects were designed to benefit (Kothari
1986; Bardhan 1984, 1988; Kohli 1987, 1988 and Dhanagre
1987). Not only did the developmental projects not benefit
them, they added new dimensions to their already disadvantaged position. As technocentric economic growth took off
and huge irrigation and hydel projects and heavy industries
took shape, thousands of people were displaced from their
original habitat. Without any comprehensive resettlement
and rehabilitation policy, displacement became the inevitable
fallout of development. As the natural resources were put to
commercial use, a large number of people directly dependent
on nature for their subsistence, lost their access to and control
over these resources. It is no surprise, then, that they have
resisted the policies formulated to bring them benefit. Thus,
while resistance to the colonial state was prompted by an
understanding that it was alien and oppressive, post-colonial
assertions are against the Indian state, whose development
logic is legitimised in the name of the people.[6] What prompts
people to question this logic and legitimacy? How do hitherto
voiceless people acquire a voice to question the state that they
have regarded as their benefactor? From where do they get the
resources to mobilise themselves? How does civil society
formulate its discourse vis-à-vis the state? Do marginalised
groups always find collective action enabling? How do these
assertions shape the democratic polity and society in which
we live?

Contemporary assertions by the marginalised to gain control over their resources reveal, on the one hand, the tenuous
relationship between the neglected citizenry and the state and,

on the other, the potential of these people to redefine and refashion this relationship. As Melucci puts it: 'The public spaces which are beginning to develop in complex societies are points of connection between political institutions and collective demands, between the functions of government and the representatives of conflict' (Melucci 1988: 259). Conflicts over natural resources, as I have pointed out earlier, are not new, but contemporary movements have added a new dimension to the struggle by articulating the issues in terms of survival of the majority, as well as by focusing on the related issues of dominance, unequal distribution of developmental benefits, sustainable development and people's involvement in decision-making.[7] These movements have given people new identities and have inspired them to imagine the kind of society they would like to live in and the kind of polity they would like to be governed by. At the same time, they have provided them with new strategies to resist forces that hinder the realisation of these ideals. Movements like the Chilika mirror this new self-reflection among people—who are they and what kind of life would they like to live? What should be their relationship with nature, with fellow human beings, with public institutions and with the state that governs them? As people collectively address these questions, they bring them into the public sphere, where they are debated, discussed and democratised.

The Chipko Movement, which heralded people's resistance for control over their sustenance resources, was by local people, mainly women, in the hills of Garhwal, Uttar Pradesh, to save their forest from commercial felling. Although a continuation of the old peasant struggle, it added a new dimension to it by raising the issue of survival, dependence and control over their resources and by directing the struggle not against any class per se but against the state (Guha 1991). It occurred in the early 1970s, a period significant for the Stockholm Conference on Environment. Chipko brought home the truth that environmental degradation and social inequalities are intrinsically linked in more than one way (ibid.; Bhatt 1991). The overuse of natural resources for commercial purposes not only deprives people of their resource base and widens the gap between the elites and the impoverished masses, it also does not afford people the choice to use their resources in a sustainable manner because people dependent on a dwindling material base for their sustenance cannot be expected to be prudent users of nature. Chipko's success was soon followed by resistance against big dams, mines and industry: in Tehri, Narmada, the Western Ghats, Kaiga and Baliapal, people began to raise their voice against the development policy of the state, against the loss of their productive resources such as forest, water and land, and against the large-scale displacement that has become a common fallout of all big development projects. These instances of local resistance have performed two significant tasks: they have amplified the voice of the marginalised against dominant interests and have shown us that the disprivileged, when mobilised, are capable of not only defining what constitutes a good life, a good society and a good polity, but also of suggesting ways to execute and actualise their ideals.

Contextualising the Resistance

Located in the Puri, Khurda and Ganjam districts of Orissa, Chilika is the largest brackish-water lake in India. It is home to large varieties of fish and plants. The lake is separated from the Bay of Bengal by long, sandy ridge, varying between 100 and 300 yards (or 91.44 m and 274.32 m) in width, with one natural opening near Arakhkuda that permits the flow of water and the migration of fish from the sea to the lake. The lake maintains a sweet-saline ecosystem during the year. It becomes sweeter (less saline) between July and December due to the inflow of floodwater and becomes more saline between January and June due to the ingress of seawater. Chilika was identified as a wetland of international importance at the Ramsar Convention held in Iran in 1971, to which India is a signatory. The Government of India has also declared Chilika as a bird sanctuary for facilitating the migration of nearly 132 species of birds from Siberia every winter.

A large number of villages around the lake are inhabited by a heterogeneous population comprising both fishermen and non-fishermen belonging to different castes. Fishing and agriculture are the two primary sources of livelihood. The fishermen belong to the lower castes and most of them are either landless or possess tiny landholdings. They are therefore entirely dependent on fishing. The non-fishermen belong to higher castes and are engaged in agriculture. However, a large number of them have also taken to fishing to supplement their income because land productivity is low due to salinity, erratic monsoon and lack of irrigation facilities. And ever since the white prawn and tiger prawn became lucrative export items, traders and other rich and influential people from outside have also taken to shrimp farming, thus depriving fishing communities of their resource base.

In earlier times, since fishing was done almost exclusively by the lower castes, it was looked down upon as a lowly occupation, shunned by the higher castes. Now that the higher castes are themselves engaged in fishing, the stigma attached to the occupation no longer exists. Nevertheless, the upper castes still maintain their distance from the lower castes. This low social status of fishermen is intensified by their low economic status. They live in conditions of poverty, there is not much education among them, and many are in debt to moneylenders, middlemen and traders, from whom they have taken loans for household expenses and for buying fishing equipment. Caste and class differences are thus very sharp in the area.

Traditional Fishing Grounds

Depending on the general slope of the land and the depth of water in the lake, the fishing grounds in Chilika can be grouped as follows:

Jano: Mostly located around the various islands of the lake, *Jano* are barricaded (with split bamboos) fisheries in shallow water and are operated from October to February.

Khati: These comprise shrimp fishing grounds where fishing is done mostly with the help of bamboo traps set in the shore areas. They operate between March and September.

Bahan: This refers to net fishing in the deeper portion of the lake. It is done throughout the year but to a lesser extent between October and December.

Dian: Confined to upland areas, *Dian* fishing grounds are operated from September to January.

Uthapani: Carried out mainly during the monsoon, *Uthapani* refers to shallow water fishing.

The fishing practices of the fishermen differ, depending on the caste group to which they belong. The *Keuta* (also known as *Kaibarta* or *Khatia*) form 68 per cent of traditional fishermen who fish with nets. *Kandara*, the second largest group, use traps—*dhaudi* and *tata*—for catching crabs and prawns. The *Tiar* use bamboo traps called *baja*. The *Karatias* use both traps and nets for fishing. In addition, there are *Nolias*—the Telugu immigrants who fish mainly in the sea and partly at the mouth of the lake and in some parts of the outer channel with dragnets and cast nets. A large number of refugees from Bangladesh have also taken up fishing as their means of livelihood, though they do not have any legal right to fish in the lake.

In the past, the different castes were required to follow their respective fishing practices and any violation of this rule was considered a serious social offence. The *Kandaras* and *Tiars* could thus use only bamboo implements like traps, while the rest used nets. The fishermen were also confined to particular fishing grounds, even if these were at a distance from the village where they lived.

Fishing Rights of the People

The traditional fishing communities trace their fishing rights to the British period. When Chilika Lake was in the hands of the kings of Parikuda and Khalikota, the fishermen could only access it by paying royalty to the king. In order to protect the interests of fishermen and eliminate the encroachment on their rights by non-fishermen and traders, the first cooperative society, the Balugaon Fishermen Cooperative Store, with 24 fisheries under it, was established in 1926 at Balugaon in Puri district. After the abolition of the estates and with fishery sources coming within the purview of the Government of Orissa in 1953, the fisheries were leased out to fishermen by the Anchal Adhikari through open auction. The non-fishermen were allowed to take a limited number of *dian* fisheries and in some cases, a few *jano* fisheries. They could also use the *bahani* areas that had not been leased by paying a nominal fee to the government.

This practice continued until 1959, when the Central Co-operative Marketing Society was established in Balugaon. This society was designed to act as an apex body that would lease the fisheries from the government and sublease them to the primary fishermen cooperatives. A dual cooperative structure was thus established to protect and regulate people's fishing rights. The Central Society leased fishery sources from the Revenue Department through the Collectorate of Puri and Ganjam, and subleased the important ones to the 48 primary cooperatives operating at that time. In areas where there was no primary society, *dian* fisheries were subleased to villages dominated by fishermen. Sources that were not taken on lease by the Central Society were auctioned by the *tehsildars* (government officials from the revenue department operating at the block level) of Puri, Krushna Prasada, Banpur and Ganjam. The Chilika reorganisation scheme thus made a clear distinction between fishermen and non-fishermen and gave the latter limited rights to the lake.

Until 1988, however, there was no clear-cut demarcation of fishing sources, type of net to be used, and the barricades to be set up to catch prawn. This made it considerably difficult for the primary societies to operate. In 1986, there was a dispute between two primary societies regarding the fixing of barricades. Fishermen in the upper region of the lake had fixed very lengthy barricades that obstructed the flow of fish to the lower regions. Following this dispute, the 1988 policy demarcated the fishery sources; it also increased the annual lease of fisheries to three years.

In 1991, the Government of Orissa issued an order that divided the fisheries in Chilika into two categories—capture and culture—without, however, adequately defining either. Capture rights were confined to fishermen and culturing was opened to non-fishermen and villages that were not members of primary societies. Since the government order did not provide any guidelines for the operation of capture and culture fisheries, the Collector was free to act according to his discretion. The policy thus created further confusion and conflict. The fishermen feared that their traditional rights were being curtailed by leasing out culture sources to non-fishermen.

Despite repeated assurance by the government that the policies were meant to safeguard the traditional rights of fishermen, they did not have the desired effect for various reasons: they were ill-defined, there was no rational or equitable distribution of fisheries, there was widespread illegal subleasing, and there were no mechanisms to prevent it. The Central Society was given limited powers and acted merely as liaison between the Revenue Department and the primary societies. It was also guilty of erratic distribution and illegal subletting. Most primary societies bypassed the Central Society and marketed directly through commissioned agents. The very purpose of a dual cooperative structure designed to protect the interests of fishermen was thus vitiated.

Initially, prawn culturing began in the peripheral landmass of Chilika. The *dian*, *uthapani* and upland *jano* fisheries that had been leased out were converted into prawn culture ponds with mud embankments. Later, the deeper area of the lake was also enclosed with bamboo poles and net.

Since the 1980s, the lake has been witnessing increased subletting of leased out fisheries by the Central and primary societies and illegal encroachment by non-fishermen and outsiders.[8] Large-scale culturing of prawns has resulted in widespread conversion of traditional fisheries into prawn culture ponds or *gheries* (barricaded space). Culture fishery requires heavy capital investment but ensures big profit. It thus serves as a lucrative moneymaking source for primary societies that sublet the fishery sources to other interested parties.

The rapidly growing business of prawn culturing threatens not only the livelihood of traditional fishermen but also the ecosystem of the lake. Thousands of fishermen and non-fishermen families have lost their livelihood due to the conversion of traditional fishing sources into culture fisheries. Litigation and prawn politics now define the lives of the people in Chilika. The large-scale presence of blockades in the water channels obstructs the free flow of water and migration of fish juveniles. It also results in the loss of grazing grounds for the fish. Further, the *gheries* act as a silt trap and accelerate the silting process. It is against this socio-economic and political background that the Government of Orissa signed an agreement with the Tatas for a joint, semi-intensive prawn culture project called the Integrated Shrimp Farm Project and allowed the Tatas an advance possession of 400 hectares of land in Chilika.

The Integrated Shrimp Farm Project

In 1986, the then Congress Government of Orissa entered into a deal with the Tata Aquatic Farms Ltd to lease 1,400 hectares of land in Chilika for prawn cultivation for a period of 15 years. The government had a 10 per cent share in the deal. The Janata Dal, which at that time had opposed the project, whistled a different tune when it came to power. It merely changed the name of the farm to Chilika Aquatic Farms Ltd and increased the government's share to 49 per cent. In December 1991, the Government of Orissa awarded the Tatas an advance lease on 400 hectares of land (from Barakudi village in Bahmagiri block to Gamhari village in Krushna Prasad block in Puri district) for prawn culture.

The project envisaged the creation of an artificial lake inside Chilika by enclosing the landmass with a 13.7 km long ring embankment. This artificial lake was to be divided into a number of ponds in which the prawns were to be nurtured and commercially reared. The project comprised the following units:

* Shrimp farm: 300 ha pond area in Chilika to produce 1,500 MT of shrimp per annum.
* Shrimp hatchery near Puri to produce 200 million post-larvae shrimp seeds.
* Shrimp feed mill to be established in due course.
* Processing plant to process 1,500 MT of shrimp for export, initially in a leased plant.

The entire output of the farm was to be processed and exported with an expected annual turnover of Rs 300 million in foreign exchange.

As a part of the extension service to small-scale farmers and cooperatives in the Chilika region, the project declared that initially, about 70 million post-larvae shrimp seeds would be made available to them along with technical advice. As the requirement for feed increased due to increase in farm areas and production, a captive feed mill were to be established in due course. The shrimp produced by the farmers would be bought by the project at a fair market price. Training, technical assistance and services would be imparted free of cost to the farmers, with the Government of Orissa providing assistance in terms of the requisite infrastructure. ISFP emphasised that the direct as well as indirect employment of the people in the project and the opening of new farms would elevate their socio-economic status.[9]

Civil Society Assertion

Though the fishing communities had been resisting the commercial use of, and the consequent loss of control over, their resources, mass mobilisation could not take place in Chilika till the ISFP took shape and the threats it posed became more visible, imminent and gigantic. The people of villages adjacent to the ISFP were aware of the project, but there was little awareness about the threats it would pose to their livelihood. In fact, the people anticipated getting a good bargain for the fish that they caught, as well as employment in the project. Thus, initially, only a few educated people in these villages were sceptical about the project. Later, Meet the Students (MTS), an informal group of students from Utkal University, Bhubaneswar (the capital of Orissa), who were actively involved in effecting social change, took the initiative to visit the villages and discuss the issue with the villagers. Chitta Ranjan Sarangi, though not a student from the university, worked closely with the MTS group and played an important role in raising people's awareness and organising them against the Tata project during the initial stage.

The MTS group comprised young people pursuing radical ideas of social change, with the aim of making people conscious of the injustices perpetrated on them by both society and the state. Later, a provincial-level students' forum called Krantadarshi Yuva Sangha (KYS) was formed to mobilise youth against the Tata project. Its core comprised students who were earlier members of MTS, and who, when they passed out of the university, joined the KYS. Thereafter, it was decided that MTS would function at the university level and KYS would work as a forum to mobilise youth against the project.

This was in August 1991. At the students' initiative, a meeting of intellectuals was convened in Bhubaneswar. Out of this meeting grew the Chilika Suraksha Parishad, which was assigned the task of mobilising public opinion regarding ISFP in the cities of Orissa, mainly in Bhubaneswar, Puri and Cuttack. It was a forum that invited the think-tanks of Oriya society to debate and discuss the issue and provide moral support to the cause that MTS was trying to promote.

Gradually, the students realised that local organisations could serve as an effective vanguard in the resistance against the project. Their grounding in local issues and the trust local people placed in them would help local organisations to carry forward the resistance more effectively. Steps were thus taken to involve the Chilika Matsyajibi Mahasangha, a mass organisation of 122 revenue villages in Chilika that works to protect the interests of fishermen. Although, due to rivalry between political parties, the organisation was more or less defunct at the time, it was revived to take up the cause of the fishermen vis-à-vis the Tata project. The Chilika Bachao Andolan (CBA) was formally launched in January 1992 to work as an extension of the Chilika Matsyajibi Mahasangha in areas adjacent to the project and spearhead the movement. Govind Behera of Gopinathpur village was nominated as the convenor of the movement.

CBA was supported by many other civil society organisations, such as the Ganatantrik Adhikar Suraksha Sangathan, an organisation based in Bhubaneswar that works to protect the democratic rights of people, and the Orissa Krushak Mahasangha (OKM), which works for the cause of farmers. B.B. Das, the president of OKM, played an important role in highlighting the environmental hazards of the project and persuaded the government to undertake a study to assess the environmental impact of ISFP. He was also instrumental in attracting the interest of the international community in the issue by campaigning that the Government of India must honour the Ramsar Convention in which Chilika Lake had been declared an endangered wetland that needed to be protected.

All these civil society initiatives and formations gave the local people's protest the form of a movement that raised economic, social, legal and environmental issues related to the project. Some of the prominent issues that the movement drew attention to were:

1. The land allotted to the ISFP was traditionally used by the neighbouring 26 villages for harvesting prawn; the shallow water collected during the monsoon was ideal for their natural breeding.
2. The threats of flood and waterlogging due to the construction of the embankment on the Bhubania canal, which forms the outlet of the lake to the sea.
3. The embankment would obstruct the movement of the fish and prawn from the brackish water to the sea during breeding season. This, in turn would hamper the natural regeneration of prawns.
4. Long-term availability of fish within the lake would be adversely affected due to the pollution caused by protein feed chemicals and pesticides.
5. The project had moved ahead without the mandatory Environment Impact Assessment.
6. The land given on lease to the ISFP was classified as reserved wetland and community pasture land. Leasing out the lake was therefore illegal, as it was not listed under property that could be leased.

The movement linked these issues with a central question on development and resource use: 'The Tata project is not the central point of attack of this people's movement. The prime focus of opposition is the policy of the government towards Chilika and its people, and the Tata project is only an instance of this policy' (Chilika Bachao Andolan and Krantadarshi Yuva Sangam).

The movement articulated the issues in the three questions it posed: (*a*) to whom does Chilika belong, the people or the state? (*b*) if big business houses enter into prawn culture, what will be the fate of the people whose only source of livelihood is fishing? and (*c*) in a situation where the commercial use of resources comes into conflict with the livelihood pursuits of the poor, what should the state's priority be?

These questions contain what I have earlier cited as notions of governance coming from the people. The movement thus helped redefine the priorities the state must keep in view when formulating and executing its development objectives. It also redefined the relationship between the state and the marginalised. At the risk of repetition, I would like to emphasise that it showed the capacity of ordinary people to refashion their relationship with the state and with other sections of society. These notions of governance do not speak merely of the administrative efficiency of the state; they reveal flaws in decision-making and the lopsided priorities of the state, and they demand that state correct its priorities based on the interests of the poor and the marginalised.

Initially, the mobilisation against ISFP was confined to a few villages adjacent to the project. On 20 September 1991, the date on which the three-year lease to the Central Cooperative Society expired, thousands of fishermen gathered in Bhubaneswar and protested in front of the Vidhan Sabha (provincial assembly), which was in session. A written memorandum was given to the Fisheries Minister, who assured the people that not even an inch of Chilika would be leased out to the Tatas. Demonstrations, meetings, dharnas and rallies at the project site and in the state capital summarise the movement's activities during this phase.

In its second phase, the movement became more broad-based and adopted a somewhat militant stance when the people broke the embankment of the project.[10] The bureaucracy and the police used brutal measures to suppress the resistance. Several people were injured as the police beat them mercilessly and many were jailed. It is important to note that in this period, the Janata Dal was in power, and given its earlier support to the movement, it was expected that it would favour the people. However, when the party came to power, it not only promoted the Tata project, it also resisted the movement.[11] Nevertheless, the protest continued and the broader environmental issues pertaining to the project began to be addressed by the movement along with livelihood issues. The threats to the lake's fragile ecosystem and to the livelihood of fishermen were used to pressure the government. In advocating the environmental aspects of the issue, emphasis was laid on India's commitment to the international community to preserve the lake. It was also repeatedly reiterated that preserving the environment is the fundamental duty of every citizen.

At this stage, disagreement regarding the leadership of the movement developed between the Chilika-based Chilika Bachao Andolan and the Bhubaneswar-based OKM.[12] Local leaders felt that by overemphasising the Ramsar Convention, B.B. Das, president of the OKM, was not only limiting the scope of the movement but also hijacking it for his own purposes. The student activists, who worked relentlessly to raise awareness about the threats posed by the project, tried hard to persuade the local people to assume leadership of the movement which, at the local level at least, was seen as a manifestation of people's initiative and strength. The point was to make people aware of their situation so that they could articulate the issue for themselves. While recognising that every mass movement does need a charismatic leader to initiate the process and articulate the issues for the masses, it is ultimately the people themselves who have to carry the process forward. Hence, the students felt, no one should claim leadership of such movements.[13]

Thereafter, Chilika Bachao Andolan confined its activities to the village level while OKM operated at the provincial, capital and national levels. At the local level, people raised issues pertaining to the loss of their livelihood resources and their control over them. OKM articulated the issues in environmental terms, linking the threat from the project to the fragile ecosystem of the lake and the livelihood of fishermen, strategically emphasising the Ramsar Convention.[14] Its aim was to stop the project. As Das said:

> To win the battle one must know where the weak point of the opposite party lies and the issue on which public opinion—local, national and international—can be created. We therefore, purposefully chose

the environmental aspects of the project because we could cite the Ramsar Convention on the one hand, and the absence of an Environmental Impact Assessment by the project on the other. Our weakness lies in the fact that we could not involve the local people as we could not use their language to further their cause.[15]

At the same time, the government was interrogated on the legality of the project by invoking the Land Settlement Act according to which Chilika is a 'reserved wetland' and therefore cannot be leased to any individual or company.

Unlike the advocacy campaign that was being waged at the provincial and national levels, away from the villagers and therefore unaffected by the inequalities and power equations prevalent at the local level, the local resistance had to not only constantly negotiate with the dynamics prevalent in the sphere of civil society but also struggle hard to keep the spirit of the resistance alive. This had significant bearing on the nature of the movement. Although primarily a fishermen's movement, non-fishermen were persuaded to join in so that it could become more broad-based. Since non-fisherman engaged in fishing as an additional source of income or in prawn cultivation for commercial purposes also perceived the project as a threat, they were eager to join the struggle. However, their solidarity was confined to resistance against the Tata project; in their daily lives, the two groups continued with their traditional rivalry. Historically exploited by the powerful and dominant non-fishermen, the fishermen were suspicious of the latter's motives. And by reiterating their claim over the fishery sources, they alienated even those non-fishermen for whom fishing had become a source of livelihood. The leaders of the Chilika Bachao Andolan tried to shield the resistance from local conflicts by persuading the fishermen that the priority was to fight the bigger enemy, i.e., the Tatas; once the battle was won, the other exploiters of fishery resources (called mini-Tatas) could be dealt with.[16]

It was only after a letter signed by 21 Members of Parliament from different political parties was given to the Prime Minister and a memorandum handed over to Kamal Nath, the then Union Minister of Environment and Forests, that the central government gave the problem some attention. The ministry of Environment and Forests issued an order banning further work on the project until an Environmental Impact Assessment Study had been conducted. The Tatas assigned this task to the Water and Power Consultancy Services (WAPCO), a Government of India undertaking, despite the movement's objections about WAPCO's credibility.

Both the Tatas and the Government of Orissa stressed the positive aspects of the project. The Chief Minister of Orissa dismissed the movement as politically motivated, the handiwork of certain local hoteliers and marine exporters. The Tatas' stand was that the project had very good foreign exchange potential and that the fishermen in the area would get a better price for their catch. It dubbed the movement as being engineered by prawn middlemen, disgruntled politicians, ill-informed bureaucrats and environmentalists. WAPCO's report gave the project a clean chit, describing it as environment-friendly with no possible adverse impact on the environment of the lake. The report was opposed and criticised by both the movement and the Union Ministry of Environment and Forests. The Ministry much to the dissatisfaction of the Government of Orissa maintained that, the project could proceed only after a proper environmental impact assessment was done by a competent body of experts. A three-member team deputed by the central government to assess the situation expressed apprehension that the effluents discharged from the ponds might affect the quality of water in the lake. Further, since the project intended to meet the entire water requirement of the farm ponds through groundwater extraction, the team feared that it would affect the availability of water in the area.

While the Government of Orissa and the Union Ministry were engaged in this tussle and while the movement was vociferously opposing the project, the Orissa High Court's judgement on the fishing rights of the fishermen in Chilika halted both intensive and semi-intensive prawn cultivation in the lake.[17] Some primary societies had filed a case against the 1991 policy of the Government of Orissa and the subsequent encroachment of the fishermen's rights. The report of the fact-finding committee (popularly known as the Das Committee) constituted to study the situation reported widespread prawn cultivation and its adverse effect on the livelihood of the people and the ecosystem of the lake. Though not directly related to the ISFP, by placing a ban on intensive and semi-intensive prawn cultivation, the High Court verdict in 1993 effectively barred the Tata project.

It may be argued that the High Court verdict was not a direct response to the movement. Nevertheless, the very fact that the resistance to the project was grounded on the same issues that the Das Committee report substantiated and that the government, by admitting the negative impact of prawn cultivation on the ecosystem of the lake and the livelihood of the people, did recognise the validity of people's protest against the project, reaffirms the strength of people's collective resistance.

The battle against the corporate house was won, but that with the mini-Tatas was soon forgotten. The temporary alliance between the fishermen and non-fishermen was broken with this victory and encroachment of the lake continued as before. The leadership was amateur and the movement episodic and of too short a duration to make people conscious of long-term goals. The rivalry between the city-based advocacy campaign and the local resistance further weakened the chances of a unified struggle, as each claimed the victory to be theirs.[18]

Civil Society and Governance: Summing Up the Argument

This case study indicates that collective assertions by the marginalised take place when the state abdicates its responsibility towards them. The insensitivity and inadequacy of governance agencies to protect the interests of marginalised groups provides the context for collective action. Civil society actions in such situations relate to concerns the state is expected to address and the effort is to reform the state and bring it back to perform the role for which it came into existence or, to use a popular expression, to not let the state off the hook. In Chilika, the protest began when the state showed insensitivity to the people by putting their livelihood resources to commercial use. Moreover, shifting the responsibility for regulating the sphere from the state to the market further accentuated the dissatisfaction and apprehension among fishermen, who could not see the Tatas, governed by a profit motive as they were, giving priority to their needs.

It is not the distinction between state and civil society but the blurring of boundaries between the two that informs their relationship and which, in turn, must inform any analysis of the interface between them. The overlap of boundaries between the state and civil society manifests in two ways. First, civil society offers resistance to the state within a state-given framework. In the case of Chilika, it was the shortcomings in the existing structure of rights and threat to the existing rights that created the grounds for civil society to raise its voice. The movement's discourse on rights defined which rights were important for whom and who should possess which rights as a matter of priority. It pointed out that the role of the state was to not merely recognise and grant these rights but to protect them as well. It upheld the state's commitment to the international community to preserve the lake and referred to the Constitution to validate the cause of environment protection as the moral duty of all citizens.

Second, civil society generally uses legally sanctioned means of protest such as dharnas, demonstrations and meetings. When challenged even by these peaceful means, the state tried to suppress the voice of civil society. And the suppression was much worse when violent means were used, such as the breaking down of the embankment. However, the operation of civil society within a state-given framework does not necessarily imply that it has to remain subservient to the state or that the framework cannot be amended. While interrogating the state within the framework it provides, collective action can significantly alter the contents of this framework.

As I have mentioned elsewhere in this chapter, civil society and the state share the same ideals of universal freedom and universal rights (Mohanty 1999). Underlying the conflict between the two, therefore, is a unity of principles. When the state deviates from its ideals, shuns its responsibilities towards its people or does not fulfil its promises, collective action emerges to fill the space vacated by the withdrawal of the state. However, it is important to note here that even in such situations civil society does not strive to replace the state; it aims at reforming the state so that it can live up to its ideals.

The movement dispelled the myth about an unproblematic ideal of civil society. Differences of opinion, conflict of interests, the language in which issues were articulated by groups, and disputes over leadership characterised this particular instance of people's mobilisation. The conflict of interest between fishermen and non-fishermen did considerable damage to the movement because while civil society needed to engage the non-fishermen in the struggle, their involvement limited the scope of the movement, which was unable to address the issues of encroachment of the lake and widespread prawn cultivation by these dominant groups. Because of this inability, the movement could not be sustained once victory over the common enemy, the Tatas, was achieved. Further, the conflict between the leaders of the advocacy campaign and those who were leading the local struggle reduced the efficacy of collective action. Although in this case, the two simultaneous campaigns helped each other, they did not succeed in forming a single, coherent ideological base or strategy. While the advocacy campaign managed to successfully negotiate with the central government, it could not engage the local people in the campaign. Besides, by using a language that was not familiar to them (the emphasis on the Ramsar

Convention), it further alienated the people from the process. Such strategies have far-reaching consequences for the sustainability of collective action: if people do not become an integral part of the struggle, they fail to internalise its intensity and the moment the immediate goal is achieved, the larger purpose of the assertion is quickly forgotten. Every new threat or challenge that surfaced would require the same amount of groundwork all over again.

While inequalities in society provide the context for collection action, they also hinder such action. In Chilika, what propelled people to act was the continued perpetuation of socio-economic inequalities. But these inequalities also limited the scope of their action. The traditional antagonism that the fishermen of Chilika harboured against non-fishermen blinded them to the fact that for poor non-fishermen, too, fishing is a source of livelihood. In other words, while assertions in civil society raise critical questions about 'public/collective good' among unequally placed marginal groups, there may not always be unanimity of opinion or interest regarding this 'collective good'.[19] This conflict of interest between two equally deprived groups has significant implications for civil society. One, how can everyday existence be democratised when groups, because of their traditional caste differences and rivalries, do not acknowledge their common fate when it comes to questioning the state? Two, given this lack of unity among the disprivileged, can assertions in civil society be effectively carried out against the powerful and the dominant? Civil society thus has to fight a two-pronged battle in its effort to promote good governance. It must strive to democratise the state and at the same time it must strive to democratise its own sphere. The context of inequality in which collective action takes place demands that civil society strive to simultaneously reform both the state and itself.

The state's response towards collective action by the marginalised can be both repressive and supportive. The governing agencies at the local and provincial levels adopted an antagonistic stand towards the movement in Chilika. By extending support to the ISFP, they opposed the movement and tried to suppress it through violence. But there was supportive response from the Union Ministry and this alliance with key functionaries strengthened the ability of civil society to interrogate and put pressure on the provincial government.

Notes

1. This study was conducted as part of IDS (Institute of Development Studies) Sussex, UK and PRIA global comparative project on Civil Society and Governance. Information for the study was collected in the form of interviews from various sources: with people from the villages adjacent to the ISFP; with students who were involved with the movement; with the leaders of the Chilika Bachao Andolan and with other civil society leaders who gave active support to the movement; with journalists who not only supported the cause but also by providing wide coverage to the movement raised public opinion; with intellectuals; and with political leaders.

2. The conceptualisation of civil society as a non-political sphere does not mean that civil society remains unaffected by the structures and dynamics of power or that there can always be a distinction between civil and political. Civil society initiatives can take a political turn, but they are not equivalent to political actions in the sense that they are neither initiated by political parties nor do they form part of the state.

3. Taylor (1991), Honneth (1993) and Issac (1993) view civil society as different from the state. See Cohen and Arato (1992) for the conceptualisation of civil society as the third sphere and for the relational aspects between the state, civil society and the market see Oommen (1996).

4. For Keane (1988a, 1988b and 1998) and Chandhoke (1995), civil society performs the important task of reforming the state. Tocqueville (1900) finds civic associations working as watchdogs in a democratic state and Putnam (1999) finds a strong linkage between civic associations and democracy. Civil society,

however, is not always conceptualised vis-à-vis the state. Walzer (1992), for instance, views civil society as the uncoerced aspect of human association.

5. Before the terms governance and democracy became popular in development vocabulary, the need to make governance more humane in existing democracies like India was emphasised by Kothari. See Kothari (1987, 1988) for a discussion on the desirability of humane governance.

6. There is a growing body of literature available on people's resistance to environmental consequences and loss of subsistence natural resources in different regions of India. See Agarwal 1985; Baviskar 1995; Bhatt 1991; Fernandes 1991; Gadgil and Guha 1994; Guha 1989, 1991; Mohanty 1995; Omvedt 1993 and Pathak 1994.

7. It is not my intention to go into the debate of whether these contemporary movements can be categorised as new social movements. Suffice it to say that because these movements are different from the earlier class-based movements that mobilised people along party lines, they reflect a distinct approach towards people's issues and herald the emergence of a new phase of collective action.

8. See the Report of the Fact Finding Committee on Chilika Fisheries, submitted to the High Court of Orissa, Cuttack on 16 August 1993, for an extensive account of the government policies relating to fishing in Chilika, the ambiguities inherent in these policies and the consequent illegal subletting of the fishery sources and illegal encroachment of the lake by outsiders.

9. See the ISFP Report of Chilika Aquatic Farms Ltd, July 1991, for a detailed account of the project.

10. For a chronological account of the movement, see Chilika Bachao Andolan and Krantadarshi Yuva Sangam (undated).

11. It is interesting to note that the Janata Dal leader Biju Patnaik had earlier taken an oath that he would rescue the people and the lake from the clutches of the Congress and the Tatas.

12. Personal interviews with the leaders of the movement. This aspect is also briefly mentioned in Chilika Bachao Andolan and Krantadarshi Yuva Sangam (1993).

13. Personal interviews with the leaders of the movement.

14. For an account of Mr Das' views, see his booklet, *Chilika: The Nature's Treasure*, giving details of the lake's ecology and the

local peoples' dependence on it for their survival, and his collection of letters—*Chilika Lake: Will It Be Allowed to Die?*

15. Personal interview.
16. This aspect of the movement was gleaned from personal interviews with the people involved in the movement and the movement's leaders.
17. See the Orissa High Court verdict on 23 November 1993 in the matter of an application under Articles 226 and 227 of the Constitution and in the matter of an application challenging the government notification dated 31 December 1991 laying down the principles of settlement of fisheries of Chilika Lake.
18. These facts were gathered during personal interviews.
19. Many authors have linked civil society with pubic good. Seligman (1995) views civil society as an ethical idea that balances between individual and public good; according to Tandon (1999) civil society represents the sum total of individual and collective initiatives for the common public good.

7

When the Voiceless Speak

A Case Study of the Chhattisgarh Mukti Morcha

Neera Chandhoke

I

The interface between governance and civil society can be easily grasped when we consider the inscription on the martyr's column at the headquarters of the Chhattisgarh Mukti Morcha (CMM) in Dalli Rajhara. The inscription commemorates the memory of 11 workers who were killed in a police firing in 1977:

> *To you all*
> *The butchers who killed you*
> *Have taken possession of the law courts*
> *We will not hand over your*
> *Murder cases, to the killers*
> *We will struggle*
> *We will battle*
> *We will win*
> *Our law courts*
> *Will punish the butchers.*

The commemoration highlights two points that should be of interest to any study on the interface between civil society and governance. First, the lines *'The butchers who killed you/Have taken possession of the law courts'* pinpoint the complete distrust with which *some* groups in civil society view the machinery of governance, in this case the judiciary. Second, the lines *'Our law courts/Will punish the butchers'* pinpoint the determination of these groups to enforce justice themselves, since organisations of government have failed to do so. In tandem, these lines also inform us that the relationship between some sections of civil society and the government is not always reciprocal or complementary, and that in may well be conflictual.

Keeping in mind these two lines from the commemoration of the martyr's several preliminary implications for the relationship between governance and some *sections* of civil society can be drawn. Let me suggest at the outset that the concept of civil society covers up more than it informs us about the nature of the sphere. Civil society is often treated in the literature as a homogeneous category that either confronts or cooperates with the state. The deep fault lines within civil society, which exist between dominant and subaltern groups, are therefore obscured. We thus need to understand that civil society is a deeply conflictive and hierarchically organised sphere wherein some groups, such as the propertied and the upper castes, form the social basis of the state, while other groups are oppressed both by the state and the dominant groups in civil society. Therefore, whereas the interests of the state and the dominant groups may well overlap, those of the subaltern groups may well challenge both sets of interests.

Take the case of Chhattisgarh. It is one of the richest regions in India in terms of resources and has witnessed massive industrialisation in the shape of the Bhilai Steel Plant (BSP) and ancillary industries. Despite this, the local people lived in absolute poverty until the arrival of Shankar Guha Niyogi, who mobilised them to fight for their rights. Work conditions were exploitative and inhuman, and since the population is mainly composed of Dalits and adivasis, it was this section that bore the brunt of exploitation. Labour from the region was recruited both by contractors and cooperative societies set up by trade union leaders as well as by the management to perform casual, menial, low-skill work for as meagre a wage as Rs 3.50 per day. The organised trade unions representing workers that had been brought in from outside the region were totally insensitive to the needs of the local unorganised labour.

Thus we find that the proprietors of the industries, who included both the state and local governments that own BSP, the private proprietors of ancillary industries, the labour contractors and the official trade unions, were all exploiting local workers. Further, the presence of a large and powerful lobby of liquor barons was instrumental in persuading workers to exchange their wages for liquor. Child labour was rampant, with young children working to sustain the family. To make matters worse, local workers and peasants were not represented by trade unions; nor were their interests represented in the wider structures of decision-making. They were simply voiceless.

The workers, however, worked just as conscientiously in the mines and industrial units as they had in their fields, not knowing that few returns would come their way.[1] The concept of contract work was alien to them and they had little awareness about such issues as working hours and job security. The region witnessed the highest number of people living in conditions of bonded labour. There were no health facilities and schools in the region were non-functional because teachers were unavailable. The condition of the people in Chhattisgarh in the 1970s, before the movement began, is a powerful indictment of the absence of governance. Though the resources of the region were appropriated in the name of development, local people lived in misery and poverty, deprived of their basic human rights, such as the right to an adequate living wage, to social reproduction and, above all, the right to live in dignity. The exploitation of natural resources over which local populations logically should have first right, their exploitation as cheap labour, the non-provision of the basic conditions of survival and general indifference to their plight as hostages of labour contractors, liquor lobbies, the management of factories and the mine owners, are telling comments on the nature of governance.

As we can see, the people in Chhattisgarh were denied their basic rights because the institutions of the state were *historically allied with* the owners of capital, powerful lobbies such as those constituted by the liquor barons, labour contractors and official trade unions. In other words, civil society in the region was deeply tainted with the biases of the wider society—biases based on class, gender and caste distinctions.

However, the fact that people in power *can be held responsible* for the ills of the weaker sections of society simply because they function on behalf of the powerful segments, is a factor that is systematically ignored or neglected by theorists of civil society and governance. Until the arrival of Shankar Guha Niyogi on the scene, the people of Chhattisgarh region, most of whom are Dalits and adivasis, were employed in mines and industrial units as casual labour and worked for a pittance under hazardous and oppressive conditions. They had to launch a wide-ranging struggle to combat the oppression and create the context for governance.

Thus, in this case, we find not only a *lack of governance* or poor governance, but also complicity between the structures of governance and other groups that represented powerful interests. In other words, we find a *political society that is responsible for governance pitted against civil society*.

Correspondingly, the concept of an overlap between the two notions of 'civil society' and 'governance' may seem to be inadequate for the purpose of understanding the problems facing large sections of the people in India. It may also prove deficient for comprehending the response of the people to exploitation and oppression.

The concept of 'governance', which in recent times has found wide favour amongst multilateral funding agencies, non-governmental organisations (NGOs) and the state, relates both to the *capacity* and *quality* of administration. The emphasis upon 'good governance', arguably, is a natural reaction to the failure of the state in India to deliver either efficient admin-istration or basic services to the people. By this logic, the causes of widespread poverty, illiteracy, homelessness and hunger can be traced both to the inefficiency of state institutions and their failure to respond to people's needs. It is therefore argued by civil society enthusiasts that if (*a*) the people are 'empowered' to demand what is rightfully theirs, and (*b*) administrative efficiency and accountability is tightened, we may find some solutions to the country's problems, notably the lack of an efficient and responsive administration. Thus the connection between governance and civil society is obvious—a vibrant and vigilant civil society can compel state institutions to per-form efficiently and with accountability. Conversely, state in-stitutions will do so if they are compelled in this direction.

Three assumptions underlie the connection made between governance and civil society. One, it is assumed that the problem lies in the *unwillingness* of government institutions to perform their tasks. If they began to respond to the demands of civil society, half the battle would be won. Two, in order to compel these institutions to perform in the manner they are meant to, we need an active and vibrant civil society, which has the capacity to *control* and *monitor* governance. And three, *if the connection* between governance and civil society is established, we will realise *good governance*.

All three of these assumptions *decontextualise* governance and civil society from the wider social, economic and political setting of society. In effect, they assume that the basic system of society, economy and politics is *sound and legitimate*, unmarked by institutionalised inequality, exploitation and general powerlessness of the people, or by the institutionalised biases on the part of those who govern. The assumption of 'soundness' implies that the wider system is legitimate and does not need to be questioned. The second assumption is that given the soundness of the system, it will deliver justice to the people *provided* that the structures of governance are marked by the characteristics just described. It is manifest that these assumptions are supremely indifferent to the existence of institutionalised power structures both in the government and society. I further suggest that these assumptions *reduce politics to administration*. That is, they *abstract* both governance and civil society from the wider social, political and economic contexts and from the power relations that constitute these contexts.

The concept of governance tends to assume that the government will be responsive to the demands of the people. But we find that institutions of government have responded in brutal ways to the struggle of civil society in Chhattisgarh. On the one hand, the movement has been met with outright coercion. Despite the fact that the movement, inspired as it is by Gandhian principles, has been non-violent, it has been repeatedly subjected to barbarous repression, often at the cost of lives. The bias of government institutions was sharply revealed when judicial courts dismissed the case against the people who had assassinated Shankar Guha Niyogi—a man who has done more than anyone else to make the people aware of their rights. At another level these institutions proved to be remarkably oppressive whenever the people of the region tried to claim their rights as citizens of independent India. For instance, the local administration worked in collusion with the industrialists, and often with criminals, to suppress worker militancy. In some cases, workers belonging to the All India Trade Union Congress (AITUC) and other unions were allowed to demonstrate but permission to do this was denied to CMM-affiliated workers.

The coercion launched by the administration on the movement is truly shocking. On 2 and 3 June 1977, the police opened fire on an agitating crowd in Rajhara, killing 11 people. In 1984, when the Rajnandgaon Kapda Mazdoor Sangh was inaugurated in the Bengal Nagpur Cotton Mills, the police fired upon workers who had gathered there in order to join the union. Another peaceful agitation against the molestation of a woman by the Central Industrial Security Force was met with violence in 1980 and one worker was killed during police firing.

The success of the movement pioneered by Niyogi alarmed the industrialists, who decided that he should not be allowed to acquire a foothold in their units. Workers who declared their association with CMM were initially warned, then tortured and finally dismissed from their jobs. In 1990, when Niyogi returned to Bhilai to organise workers in the ancillary industries, he named five groups of industrialists who were regularly violating labour laws—Kailashpati Kedia of Kedia Distilleries, the Shahs of the Simplex group of industries, B.R. Jain of Bhilai Engineering Corporation (BEC), the Guptas of Beekay and the Kehtawats of Bhilai Wires. But the government did not act upon this information. During the one-year strike in Tata's Associated Cement Company (ACC) in Jamul area of the Bhilai Industrial Estate in 1990, about 12 union leaders were stabbed, 2,000 workers were jailed, while others were brutally beaten.

This large-scale coercion, supported by the administration and police, came to a flashpoint in 1991. Following the success of the ACC contract workers in July, the Progressive Engineering Workers Union (PEWU) in Bhilai organised a rally that drew a tremendous response. The respective managements began to dismiss workers who had participated in the rally. On 2 October 1990, the union proposed that workers should organise a rally, but the administration refused them permission to do so. The venue was shifted to Raipur and the rally was a colossal success. Again, a large number of workers were dismissed. By June 1992, about 4,200 workers had been fired.

In the meantime, on 4 February 1991, Niyogi was arrested on the ground that he had not presented himself for the court hearings in Balod and Rajnandgaon in connection with cases that had been going on for four to five years. On 27 March, he was released, following a directive by the Madhya Pradesh High Court. On 29 April, he forwarded a letter he had received, detailing a conspiracy to eliminate him, to the police of Rajhara. On 4 July, he received another letter informing him that Rs 1.5 lakh had been given to local criminals to assassinate him. He forwarded this letter to the police as well.

In September, about 250 workers from Bhilai reached Delhi to protest against the high-handedness of the industrialists. A delegation headed by Niyogi met the President and handed him a petition containing 50,000 signatures, which demanded protection of their fundamental rights to life and freedom of expression, as well as their right to form trade unions. The delegation also met the Prime Minister and opposition leaders with similar petitions. Barely 10 days after his return from Delhi, Niyogi was shot dead in Bhilai on the morning of 28 September 1991.

The CMM held the Patwa government, the ruling party and the industrialists of Bhilai responsible for the assassination of their leader. The FIR lodged by Asha Niyogi, Niyogi's wife, accused nine industrialists, including Kailashpati Kedia, Moolchand Shah, Naveen Shah and Chanderkant Shah of the Simplex group of industries. Later, it became clear that the industrialists, liquor barons and the politicians had hired killers to assassinate the labour leader. After repeated protests by the members of CMM, the case was handed over the Central Bureau of Investigation. The results are well known: whereas the hired assassin Paltan Mallah was sentenced to death, industrialists Moolchand Shah and Chanderkant Shah were sentenced to imprisonment along with three others. Later, however, the MP High Court acquitted all the accused on the ground of insufficient evidence. The CMM has appealed to the Supreme Court against this decision of the High Court.

In the meanwhile, repression continued. On 1 July 1992, over 5,000 workers, who had organised the blockade of the Bombay-Calcutta railway line, were attacked and fired upon by the police. Thirteen workers, three others and a police inspector were killed and hundreds of the blockaders injured. On the same date, the police opened fire on more than 3,000 workers in Bhilai, killing 20 and injuring over 150, many of them seriously. This was done at the behest of the Bharatiya Janata Party (BJP) government headed by Chief Minister Sunderlal Patwa. Two years earlier, workers had been killed in Dalli Rajhara when they protested against privatisation. On 23 May 1997, six workers were killed during a firing in Maihar district, Satna. All that these workers were demanding was that the government apprehend the killers of labour leader Ramesh Tiwari, who had been murdered by a factory manager and a security guard. On 25 May 1997, Mohan Rathore, a journalist, was killed.

Despite the fact that the movement, inspired as it is by the Gandhian principles, has been non-violent, it has been subjected to brutal repression. One can mention several other instances of police brutality and bureaucratic apathy here towards the plight of the people here, but the point I hope is clear. Despite the fact that CMM used only non-violent means of protest, such as peaceful demonstrations, dharnas, strikes, morchas and petitions—all of which are permissible in civil society—their protests were savagely put down. During a conversation with one of CMM's leaders, I wondered whether it was not legitimate to use violence in a society where the regime ritually used violence against its own people. His answer was an emphatic no; violence, he argued, would impoverish the movement and denude it of any spirit or commitment.[2]

The administration has been equally hostile to other initiatives taken up by CMM. As the movement puts it:

> Ideally, the government should encourage such social initiatives. But here, the local administration tries everything to thwart our initiatives. They do not ensure continuous power supply to our hospital. They create technical problems in the registration of students. In general, their attitude is quite antagonistic.... [The politicians, too,] do everything to weaken us. They indulge in false propaganda. When we protested against mechanisation of the mines, they said that we were hindering the development process. Our presence is a threat to them.

Here we witness that structures of government, far from being responsive to initiatives in civil society, actual hinder civil society organisations when they protest against injustice.

On some occasions, however, the judiciary has been fair to Niyogi and to the struggle. In 1990, Niyogi was jailed for two months on the ground that he had failed to appear before the court on several occasions in reference to various criminal cases against him. Releasing him on bail, Justice Gulab Singh Gupta of the MP High Court said that the offence for which he was being tried was bailable.

> He has remained absent on many occasions for which he had made applications dispensing with his presence. These applications were allowed.... If the courts were not happy with his remaining absent, they should not have exempted him from personal appearance.

Attempts to extern him from the five districts of Chhattisgarh were further neutralised by the MP High Court on 9 August 1991, which granted an *ex parte* injunction on a writ petition filed by Niyogi. Thus, while the coercive institutions of the government have tried to repress the movement, the judiciary has on occasion played fair and upheld the rights of the local people in Chhattisgarh.

The kind of repression that has been launched upon the CMM holds important implications for the basic assumption that civil society will be able to effect changes in the style and mode of governance *within the given context*. An essential prerequisite for the ability of civil society to influence the state may be a *redefinition of the context itself.* And this is precisely what we find in the region of Chhattisgarh, as the movement has not only taken upon itself to perform whatever functions the government should be performing, such as providing education, health services and a living wage, it has also undertaken the task of mobilising the people to struggle against the unequal and oppressive context of social, economic and political power in the region.

The struggle of civil society in this area goes far beyond what the theories tell us. These theories concentrate on the carving out of a space within state power where people, through associational life, are able to forge public opinion that can hold state power accountable and enforce governance. The CMM, on the other hand, has shown us that in certain conditions, *nothing is possible without struggle*, and if the government still does not respond, civil society should turn its back upon the state and concentrate on self-help and building solidarity. To rephrase the point, basic theories of governance tell us that the government has to be accountable and responsive to the people. But what happens when governments fail to be so? In such cases, it is manifest that the people have to establish structures of good governance themselves.

Finally, civil society is not an undifferentiated or homogeneous sphere. It is not only deeply divided but also hierarchical in nature. Therefore, whereas some sections of this sphere have access to the structures of governance, others are not only denied access, but these structures are also loaded against them. Given this, I suggest that civil society be studied from the point of view of the most disprivileged, taking the notion of disprivilege to indicate those groups in civil society that are oppressed by the institutions and the structures of governance. Additionally, it is possible that the dominant groups in civil society control the institutions and structures of governance, which results in a battle within civil society—a battle between the dominant and the subaltern groups.

In fact, the struggle of the CMM against the state and some sections of civil society has given rise to one of the most important and creative social movements in contemporary India, and brought to the fore one of the major issues of governance—the responsiveness and accountability of governments. In other words, since the context within which people could influence public policy was simply missing, the people of the region took it upon themselves to redefine the context through struggle. This may well alter the perspective of those who see an uncomplicated overlap between civil society and political society.

II

History of the Movement

Introduction

At this point, it may be worthwhile to revisit the main assumptions that underlay the project of the postcolonial state in India in order to understand the importance of the alternatives that CMM has thrown up. Partly inspired by the Statist tradition of the colonial state, and almost wholly by the modernising impulse of the freedom movement, the postcolonial state took upon itself the awesome task of transforming society and shaping it in the modern mode.

In retrospect, the dominant assumptions that underlay the project were not too complimentary to the Indian people. People, it was widely touted by the modernisation theory that saw its heyday during the 1950s and 1960s, were just so much clay that could be moulded by ambitious leadership. Out of this clay would be forged the modern Indian nation. In time, this assumption took on the formidable avatar of the modernising elite and the corresponding ideology of development. The assumption, it is needless to say, rendered those very populations that had mobilised on an awe-inspiring scale during the freedom movement, into so many subjects who were to be acted upon. Depriving the Indian people of agency, the developmental ideology aimed to create a society in the image of societies of the advanced capitalist world.

In the process, the overpowering seduction of development that translated as modernisation somewhat deliberately overlooked the impact of industrialisation in countries such as England—destruction of the environment, expropriation of people from their resources, widespread proletarianisation, exploitation and the resultant pain and misery that has been chronicled in such evocative detail by Karl Marx. In India, where most of the people lived off the land, the appropriation of resources for purposes of development meant that people were stripped of their means of subsistence and left to the unkind mercy of the market.

In retrospect, the havoc that development or modernisation wreaked on some sections of the people and some regions of the country is truly terrifying. It denied people control over their own resources, it garnered these resources for use in other parts of the country and for other sections of the population, and it brought devastation to local populations. Still more frightening is the total insensitivity with which bureaucrats, politicians, the propertied classes and all those who made a living through forging alliances with them, dealt with local populations. None of the attributes of what has come to be known as good governance marked their transactions with local populations. The agencies of the state proved to be repressive, inefficient, opaque and unaccountable, even in the simple tasks of governance. This more than evident when we consider the case of Chhattisgarh.

Phases of the Movement

Phase I: The Beginning of the Struggle

When the Bhilai Steel Plant was inaugurated, the Indian government promised both industrialisation as well as jobs for the local people. Yet, out of the roughly 70,000 workers employed in the plant, less than 10 per cent were local; most of them were brought in from outside. Manual labour for the Bhilai Steel Plant and other industrial units was provided by contractors who recruited labour at very low rates. Most of the local people performed casual manual and menial work under hazardous conditions in mines, factories and the ancillary industries that had mushroomed to supply components to the factories. No health facilities were provided for the workers, and wage levels were far lower than those prescribed by various government regulations. Only core workers were paid regularly. Payment of wages to the daily casual workforce was erratic and much below the prescribed minimum wage.

The issue of low wages and exploitative work conditions should logically have been taken up by the trade unions. Yet the AITUC, which took up issues relating to the regular workforce, systematically neglected the problems of the casual workers, who lived and worked in degrading conditions. When workers agitated for better wages, a cooperative committee system was introduced, but it proved ineffective in ameliorating their condition. It is in this context that Shankar Guha Niyogi, who came to work in the BSP in 1961 as an engineering apprentice at the Coke Oven Plant (where he worked till 1968), launched the struggle. Deeply moved by the condition of the casual workers, he founded the Blast Furnace Action Committee with 16 members and organised a number of strikes on the issue of remuneration.[3]

For this reason, in 1968 the management dismissed him on the charge of conspiracy. Niyogi, however, continued with his political mobilisation and published a weekly magazine called *Sphuling* for about seven to eight months in order to expose the anti-worker character of the management. An encounter with the Naxal 'Spring Thunder' persuaded Niyogi to join the Communist Party of India (Marxist-Leninist) (CPI [M-L]) in 1969, but his propensity for independent and constructive criticism got him expelled from the party. This led him to rethink the aims and strategies of the struggle and he subsequently decided to live with the people and organise them politically.

He worked for some time in the fields of Bastar, where he launched a struggle against middlemen who profited from the sale of meat by the villagers to urban areas. He mobilised the people to directly sell their agricultural produce, poultry and meat to the cities. He also founded a newspaper for the area.

As his career as a political activist became known to the police, he was subjected to repeated coercion. He was imprisoned in the Jagdalpur jail from 1970 to 1971. This was the beginning of several trips to the jail, where his longest spell was during the Emergency, from 1975 to 1976. Subsequently, he worked for some time in Danitola, crushing quartzite stone in the mines. Here, he began to mobilise workers under the banner of AITUC, simultaneously establishing contact with the political activists in Dalli Rajhara. Danitola became the site for his experiments in 'trade unionism with a difference'. Arrested during the Emergency under Maintenance of Internal Security Act (MISA) but released after 14 months, he continued to be harassed by politicians at the behest of the powerful lobbies that had been looting the area for their own profit.

In 1990, for instance, he was externed from the districts of Chhattisgarh under the Externment Act. In 1991, he was imprisoned because he had failed to appear before the court for various trumped-up charges. The industrialists and other mafias who ruled the area, tried their best to ensure that he was either jailed or that he left the region. Though he was repeatedly subjected to calumny, to charges of absconding and of marrying a tribal girl by the liquor barons, labour contractors, industrialists and politicians, Niyogi nevertheless managed to institute a spectacular movement in the area and transform the people of Chhattisgarh into political aware citizens. In time, a workers' agitation for increased wages became a movement for a 'New Chhattisgarh for a New India'. How this happened constitutes the most exciting saga in the history of independent India.

Phase II

During the last days of the Emergency, at least 10,000 workers of Dalli Rajhara revolted against the local trade union leadership of the AITUC and the Indian National Trade Union

Congress (INTUC) on the issue of equal bonus for regular as well as contract labour. During negotiations with the management, it was decided that workers belonging to the regular trade unions would be awarded a bonus of Rs 370, while the casual workers would get only Rs 70. When questioned, both unions blamed each other. This naturally led to resentment and on 2 March 1977, the contract labour in BSP announced a general strike even as it realised that the existing unions were incapable of representing their interests. On 3 March 1977, workers gathered in the Lal Maidan, where the historic process of forming a labour organisation began. On 23 March, an agreement was reached between the management, administration and contractors on the one hand, and the workers under the leadership of Banshilal Sahoo on the other. Under this agreement, workers rejected the INTUC and AITUC leadership and asserted their right to form an independent trade union. In the meantime, it was learnt that Niyogi had been released from prison and a delegation was sent to meet him and request him to lead the new union.

Niyogi reached Dalli Rajhara on 25 March and began to organise the people to support the strike. At the same time, he registered the Chhattisgarh Mines Shramik Sangh (CMSS) in Indore. This organisation was to sponsor an entirely new and different kind of trade unionism. Its red and green flag represented solidarity between industrial labour and the peasants. In May 1977, the CMSS put forth an 18-point charter before the management, of which the most important clause demanded increased wages for transport workers and ideal or fallback wages, including bonus and other facilities, for contract labour. ('Ideal wages' are payments made in the case of non-availability of work in the mines and therefore represent job security.) CMSS inaugurated its political career with some success, since in the last week of May the management negotiated a settlement with the movement. But the agreement was not honoured on payday, and the management brought in the police to deal with the striking workers. CMSS responded by organising a massive rally against police coercion, but on

2 June 1977, Niyogi was arrested. When workers demonstrated against the arrest, the police opened fire killing 11
people, including one woman and one child.

The struggle intensified after the incident and the 57-day
strike was called off only after Niyogi's release and the acceptance by management of the workers' demands. Meanwhile,
the movement spread to other mines in Danitola and Hirri.
Concurrently, Niyogi's release from prison signified another
phase of the strike. In November 1977, the workers of Dalli
Rajhara, Danitola and Hirri struck work for 56 days. In the
face of intense pressure, the management had no option but
to concede to the demands of the CMSS and the movement
tasted its first real success, which it had achieved without the
backing of trade unions.

Phase III

By the beginning of the 1990s, CMM had developed into a
well-organised trade union. On the whole, the experience of
mobilising the miners had been successful and Niyogi turned
his attention to other areas in the region that were marked by
the exploitation of workers. By 1990, the casual workers in the
auxiliary industries around Bhilai were determined to fight for
better working conditions. For example, the Simplex group,
which is a major supplier of the Steel Authority of India
Limited (SAIL), owns seven units in the area. In 1990, these
units employed approximately 2,000 workers. Of these, only
105 were regular wage labour. The rest were paid about Rs 500
to Rs 600 a month, a wage that is grossly insufficient. Due to
lack of proper security measures, the accident rate in the units
was also high. But the existing trade unions served the interests
of the employers and failed to represent the needs of the
workers. Further, the industrialists employed local goons in the
guise of contractors to keep worker discontent in check.

The experience of the 15,000 workers in Dalli Rajhara
inspired the workers in the auxiliary industries of Bhilai to

organise themselves into a trade union. In March 1990, 70 contract workers of ACC went on strike to demand better working conditions and other facilities. The management tried to break the strike by bringing in goons and the recognised INTUC union, but failed. Various unions affiliated to CMM supported the strike and Niyogi went on an indefinite hunger strike. Finally, the management conceded and according to the settlement, contract workers were guaranteed work 20 days a month, 20 per cent of the profit as bonus, and other facilities. The success of this strike inspired workers in industrial units in other areas to also associate themselves with CMM, which had displayed a remarkable capacity to change the fate of contract workers.

On 2 October 1990, Niyogi called a meeting of people who were sympathetic to the struggle of the workers of Bhilai in order to launch a mass movement. The BJP government in the state banned the meeting, which was then shifted to Raipur. About 30,000 people attended, including workers from Delhi and Calcutta as well as tribals from Abujhmar. Marching in the rain, activists and sympathisers declared their solidarity with the movement begun by Niyogi, who urged them to stand up and fight (Dutta 1992).

Phase IV: Expanding the Domain of Struggle

The founding of CMSS through a process of sustained struggle bred a high degree of commitment among the workers. On various occasions, the management tried to make them renounce their union and return to work, as for instance in 1991, when Niyogi was once again in prison. The workers, however, held fast to their demands and to their commitment.

Till 1977, the movement was no different from other trade unions. Even so, the gains made by CMMS were enormous. Initially, it managed to raise the daily wage from Rs 3.50 to Rs 7 and subsequently to Rs 80, which is the highest daily wage in the country. But Niyogi, then in Dalli Rajhara—an area rich in iron ore—realised that improvement in wages was not enough. A radical movement, he believed, had to reach out in two directions. One, the true character of the Indian state had to be exposed, and two, the movement had to concentrate on internal reform by focusing on, say, liquor consumption. Most of the daily wages were spent on liquor, of which the liquor barons steadfastly pushed up sales. Niyogi realised that the movement for decent work conditions had to be tied to a movement for internal reform. Otherwise the gains of the movement in the workplace would be neutralised by other exploitative conditions in the household. It is in this context that he launched the anti-liquor movement.

In 1976, the much-acclaimed anti-liquor movement led by women was to overwhelm the region, much to the dismay of the liquor lobby. Liquor shops were banned, people were discouraged from visiting them and social sanctions were imposed upon those who did. Far-reaching mobilisation on the issue rocked the area. The anti-liquor agitation achieved a great measure of success, setting an example for other such mobilisations. Niyogi was soon to clash with the most powerful liquor contractor of Chhattisgarh—Surjit Singh Bhatia— who operated under the protection of the Congress-I industries minister, Jhumul Lal Bhedia. He received several threats to his life, as did some of his colleagues.

This movement signified but the beginning of a struggle for comprehensive and far-reaching strategies that in time transformed the life of the people of Chhattisgarh. It aimed to take into consideration every aspect of the life and work of the poor adivasis and Dalits. In time, it was to cover such significant issues such as environment and the evolution of a mechanisation programme that would balance technology and human energy. Other aspects of the movement were directed to the issues of appropriate technology, gender relations and the abolition of exploitative work conditions. All this culminated in the formation of the CMM—a federation of about 20 organisations—in 1978–79 by the people of Dalli Rajhara.

Phase V: Formation of Chhattisgarh Mukti Morcha

The formation of CMM represented the culmination of a struggle that had recognised that any movement for workers needs to integrate both their living and working conditions. It was not enough for workers to struggle for a raise in wages; it was equally important for them to change their life conditions. The CMM held that workers' unions should move away from focusing on just economic issues to encompass other spheres that touch the life of the working classes. And since the government was not performing the duties it is expected to perform in, for instance, the areas of education and health, the members of CMM decided to organise these services themselves. In time, CMM brought within its fold bonded labour, textile mill workers, activists against child labour and abused women. Lakhs of people joined the movement that was meant to ameliorate the conditions of Dalits and adivasis, who were being exploited by a combination of liquor lobbies, the management of the mines and factories, contractors and the government. In doing so, the movement sent an important message, notably that *where governance fails to deliver justice to the people, the people, through the process of struggle, establish the preconditions of justice for themselves. Ineffective governance was challenged by the mobilisation of civil society to secure the basic conditions of life and dignity for its inhabitants.*

In 1984, Niyogi moved to Rajnandgaon to organise the workers in the Bengal Nagpur Cotton (BNC) Mills, the oldest textile mill in Chhattisgarh. The police opened fire on the striking workers, killing four members of the newly formed Rajnandgaon Kapda Mazdoor Sangh on 12 September 1984, but the struggle proved victorious. With the help of the National Textile Corporation, the BNC Mills won the prestigious best performance award. In 1990, Niyogi returned to Bhilai after 22 years to complete the work of unionising labour in the ancillary industries around the Bhilai Steel Plant.

Over almost 25 years, CMM's struggle under Niyogi's leadership concentrated on securing conditions within which individuals, who were practically invisible as far as governance was concerned, could live in dignity. Together, the rise in daily wages and the banning of liquor resulted in higher levels of nutrition and a higher standard of living. Workers now live in pucca houses and can afford green vegetables and fruit. Households are able to store grain and vegetables and afford clothing and cleanliness because they have access to funds that were earlier frittered away on drink. The ban on the consumption of liquor has also eradicated what is the scourge of rural India—indebtedness. People are now able to save in banks small amounts of money.

Phase VI: Recent Phase of the Struggle

In the aftermath of Niyogi's death, CMM focused on two main issues: carrying out an agitation against the MP High Court's decision to set aside the conviction and death sentence on Niyogi's assassins, and furthering Niyogi's concept of *Sangharsh aur Nirman* by paying attention to all aspects of the lives of the marginalised.

In the first half of 1999, CMM held a camp in Jamul (Bhilai), where members distributed ration cards to over 500 families. The acquisition of a ration card, it may be noted, usually involves a great deal of harassment in the form of bribes and repeated trips to the concerned authorities. During the same period, CMM took up causes related to the most vulnerable sections of the population: senior citizens, widows and handicapped persons. These sections rarely receive the benefits meant for them, such as pensions. CMM invited complaints from indebted beneficiaries and then acted on them. A *mukhiya*—Santosh Das—who was deputed for the job, found that more than a lakh of rupees that had been sanctioned for pensions, had not been distributed. Das successfully ensured that this money was disbursed among the intended beneficiaries.

In Pendri village of Rajnandgaon district, a liquor shop that was opened in close proximity to the district school. The CMM successfully agitated for its closure, but the shop opened at another location. CMM activists are now protesting against the reopening of the shop and lobbying for the provision of basic amenities to the inhabitants of the village.

CMM has now expanded its constituency from workers to also cover marginal farmers. In 1998, the polluted waters of the Kamal solvent factory destroyed the crop of 13 farmers of Khuteri village in Tedesara area. The factory management agreed to compensate the farmers, but no money was disbursed despite repeated written requests. The Members of Parliament (MPs) and Members of the Legislative Assembly (MLAs) of the area also showed little interest in the matter. CMM took up the farmers' cause and organised protest marches as well as sent written complaints to the authorities. Finally, a settlement was reached in July 1999, whereby the farmers received Rs 38,000 per acre as compensation. In addition, the factory management promised to repair the polluted water storage system.

In 1992, the government had acquired farming lands in the Bafara district of Khaira development block. However, no compensation was forthcoming to the farmers until CMM helped them fight their case. Finally, on 12 May 1999, they succeeded in receiving compensation.

CMM continues with its work of mobilisation by organising massive rallies on Martyrs' Day (1 July) and Shaheed Diwas (28 September). It has also expanded it struggle to fight against all forms of injustice, with the Nyayaagrah movement being initiated for just this purpose. Through the organisation of rallies, including bicycle rallies, and street corner meetings, CMM has made the following demands:

1. As promised by both the Congress and the BJP, the farmers of the region be granted Rs 5,000 per acre as drought relief. And at least one person per family be guaranteed employment.

2. Although electricity rates have been increased, no dues are collected from the industrialists. CMM demands that these dues be collected and electricity rates be reduced to their earlier levels.
3. CMM continues to demand that the Niyogi's assassins be punished; the case is now in the Supreme Court.
4. The movement has also raised the demand that 4,200 workers of the BSP, who were dismissed, be given back their jobs.

On 28 September 1999, Niyogi's death anniversary, CMM organised protests against the World Trade Organisation (WTO), which it sees as anti-poor, the concept of free trade propagated by it and what CMM considers its cultural invasion. Rallies were organised in Dalli Rajhara, Tedesra, Lohara, Bhilai, Rajnandgaon and Guroor.

III

Self-governance and its Influence on Public Policy Relating to Workers: Organising Civil Society

Since the government has failed in its basic task of providing the people with amenities, CMM has taken this job upon itself in every area that touches the lives of the people.

Education

The basic task of governance should be to provide people with the preconditions of a dignified life, however rudimentary they may be. But the government in the Chhattisgarh region had not performed even this basic task. Therefore, the people went ahead and not only established schools but also provided teachers who would teach in these schools.[4]

Immediately after its formation, CMM advised colony *mukhiyas* to open primary schools for the children of contract workers. At that time, Bhilai Steel Plant was operating only 22 schools in the labour camps, and the children of contract workers were unable to get admission in these schools. CMM's colony committees therefore decided to set up and run primary schools, the infrastructure for which was provided by CMM. Schools were set up in Bhagoli, Para, Pandari, Dalli, Ramnagar, Kelabaadi, Rajwara and Kande. This had some influence upon the government and in the next three years, all schools except one were taken over by the government's tribal welfare department.

A workers' cooperative committee of the union still runs the Hemant School, which has five teachers and around 250 students. Over 95 per cent of the students belong to adivasi and Dalit communities and more than 60 per cent of them are girls. The workers—many of whom are unemployed— have recently started a primary school in Veergaon Ural. Called the Shaheed School, it is being run with the support of CMM, which has also helped workers to build a middle school in Pathratola.

When the government did not respond to the people's demand for a high school, CMM built its first secondary school that began functioning in 1994. Named after Lata Shankar Guha Niyogi and run by the Pragatisheel Gramin Shikshak Samiti, the school has classes up to Standard X, with three teachers and 80 students. It also now has its own build-ing, which has been built by the villagers with CMM support. Though it currently follows the syllabus prescribed by the state government, CMM hopes to change it and make it more relevant.

Health

The Chhattisgarh area was notorious for its lack of health facilities. In December 1977, due to the negligence of the BSP doctors, Kushum Bai, the Vice President of CMM, died during childbirth. The workers were naturally resentful, and this resentment translated into a determination to prevent the repetition of similar occurrences in the future. They therefore decided to set up a hospital and initiate a health awareness programme. Since no qualified doctors were available in the area, about 100 volunteers constituted a people's health committee. In 1981, CMM initiated a 'Struggle for Health' programme that was financed by the union office and the garage. On 25 August, pamphlets were distributed by the workers, which raised eight major health issues, including elimination of tuberculosis, safe pregnancy and healthy nutrition for children. The pamphlet pledged to build a hospital, conduct health awareness programmes among the peasants and workers and train health workers.

This later culminated in the setting up of Sahid Hospital in Dalli Rajhara on 3 June 1983. The hospital which was inaugurated by a senior worker Sri Lahar Singh, and an old farmer, Sri Halal Khor, was built by the workers themselves. Initially it was a 15 bed hospital equipped with modern laboratories, an operation theatre and an ambulance. It has now expanded into a 60-bed hospital and the construction of another ward with 15 beds is almost complete.

The establishment of the hospital inaugurated a two-pronged health programme. First, the programme emphasised the scientific treatment of all illnesses. At the same time, it launched an awareness drive—the Jan Chetna. In addition, the programme publishes various books that give information on health and disseminates information on preventive measures. The hospital also has a training centre and provides medical facilities at reasonable rates, making health available to all. Shahid Hospital is financed by the workers and peasants, who pay a fee Re 1 for outpatient services and Rs 20 to Rs 30 for other medical services that include X-rays and minor opera-tions. The income is used for subsidising treatment and for other minor expenditure. Any extra expenditure is borne by CMM, which has also donated a truck to the hospital. Shahid Hospital has more or less achieved financial self-sufficiency and seeks a grant from CMM only in extraordinary situations.

The hospital has three doctors and 30 assistant staff. A voluntary team of six health workers is responsible for the management and health education activities. Free medicine is provided to the people, with doctors confining medication to the 120 drugs listed by the World Health Organisation (WHO). It also has a training programme for assistant staff. The doctors in this hospital take the trouble to explain the cause, nature and the cure for a malady to their patients in comprehensive lan-guage. As Dr Raju, one of the doctors, says: 'One factor makes all the difference. We are not here to earn a livelihood; we are here to make a difference in their lives. Moreover, their trust in the hospital makes us even more responsible.'[5]

The hospital's rate of successful treatment is reported to be phenomenal, even by Western standards. Research is con-ducted to develop cheap and locally available knowledge for remedies. For instance, the hospital has developed indigenous drugs for the treatment of jaundice and prostrate-related prob-lems. In place of an oral dehydration solution, the hospital prescribes *pasia* that is water containing rice starch, because it is easily available in every household. Since the region does not have access to safe drinking water, diarrhoea is a common ailment. The health awareness campaign has achieved consid-erable success in reducing deaths due to diarrhoea. Dr Raju claims that has been no report of any death due to diarrhoea since 1984. The hospital also undertakes regular vaccination drives and organises camps in interior areas when necessary.

Khiw Lal Patel, a volunteer health worker in the hospital, pointed out that the struggle for health is against the use of medical knowledge to make money. Since most doctors use their knowledge for personal gain, few doctors are found in rural areas. People therefore have to rely on quacks.[6] The most notable success of the health awareness campaign, however, is that *it has firmly located the problem of health in the social and economic context.* As Dr Raju points out: 'We mostly treat maladies caused by poverty. Eliminating poverty is the most effective preventive measure we can have.'

Establishment of the Shahid Garage

After a struggle with private garage owners, the movement established the Shahid Garage as well as a training centre in 1982. The centre's goal was to both train mechanics as well as pay them for the work they put in. Before the establishment of the garage, young boys worked in privately owned garages for long hours with meagre returns. When they struck work at Niyogi's suggestion, the owners fired them all. This experience motivated CMM to set up its own garage, which generates financial resources of about Rs 2,500 per month for the movement. The rest of the earnings are disbursed among the workers. It was proposed that the garage and training centre be converted into a polytechnic, but the MP government rejected the proposal.

Release of Bonded Labour

Together with the Raipur Churches Development and Relief Committee, CMM also took up the issue of bonded labour. It petitioned the Supreme Court in 1983 and 1988 for the release of bonded labour. Appeals to the judiciary were accompanied by dharnas on the streets of Bhopal and Delhi, and protest marches to focus on the plight of bonded labour. The release of 5,000 bonded labourers in accordance with a Supreme Court decision in 1988 enlarged the social base as well as the range of issues taken up by the movement.

CMM consistently works for the rehabilitation of the workers once they are released. After receiving training at the polytechnics that have been set up for the purpose, the trainees are provided with jobs. Apart from monitoring the rehabilitation of labour that was formerly bonded, CMM also focuses on exposing corrupt government officials in charge of rehabilitation. Along with other organisations, it has fought to ensure that the released workers are given a home to stay in, enough money to buy productive assets, and enough land to grow subsistence crops.

CMM also oversees the government's poverty alleviation programmes to ensure that people are given their due. If land has been granted to the released workers, it supervises the issuing of *pattas*. Released labour is encouraged to form unions and CMM is currently planning to fight for their land rights.

Rehabilitating Slum Dwellers

CMM has also taken up the problems of slum dwellers in Raipur. It supervises their rehabilitation through programmes initiated by the state government and ensures that *pattas* are given wherever land has been granted. It also makes sure that the slum dwellers are not relocated in areas that are too far from their place of work.

Women's Rights

Women's rights have become an important part of CMM's work. A Mahila Panchayat has been set up to deal with problems relating to women on an individual case basis. The cases range from rape to desertion, to dowry and domestic harassment.[7]

Consciousness Raising

Consciousness raising measures are undertaken to make the workers politically aware. For instance, CMM's weekly newspaper publishes articles on international liberation movements. In the late 1980s, for example, members of the CMM were fully aware of the South African liberation struggle. Intensive discussions took place when the governments in the East European bloc fell in 1989. The members are well informed about a range of issues—for example, the problems of multinational companies, of mechanisation of industry and of capital flowing into the area without benefiting local inhabitants.

Struggle Against Mechanisation[8]

At a time when mechanisation threatened livelihoods, CMM published several articles that sought to balance labour with technology in its now famous movement against mechanisation CMM's struggle had barely begun to produce results when nearly 10,000 workers were dismissed due to the mechanisation of the iron ore Bailadila mines in Bastar. Some of these mines operated under the National Mineral Development Corporation, while others were owned by contractors and included the Bora, Ashok Mining and Bharat companies. Here, miners worked 12 hours a day for a meagre Rs 3 per day. The two national trade unions—the Metal and Mines Trade Union associated with INTUC, and the United Mines Workers Union associated with AITUC—were neither able to bring about changes in the lives of the workers nor to resist mechanisation.

Until 31 March 1978, the mines owned by the companies used manual labour. The contract of Ashok Mining company workers was expiring on this date, and in order to mechanise the mines, it was not renewed. INTUC supported the management's mechanisation plan, while AITUC was opposed to it. On 11 March, miners working for Bora also joined the agitation, but the upper ranks of union leadership did not support them. As the agitation intensified, coercion correspondingly mounted. The police fired upon the workers, burnt their homes and raped their women. Eleven workers were killed in the firing. In the aftermath of this experience, CMM published a booklet about the experience of Bailadila, focusing on the problem of replacing labour by machines. It also suggested alternatives. This booklet formed the basis of CMM's drive against mechanisation and for the suggested alternative of semi-mechanisation.

Mechanisation historically has been used to not only upgrade production but also as a tool to deal with recalcitrant workers. CMM argued that the goal of any industry should be the employment of people. Machines should be used only in cases where human beings cannot perform the task, or when workers are not available. In addition, CMM claimed that mechanisation is not profitable for the management, either financially or qualitatively.

The various managements on the other hand, argued the case for mechanisation on the following grounds:

1. The quality of the iron ore produced by manual labour is not good enough for blast furnaces.
2. The production costs of mechanised mines are lower than that of mines operated by manual labour.
3. A large quantity of iron ore has to be dumped due to non-utilisation by BSP.

To these points, CMM responded by pointing out that:

(a) Since its establishment BSP has been utilising the iron ore produced through manual labour, and its performance in terms of production and profit has been better than that of other steel plants in the country. The manual mines of Bailadila have supplied iron ore to Japanese steel plants and there has been no complaint.
(b) The blast furnaces are damaged not because of the poor quality of iron ore but because of malfunctioning due to lack of proper maintenance.
(c) As far as production costs are concerned, CMM has proved that manual production is not costlier than mechanical production. Further, since only 3 per cent of

the production cost is spent on iron ore, even if it is reduced, it will not make any difference to the overall production costs.

(d) The policy for steel, rather than the workers, is responsible for the non-utilisation of iron ore by the BSP.

(e) By comparing the performance of manual with mechanised mines, CMM has shown that in no way can manual mines be described as inferior.

CMM had reason to be concerned about the mechanisation of mines. The introduction of gigantic shovels, the replacement of small drilling machines by larger ones, and of small trucks by large dumpers, meant that loaders, blasting and drilling workers, helpers and mechanics would be out of jobs. However, rather than rejecting mechanisation, CMM suggested semi-mechanisation. A crushing plant, it argued, should be established on the lower part of the hill so that it could process the iron ore and only processed iron ore should be transported to the BSP. (Earlier, iron ore was transported by trucks to railway sidings, from where it was sent to the BSP.) But the workers of drilling, blasting, raising, loading and transportation should remain as before. Semi-mechanisation would cost less in iron ore raising.

After a long agitation, the BSP management agreed to the plan, with the proviso that the situation be reappraised after two years. However, the technocrats of BSP have continued to press for mechanisation and this causes some unease, since the rate of migration from the region is low. People would prefer to stay in the area, but to do this they need to find work. CMM has prepared an alternative industrial policy that stresses labour-intensive industrial development and a self-reliant economy. But it seems to be fighting a losing battle because factory management has altered under privatisation and globalisation. No new recruitment is taking place and factory managements are waiting for the present workforce to retire. The thinning out of the workforce is further ensured through voluntary retirement schemes.

This is the most important challenge for CMM, since the region has shown a low rate of outmigration. People want to stay on in Chhattisgarh rather than look for work in other parts of the country. The dismissal of workers, which will logically follow mechanisation, will thus have a major impact on employment opportunities within the region.

Environment

The CMM has charted out alternatives to policies proposed by the state in every sphere. On the issue of environment CMM believes that local people must have ownership rights over the forests on which they are dependent for many of the subsistence needs. Forests, instead of being exploited for commercial purpose, are to be seen as people's subsistence resource.

This perspective is tied to alternate notions of development. As Janaklal Thakur, the current president of the Morcha argues, CMM is against the existing concept of development in which local people and resources are exploited to develop something about which they know nothing.

> I am perplexed when I hear that all this is done for the sake of nation-building and national development. I can't understand where is this nation when Chhattisgarh and other such regions and their people are not its part. I think this concept of development is flawed and that it has taken its toll on regions like Chhattisgarh. We want a development that is people-oriented; in which the goal is to uplift the living standards of the people through local resources, not the exploitation of local resources through them.[9]

The idea that people have the first right over natural resources challenges the right of the Indian state to garner resources wherever they are found, and its complete insensitivity to the needs of local people. Equally, the idea that development should be people-oriented mounts a powerful challenge to existing ideas on the subject. For instance, CMM demands the participation of the people in decision-making processes. Thakur argues that local people have hardly any say and therefore decisions relating to development are supremely insensitive to the cause of the workers, especially to the fact that local people should be given employment whenever a new plant is set up.

> This does not mean that I am against people from outside coming here. In fact, we have a large number of workers from various parts of the country and they are not responsible for the exploitation. They spend their earnings here and therefore contribute to the development of the region. We are against both the system and the people who benefit from the people and the resources but do not contribute to the development of the region.[10]

The spokespersons of the movement believe in people's rights and in their final authority; their attempt is to ensure that these rights are not taken away by anyone, including the government.

IV

Political Society and Civil Society

After the formation of the National Front government in Delhi in 1989, Niyogi was asked whether he expected anything different from the new dispensation. His answer was a clear indication of the wariness with which this civil society organisation regards political society. He said:

> The anti-people system is still there even after the election and formation of the new government. This way there is no difference between the previous Congress government and the new National Front government. The present political situation, however, is more

conducive for the movement because unlike the Congress Party, which represents the reactionary forces of society, the National Front is a combination of various classes of society. It would be difficult for the Front government to act swiftly against progressive movements. Thus it is time for the working classes and the democratic forces to work together.[11.]

Participation in Elections[12]

The CMM has adopted the policy of participating directly in government in order to effect a change in the very basis of representative institutions. As the president of CMM argues, the present system of governance holds no meaning for the poor and oppressed people of India:

> The futility and 'issuelessness' of elections is a major issue for us. We see no difference on the fundamental issues among major political parties of the country. We want issue-based elections. In this election we are going to raise the issues of irrigation policy, employment policy, increasing rates of electricity and other such issues.[13]

In 1984, CMM won the prestigious reserved seat of Dondi Lohara. Janaklal Thakur, who is also a local tribal leader, won the seat. However it is interesting to note that though CMM has been involved in the electoral process since 1977, and though it has fielded candidates,[14] *winning elections has never been its objective.* The movement has used elections to heighten people's awareness about the shortcomings of the present political system. Accordingly, CMM has spelt out a series of issues that have not been addressed by political parties: basic rights such as the right to work, unemployment, irrigation policy and India's membership in the WTO. The people are called upon *to vote out* parties that have taken away their right to work.

In addition, CMM has tried to demonstrate by example that accountability should be an integral part of electoral politics. In 1990, for instance, the 13 candidates it fielded took the following oath in the name of Veer Narain Singh, Bhagat Singh and Nelson Mandela:

- We will serve the people till our last breath and work for a social system free from exploitation.
- We will keep our honesty intact against any temptation.
- People's organisations are the fountain of power. Therefore, we will strengthen people's organisations.
- We will further the cause of scientific education and work for qualitative change in the country.
- We will not accept any gift from anyone; we will honour women and refrain from taking intoxicating drugs. We will lead a simple life and will always be ready to relinquish our post in the interests of the organisation and on demand by the people.
- We will not take our differences to the people before clearing doubts within the organisation.
- In order to nurture fresh leadership, we will not contest elections again.
- We will work for the public and refrain from private ambition.
- We will keep up the dignity of the martyrs of Dalli Rajhara and Rajnandgaon and follow the path shown by them.

V

Ideology and Organisation of the Movement

The CMM has made three issues its main planks. First, it insists on the full participation of the peasants and the landless. Second, it places great emphasis on the participation of women. And third, Niyogi believed that a social construction programme must be launched to make the movement self-reliant and comprehensive. Social engagement is constructive, he argued, and constructive action can be achieved only through social struggles. The slogan he gave to the people was *Sangharsh aur Nirman.*

At the same time, the members of CMM have made common cause with the peasants and worker in the rest of the country as well. They have highlighted the following issue as being of particular importance: employment for the 18 crore (180 million) unemployed in the country; checking migration from rural areas; controlling prices; and restoring normalcy in Kashmir through the withdrawal of the armed forces. CMM demands that people living in tribal regions be provided with essential commodities, that violence and sex-based consumer culture be checked, that the devaluation of the rupee be halted and that the country end its dependence on foreign debt and become self-sufficient.

Early in its life, the movement realised that it was not enough to spout political platitudes. It was equally important to institutionalise the programmes, ideology and aims of the movement. In 1978, CMM established 17 wings, each with a different responsibility: trade unions, peasants, education, health, sports, anti-liquor culture, *mohalla* and colony welfare, women's issues, mess facility, law, libraries, *parcha* distribution, water, fallback wages, building and construction. Eight trade unions function within CMM—the CMSS, the Rajnandgaon Kapda Mazdoor Sangh, the Chhattisgarh Chemical Mill Mazdoor Sangh, the Pragatisheel Cement Shramik Sangh, the Chhattisgarh Gramin Sangh and the Chhattisgarh Shramik Sangh.

In 1977, the first union issued a seven-point programme that outlines the philosophy of all the unions. The preface of the programme states: 'We are fighting for the society, not for individual interests.' The seven points of the programme are as follows:

1. Struggle against the capitalist classes.
2. Social production and social ownership of the means of production.

3. Democracy within the organisation as well as in the wider society.
4. The construction of a people's culture.
5. Gender equality as well as unity among men and women to fight injustice and exploitation.
6. Environmental protection, which mobilises people to fight against the exploitation of natural resources.
7. World peace and disarmament.

The CMM has published widely on its understanding of contemporary politics and economics in the form of pamphlets and a weekly newspaper, the *Mitan*, which is edited by the workers themselves. Widely circulated in the area, the *Mitan* focuses on issues of common concern through a variety of measures, such as cartoon features. The language of the newspaper is Chhattisgarhi.

The Nava-Anjor, as the cultural wing of the Morcha, strengthens the grassroots culture of the region through street plays, folk songs and other activities. In 1988, the youth wing of the Morcha—the Pragatisheel Yuva Sangh—was set up to mobilise youth on the issue of their rights and exploitation. It has charted out a 10-point programme that sets out its objectives of struggling for a just society. Also established in 1988 was the Chhattisgarh Students' Federation, which has two objectives. One is to mobilise students to fight against the exploitation of the region and construct a new Chhattisgarh. The second is to work out a new educational policy based on a critique of the present educational policies, the accent being on a grassroots-oriented, self-reliant and creative policy.

The women's wing of the Morcha, the Mahila Mukti Morcha, constitutes an important aspect of the movement. It lays emphasis on the participation of women and on the need to solve issues concerning themselves. Women are represented in all negotiations with the management of industrial units. In 1978, women played a decisive role in the anti-liquor agitation, the logical culmination of which was the establishment of the women's wing in 1979 with the following objectives:

1. to enhance the capacity of women for leadership;
2. to oppose the exploitation of women;
3. to support the struggle of other exploited sectors of society;
4. to oppose capitalist exploitation; and
5. to construct new values among the working classes.

The women's struggle is part of a wider struggle against exploitation. Sudha, a women's activist, says that CMM takes on women's issues not apart from but in tandem with other issues pertaining to exploitation.[15]

CMM and Other Social Movements

Niyogi was concerned with putting forth a national alternative by uniting various social movements from different regions in the country and some initiatives were taken in this respect. In order to chalk out alternative development models, CMM met with representatives of six organisations—the Bandhua Mukti Morcha, Narmada Bachao Andolan (NBA), the Bhopal Gas Peedith Mahila, Udyog Sansthan, the Uttarakhand Sangharsh Vahini and the Shoshit Samaj Dal—in New Delhi, where it was jointly resolved that closer linkages with like-minded organisations were needed to confront the growing challenge from capitalist, communal and reactionary forces in the country.

CMM is concerned with struggles both at the national and international levels. It has supported the struggle of the victims of the Bhopal gas tragedy, joined hands with the Bandhua Mukti Morcha for the rehabilitation of released bonded labour, and has shown solidarity with NBA in its struggle against the building of the Narmada dam. It was also one of the organisers of the massive farmers' rally held in Delhi to protest against the Dunkel project in September 1988.

However, the CMM is also very clear that every social movement operates within a very specific context and that the model evolved by them may not be applicable in other contexts. It is thus against the idea of merging various social movements into one national organisation. Instead, it would prefer a common platform where movements can share their experiences and learn from each other.

VI

Implications for the Civil Society—Governance Interface

Two factors differentiate CMM from other civil society organisations. One is that it recognised that a transformation of the social, economic and political contexts was necessary before good governance could be established. Within the given context, the structures of governance were completely insensitive to the needs of the poorest sections of the people. Their interests were just not represented in the institutions of governance. In fact, the administration was actively conniving with dominant groups in the region to oppress the people. Civil society therefore had to organise itself in the form of a movement, which struggled against oppression and injustice through peaceful means.

The second factor is that, unlike CMM, not all civil society organisations are in a position to make an impact on governance. Whereas groups that possess economic and social clout can impact the administration to some degree and make it responsive to their demands, other groups whose members belong to the poor and oppressed sections of society are voiceless. And third, since civil society is itself a deeply divided and fragmented sphere, impoverished groups have to battle both the administration as well as dominant groups within civil society to realise their ends.

What is more important is that groups of society's dis-privileged sections are capable of throwing up alternatives to existing policies as well as institutionalising those that are more sensitive to the their needs. The overlap between governance and civil society can therefore be conflictive. However, we can only realise this when we locate the civil society and governance argument in the wider context of social and economic relationships and recognise that these relationships are marked by power. Both governance and civil society thus embody the themes of power and resistance to power in society, the polity and the economy.

What marks CMM as an organisation of civil society is that it is a movement that has radically challenged all established notions of the relationship between governance and civil society.

Achievements of the CMM

CMM has a membership that runs into thousands and a support base that runs into lakhs throughout the region of Chhattisgarh, with its main base remaining the contract labour in the Dalli Rajhara iron ore mines.

One of the finest achievements of the Morcha has been to integrate the work, home and cultural lives of the people. Moving away from a narrow economics perspective, which has proved to be the bane of most trade unions, CMM created solidarity among the dispossessed and forged bonds of understanding with other movements. As a movement, CMM is open-ended and responsive to the issues and problems of the masses, both within the region and outside it.

By taking up the issue of bonded labour, the problems of slum dwellers, mechanisation, child labour, anti-social practices such as liquor consumption, and the status of women, CMM has fashioned a wide-ranging programme of social transformation that outstrips current notions of governance and civil society.

In an important breakthrough, CMM has effected major changes in the whole idea of citizenship. For instance, in 1991, the people of the region demanded autonomy. According to CMM, this meant geographical as well as socio-economic autonomy, autonomy to chart out paths of sustainable development and autonomy for all the downtrodden people of the region. This view contrasts sharply with that of social movements that are based on chauvinism and exclusiveness. Chhattisgarh has now become a separate state, largely due to the efforts of CMM.

But the members of CMM have gone one step further: they have charted out a new meaning of what it means to be a Chhattisgarhi citizen. According to CMM, a Chhattisgarhi citizen is one who works in the region and who does not exploit either the resources or the people for his/her personal benefit. Citizenship can thus be conceptualised on the basis of productive labour and non-exploitation. It does not matter if the person belongs to a different part of India and does not speak Chhattisgarhi. Correspondingly, the enemies of Chhattisgarh are those who exploit the people and natural resources of the area for private gain, even if they have been born in the area and speak the language. This is in stark contrast to other social movements in the country, which are based on exclusiveness. It is also in contrast to the official definition of citizenship in India. In effect, this particular conceptualisation has outstripped existing structures of social and political power, for it connects the demand for autonomy with fundamental policy changes. As the president of CMM said: 'We are not against a separate Chhattisgarh, but we a want a new Chhattisgarh.'

CMM as a Civil Society Organisation

The main problem with CMM is that it did not build links with other trade unions in the area. The Bhilai Steel Plants employs about 50,000 workers and other public sector enterprises employ a number of workers who have been organised into trade unions. Had they acted together, they could have countered the onslaught of the government. However, largely due to the fact that the organised trade unions were indifferent to the plight of the unorganised sector, the 'CMM reacted to the narrow-minded self-centredness of the public sector permanent workers with another variety of sectarianism which pitted the Chhattisgarhi unorganised worker against the '*pardeshiya*' organised outsiders' (Monteiro 1998: 163–64). What CMM failed to realise, argues Monteiro, is that when the struggle becomes larger and tougher, class-consciousness and broader organisation become indispensable.

VII

Conclusion

The southeastern part of Madhya Pradesh known as Chhattisgarh sharply reveals the lack of governance in major parts of India. Whereas this region has witnessed industrialisation to a considerable extent, it continues to be the poorest in the state as well as the poorest in the country. The stark contrast between the presence of a remarkable amount of resources, which have been exploited for the benefit of other parts of the country, and the deprivation of the people, in time bred its own consequences. This was the emergence and the consolidation of CMM, which initially began as a workers' strike and developed into one of the most remarkable movements in contemporary India. The movement has, in effect, shouldered the tasks of governance even as it has taken on the responsibility of providing services to the people.

But CMM has gone further than just delivering services, which normally fall within the provenance of governmental activities. It not only launched a movement for people's health, it also set up a hospital when the state failed to provide one. It not only fought for better wages, it also initiated a movement against the consumption of liquor. Further, it has fought for the abolition of bonded labour, overseen the rehabilitation of released labourers, set up various wings to deal with different issues, and inculcated and developed immense political consciousness among its members. Not only did the movement do all this, it charted out new definitions for both a desirable Chhattisgarh and a desirable Chhattisgarh citizen.

The forging of the movement involved a deep-rooted struggle against all the vested interests that in tandem had exploited both the people and the natural resources of the region in the post-independence period. In time, through the process of struggle, the people of Chhattisgarh won for themselves not only the basic conditions within which they could live in dignity, but also redefined the aim of the movement as building a 'New Chhattisgarh for a New India'.

There appears to be a deep-rooted contradiction between the assumptions of the civil society argument and the experience of the people of Chhattisgarh. CMM has had to conceptualise a new civil society in order to conceptualise good governance. In other words, a combination of historical circumstances prompted CMM to conceive of new and wider social, economic and political structures, within which a civil society can function and within which structures of good governance are conceivable.

It is this creative aspect of the movement that sets it apart from other civil society organisation—pressure groups that work within the framework provided by the state or social movements that deal with single issues. CMM's movement has gone far beyond most of the state-inspired meanings that pervade notions of good governance simply because it has demanded and effected a structural change in society.

From this examination of the lack of governance in the most exploited part of the country it becomes clear that existing conceptualisations of the overplap between governance and civil society, which have overtaken imaginations and intellectual energies, may prove inadequate when it comes to understanding the dynamics of civil society in India.

Notes

1. Personal interview.
2. Conversation with Anoop Singh of CMM.
3. The workers of the Hirri dolomite mines of the Bhilai Steel Plant achieved their first victory when the management conceded their demand of regularising the workforce, which had hitherto functioned under the contract system of cooperative committees.
4. This section is based on Illina Sen's 'Schooli Shiksha aur Jan Siksan' in *Sangharsh Aur Nirman*, edited by Anil Sadgopal (date not available) as well as material collected during the field trip.
5. Personal interview.
6. Interview.
7. Based on the article 'Lal-Hare Jhande ka Sanghatan' in Sadagopal (date not available. 374–83) and the field trip.
8. Based on the May 1978 essay by CMM that was reproduced in Sadagopal (date not available); Niyogi, 'Mines Mechanisation and People', and 'What is the Problem of Iron Ore Mines in Dalli Rajhara (ibid.) and Niyogi and Anoop Singh', Alternative Industrial Policy (ibid.).
9. Personal interview with Janaklal Thakur, President of CMM and former MLA. Thakur was a transport worker at the time when CMMS was formed.
10. Ibid.
11. Interview with the journalist Kushaldev Nath in the beginning of 1990.
12. The CMM is a registered regional party.
13. Interview with Janaklal Thakur, field trip.
14. Barely a month of its formation, CMM fielded two independent candidates to contest the assembly elections in May–June 1977. In 1980, the CMM President, Janaklal Thakur, contested from the Dalli Rajhara constituency and was elected. In 1989, he contested from the Kanker parliamentary constituency. In March

1990, CMM fielded 13 candidates for various seats in the region. Again, in 1993, Janaklal Thakur represented the Dondi Lohara seat in the assembly. In 1998, he was defeated in the assembly elections by a slender margin. In the just concluded Parliamentary elections, CMM fielded Anjor Singh Thakur—the peasant leader and Vice President of the organisation—from Kanker. He managed to get more than 15,000 votes but was defeated.

15. Interview.

8

Democratic Governance, Civil Society and Dalit Protest

Sudha Pai and Ram Narayan

In recent years there has been an upsurge in the volume and intensity of civil society articulation against the Indian state, bringing into sharp focus some neglected aspects of democratic governance. The reason for this has been the acceleration of the democratisation process leading to heightened political consciousness, paralleled by a critique of the existing structures, practices and policies of governance. With a decline in the capacity of the state to provide adequate governance, two kinds of civil society initiatives have emerged: movements of the poor, oppressed and marginalised sections such as Dalits, tribals and women; and second, non-governmental organisations (NGOs) reflecting the disillusionment of the middle classes with electoral politics, corrupt politicians and the inability of the state to undertake the tasks of development.[1]

Our study deals with the first kind of movement. Its main objective is to examine the interface between civil society and governance in a non-Western society with deeply entrenched hierarchical divisions, in the context of Dalit protest against the state's failure to protect their life and self-respect from the violence perpetrated by the police, the bureaucratic apparatus and the upper castes. We do this by examining the widespread and intense protest under the leadership of a prominent Dalit association—the Rashtriya Soshit Morcha (RSM)—following the removal of Ambedkar's statue in Shergarhi by the Meerut city administration and the consequent police firing on 29 March 1994.

In the days following the incident, the RSM raised fundamental issues of governance such as state violence against disadvantaged groups and provision of justice for them. While initially the state government, headed by a coalition of two parties committed to the establishment of a *bahujan samaj*, upheld the need to maintain law and order and supported the actions taken by the police and city administration, it finally had to agree to the demands of local Dalit associations, which resulted in the transfer of many police personnel and the reinstallation of the statue.

The study also demonstrates on the basis of the empirical material examined that, unlike in Western Europe, civil society in non-Western societies like India is a deeply divided and hierarchical domain. The result is that democratic governance is often denied to disadvantaged and marginalised groups like the Dalits. Associational life is also limited to social groups with little trust or interaction between them, due mainly to lack of social transformation and the continuation of traditional social values. We argue that the democratisation of civil society, leading to the establishment of a state that can provide effective governance for all citizens, is possible even in such a situation. But it can only come about through prolonged and intense contestation and struggle by disadvantaged social groups, such that was witnessed in western Uttar Pradesh (UP).

Civil Society and Governance in the Indian Context

The term civil society has been variously conceptualised as a movement against a hegemonic or authoritarian state

(O'Donnell and Schmitter 1986); a 'third realm', autonomous of the state (Taylor 1991; Cohen and Arato 1992); an ethical idea that harmonises individual and public good (Seligman 1992); a voluntary sector (Van Til 1988); and an arena of dense networks and associational life contributing to democratic life (Putnam 1993). As these definitions arise mainly out of an examination of civil society in the industrial societies of Western Europe, with its characteristic of modern associational life based on equality, autonomy, recognised rights, duties of members and other such principles, the application of this concept to non-Western societies needs to be done with care and after rigorous analysis.

As our study deals with Dalit protest against the state, the framework of civil society versus the state is relevant.[2] However, the relationship between civil society and the state is different in India from that in the West, due to the different historical paths travelled by these societies. In India, the two are very closely intertwined. Due to our colonial legacy, the centrality of the state, both in maintenance of order and development, makes it overdeveloped and relatively autonomous of society. Dalit assertion, which underlay the violence that took place in Meerut in March–April 1994, was certainly a product of mobilisation by leaders emerging from within civil society. But *equally*, and perhaps *more importantly*, it was also a product of the state's activities since independence, such as the provision of welfare, protective discrimination and a democratic space in which a new generation of Dalit leaders thrown up by these activities could make their discontent felt.

The clash between the Dalits and caste Hindus was related both to their *cultural* and *economic* interests. In the West, the state, market and civil society emerged successively, with each acquiring a certain level of autonomy. India, on the other hand, drew heavily upon the socialist model available at the time of decolonisation, thereby establishing the state's control over the economy. Despite structural adjustment in the 1990s, the state still retains substantial control over the market. Moreover, by adopting the concept of 'distributive justice', the state attempted to retain its centrality by not only initiating planned development but also launching and sustaining civil society (Oommen 1996). As a result, abstracting civil society from the state, economy and society is not fruitful for an understanding of the processes that occur in any of these arenas.

In addition, political actors often hold interchangeable roles, straddling both civil society and the state. Political leaders who head a social movement within civil society may also wield power in the state, making it necessary for them to play a dual role.[3] Political parties also simultaneously straddle civil society and political society, playing a role in both. Thus, there are significant interconnections and the boundaries between civil society and the state are fuzzy as compared to the West.

The difference in the relationship between the state and civil society in non-Western societies like India and those in the West is not merely structural but normative as well. First, the attempt to establish a civil society in India is recent, beginning in the colonial period. As a result, traditional values and attitudes arising from its segmented and hierarchical society, as well as modern values based on equality, rights and justice that are enshrined in the Constitution coexist in uneasy relationship.[4] Particularly relevant to our study is the existence of caste hierarchy, due to which civil society in India is a *complex space* where different caste groups with differing social values and ritual status often come into conflict, as much with each other as with the state. Moreover, due to rapid social change, the relationship between these social groups is unstable and fluid, making civil society an arena of contestation among them.

Second, the democratic state is usually understood as an impartial arbiter between equal citizens as it gains legitimacy from them. However, it often fails to be impartial between civil sectors when its population is heterogeneous. This is especially true in the day-to-day functioning of its bureaucracy.

Third, since our study deals with Dalits, a historically oppressed and marginalised group, it is necessary to simultaneously problematise their position in civil society and their relationship with the state, both of which create problems for governance. Until recently, persons manning the state belonged to the upper or middle castes, who were insensitive to the special needs of the lower castes. Historically, Dalits were excluded from civil (Hindu) society and it was only during colonial rule that the rights to education and vote were extended to them. After independence, under the auspices of the Nehruvian agenda, the government launched an attack on the caste system through such measures as abolition of untouchability, positive discrimination and welfarism. However, despite the establishment of a democratic framework, civil society in India remained elitist, exclusive of the lower orders. In Hegelian terms, it was a 'bourgeois society' limited to a few 'proper citizens' (Chatterjee 1999: 11). It is only since the 1980s, with rapid democratisation and the rise of lower-caste political parties like the Bahujan Samaj Party (BSP) that this exclusion has been militantly questioned, leading to conflict.

Fourth, as we examine the role of a Dalit association that provided leadership to the protest movement, the notion of civil society as a sector in which associational life takes place, promoting democratic values in the Tocquevillean sense, is also relevant. This would imply the existence of an arena within civil society that is autonomous of the state and to which all citizens have free and equal access for discussion and dialogue. However, in the absence of democratic values and equality among social groups, this aspect of civil society has yet to strike deep roots in India.

The term 'governance' is equally problematic and needs to be defined in the Indian context. Traditionally, governance meant maintenance of order and protection of the life and property of citizens by the state and the citizens, in turn, granted legitimacy to the state. However, today it is used in a much broader sense and refers to a new 'process' or 'style' of governing in which the state shares the responsibilities—including those in the social and economic field—with institutions and actors placed within the private and voluntary sector. Such a definition introduces a change in the long-standing balance between the state and civil society; it shrinks the arena of the former, giving more space and responsibility to the latter (Stoker 1998: 17–27). However, in countries like India, in the absence of a homogeneous, strong and democratic civil society that can assume some of the responsibilities of governance, the state continues to play a central role. As our study shows, *Dalit citizens* as a disadvantaged group *expect the state to provide them 'justice'*, i.e., protection against all forms of discrimination and caste-based atrocities. And when the state fails to deliver this, they are quick to oppose it. In disputes between lower- and upper-caste groups over issues such as land, erection of Ambedkar's statues, payment of minimum wages, the practice of untouchability, etc., the state must act—and be seen to act—as an impartial mediator favouring neither side. The Dalit leaders of the RSM raised two related issues of *violence* and *justice*, which can be seen as key themes in defining and understanding the relationship between civil society and the state that is responsible for providing governance. Hence, the interface between the two and the ensuing implications for governance are different in non-Western societies.

This chapter is divided into four parts. Part I briefly describes the phenomenon of Dalit assertion in western UP, particularly in Meerut district, both historically and specifically in the 1990s. This section provides the background to our study in Part II of RSM—one among many Dalit associations within civil society in Meerut city committed to looking after the interests of Dalits and protecting them against oppression and economic and cultural exploitation by both caste Hindus and the instruments of the state: the police, bureaucracy and the courts. Part III builds, based on newspaper reports and interviews with Dalit leaders, a detailed narrative of the Shergarhi incident and the roles played by the police, magisterial bureaucracy, media and Dalit associations. It also highlights the centrality of RSM in upholding Dalit interests. Part IV deals with the response of the state government, in particular that of the BSP, one of the partners in the ruling coalition. In the light of the empirical data presented, the conclusion returns to a discussion of the interface between civil society and governance in India.

I

'New Forms' of Dalit Assertion

The western districts of UP, especially Meerut,[5] have a history of Dalit consciousness and activism since the late colonial period. The *chamar-jatavs*,[6] who form the most numerous sub-caste among the Dalits in this region, have been the most identity-conscious and upwardly mobile group, feared and respected by other Scheduled Caste (SC) groups in UP. The Schedule Caste Federation (SCF) between 1945 and 1948 (Duncan 1979; Narayan 1996) and the Republican Party of India (RPI) between 1956 and 1969 (Brass 1968; Lynch 1969) were both active here and, despite their failure to institutionalise themselves as political parties, contributed to the creation of identity consciousness and politicisation. The RPI movement in the 1960s was very active in the Hastinapur (village) Assembly constituency, close to Meerut city, and in 1982, the *Jatav Mahasabha* was set up in Maithena Inder Singh,[7] a large, Dalit-majority village about 20 km from Meerut.

However, we argue that despite the region's long history of Dalit consciousness, assertion in the 1980s and 1990s was a *qualitatively new phenomenon*, different from protest in the 1960s and 1970s—an important factor that underlies our selection of this district. Since the mid-1980s, Meerut district has experienced a rising wave of Dalit assertion, leading to a number of incidents ignited by caste atrocities. A study based on police reports divides the districts in UP into two categories: 20 districts where atrocities against Dalits are very high and 23 where they are fewer. What is important for us is that Meerut district heads the first category, followed by some other western districts (Prasad 1995: 104). From the mid-1980s, the Dalit movement here entered a period of revolt, a new form of political assertion that came after many years of fragmentation and cooption by the Congress in UP. This assertion *was a product of deep and increasing discontent with the state's failure to provide protection to the life and property of Dalits, improve their socio-economic condition and end the practice of untouchability.* The reasons for the assertion lay in the changes that the region witnessed since independence. First, it was a result of the process of democratisation of the Indian polity, leading to greater consciousness of their low-caste identity and higher levels of politicisation. Second, the state's policy of protective discrimination resulted in the rise of a post-independence, educated, upwardly mobile Dalit generation, who were the vanguard of the new assertiveness and were involved in the establishment of associations in Meerut city. Third, the sustained economic development that took place in these districts over a long period of time made the condition of the *jatavs* here (as in the colonial period)[8] much better than in other parts of the state. This provided the *jatavs* the potential to challenge the oppression of the traditionally landowning castes—the *rajputs, jats* and *gujjars*—who, until very recently, maintained an oppressive socio-economic hold over them.[9]

Due to these developments, Dalit assertion in Meerut district has taken 'new forms'[10] at the grassroots level, such as a desire for education that would enable them to compete with the upper castes in all walks of life, reading Dalit literature, installing statues of Ambedkar and forming Dalit associations (with which we are concerned here). These socio-political activities are independent of the BSP, a militant Dalit party formed in 1984; in fact, they are often critical of and antithetical to it. They are part of an older grassroots process in the region that occurred during the 1960s, that of Ambedkarisation, i.e., the tremendous growth in awareness among Dalits, particularly the *jatavs*, in parts of western UP about the ideas and life of Babasaheb Ambedkar, which has been revived by a new generation (Singh 1998).

It is also necessary to explain why the Shergarhi incident of 1984—in which the police removed a statue of Ambedkar leading to violent protest—has been selected instead of any one of the many cases of Dalit protest that took place in Meerut in the 1990s. In recent years, oppression and exploitation of Dalits based on *ritual untouchability* have been replaced by other forms of caste atrocities, the breaking/removing of the Ambedkar statues being one of them.[11] The latter is used by caste Hindus to humiliate and suppress attempts by Dalits to improve their social and economic position. Ambedkar's statue has great symbolic and cultural significance for Dalits all over India, which explains the violence on its removal.[12] Moreover, there is a special *cultural* relationship between Ambedkar and the *jatavs* of western UP. He is seen as a person who was able to provide protective discrimination for the Dalits in the Constitution. This relationship is enhanced by the fact that he himself was a Dalit, because the *jatavs* believe that only a Dalit can understand their problems and achieve *empathy* with them. All offices of Dalit associations, panchayat *ghars* and Dalit homes in western UP have statues or photographs of Ambedkar. He is held in great reverence by them; as Owen Lynch writing on Agra in the 1960s remarked, for the Dalits he is a god and is worshipped as one (Lynch 1969). While exploring the roots of Dalit consciousness, Zelliot comments on this overpowering image of Ambedkar:

> The meaning of this symbol, of the statue or the photo, grows from the life and work of B.R. Ambedkar. The image is always clad in a Western suit, white shirt, red tie, pen in pocket, book in hand. The image usually represents Ambedkar with an upraised arm, teaching or declaring the message of courage and equality. It stands erect, unmoving. This is what the image represents: education, success, contribution to the political world of India, courage, empowerment through reservations, protections through relationship to government, 'one of us' who was not only important personally, but was important to India. The book Ambedkar carries is the Constitution,

and his role as chairman of the drafting committee has assumed great importance and symbolic value. He is without specific caste. He is the dalit of dalits. He has no identity as a Maharashtrian. He is all India (Zelliot 1998).

Although the installation of Ambedkar's statue has socio-cultural meanings and is an identity marker, in recent years it has had important political repercussions. During the late 1980s and 1990s, leaders of the BSP, particularly Mayawati, used it as a tool for political mobilisation and identity building in the countryside. Criticising Gandhi and other Congress leaders as representing the upper castes and installing statues of Ambedkar, who is depicted as the messiah of the Dalits, helped the party to create an alternative space for itself during the period of Congress decline, leading to conflict and violence between the caste Hindus and the Dalits. Mayawati's political slogan since the early 1990s—*jo zameen sarakari hai, woh zameen hamari hai*[13]—has been taken literally and used by villagers to set up statues on vacant government land leading to accusations of land-grabbing by the upper castes. It is reported that during her brief tenure as Chief Minister in 1997, Mayawati installed 15,000 Ambedkar statues all over UP (Sethi 1997). The Shergarhi incident is the most important instance of its kind in UP, leading to large-scale violence, police firing and a judicial inquiry.

II

Soshit Dalit Associations in Meerut and the Rashtriya Morcha

As described in the previous section, by 1994 the socio-economic and political changes in the Meerut region led to the rise of a number of Dalit associations, many of which still exist today or have been replaced by similar new ones.[14] They fall into three broad types: traditional, modern and political. The first consists of panchayats or *mahasabhas* in the villages surrounding Meerut city. These associations generally meet whenever there is a common problem confronting Dalit society or an instance of atrocity against them. The meetings are not, as in the past, organised by 'caste leaders' but by educated *pradhans* of villages that have a large Dalit population (of which there are many in Meerut district) and are held in panchayat *bhawans* or Ambedkar schools that can be found all over the region. Apart from panchayats, almost all villages have an Ambedkar Sudhar Samiti that helps Dalits solve their daily problems and provides them with a platform for common action. These associations form a network that enables quick mobilisation, as was seen during the Shergarhi incident when large numbers of Dalits from all over UP converged in Meerut city to support local Dalits.

The second type consists of 'modern', voluntary and, in some cases, registered associations of Dalits set up by educated Dalit leaders—lawyers or teachers—in Meerut city. A few associations of this type that existed in Meerut in 1994 were the Samukhya Dalit Morcha, the Bhawan Nirman and Bhatti (kilns) Mazdoor Union, the Akhil Bharatiya Jan Kalyan Ambedkar Sudhar Samiti, the Rashtriya Soshit Morcha (RSM), the Dalit Siksha Andolan and the Ambedkar Uthhan Parishad.[15] Formed in the early 1990s, they were established to protect the interests of Dalits. It was increasingly being felt that the state was not interested in doing this, controlled as it was by the upper castes and the political parties that represented them. Products of social and political awakening and increasing literacy and prosperity among Dalits, particularly *jatavs*, these are independent associations set up by Dalits for Dalits. They can be said to fall within the ambit of civil society, although individual members may support political parties. For example, while these associations were not set up by, say, the BSP, links of two types with the BSP do exist in many of them. First, there is overlapping membership—there have been times when members of these associations have moved to the BSP; and second, many of these associations are supporters of the BSP and actively campaign for it during elections. Of the associations just listed, only the RSM, the Dalit Siksha Andolan and the Bhatti Mazdoor Union exist even today, probably because they managed to carve out their own goals and an identity that was independent of any political party.[16]

The third type consists of associations that are attached to political parties but that have an independent leadership and following, such as the Dalit Sena (DS), the Ambedkar Sewa Dal and the Anusuchit Jati Morcha. These associations are not based in Meerut. They become active whenever and wherever atrocities against Dalits take place. Of these, the DS, set up by Ram Vilas Paswan, a Dalit political leader who was a minister in the V.P. Singh government in 1989 and the general secretary of the Janata Dal (JD) in 1994, played an important role in the Shergarhi incident.[17] The Sena has a base in both UP and Bihar, but it is also an adjunct of the JD. But of the many associations that were involved in organising Dalits during the Shergarhi incident, we have selected RSM for study as it played a central role in upholding the interests of the Dalits at that time. Dharampal Singh, the leader of RSM, is even today regarded as one of the most respected Dalit leaders in Meerut city.

Set up in 1992, the RSM[18] is a non-political, autonomous association for the SCs, STs and the poor. The immediate context for its formation was the increasing number of atrocities and violent attacks against the Dalits in the Meerut region, the growing realisation that the present polity had failed them, increasing intolerance of their abusive treatment by both the state and the upper castes, and the need of an association to protect their interests. Formed by 'Comrade' Dharampal Singh, an advocate who was a member of the Communist Party of India (Marxist) (CPI [M]) from an early age until the mid-1980s. Realising that caste and not class—as emphasised by the left—was the real basis of Indian society, Singh decided to help his less fortunate caste brethren by involving himself in issues concerning the Dalits. As an advocate in Meerut High Court and an elderly and respected member of his community, he was well placed to do this.[19] Vijaypal Singh, a young RSM leader who is a resident of Shergarhi and also an advocate in Meerut, elected to assist him in this task. The association has a president, a general secretary, a number of vice-presidents and members spread throughout Meerut district.

The question of whether the RSM can be described as a civil society organisation (CSO) is debatable and is discussed in the concluding section of this chapter. It is an association whose main aim is to protect the interests of Dalits and others who are oppressed. The RSM believes that the polity is being used to grab power and indulge in corruption. Its leaders argue that the Constitution provides for the right to life, and yet Dalits have been deprived of this right, their women and property are not safe, their marriage processions are stopped, they are economically dependent on others and, most important, constantly suffer the stigma of untouchability. RSM describes the present condition of Dalits as 'unfreedom', its slogan being 'khoon do, azadi lo' (give blood, take freedom). Associations like RSM, while having a permanent presence, become very active when incidents of atrocities against Dalits take place. Apart from providing legal aid and some social services to the community, the association's main activity in the political field has been to hold large rallies on issues of importance to the Dalit community. By doing this, it has tried to pressure the government of the day to attend to these problems.

All RSM's activities have centred on three main demands. A key demand is security for the life and property of Dalits. RSM's leaders claim that the police are concerned only with the security of caste Hindus. Dalits, therefore, need to take steps to ensure their own safety and every Dalit village and neighbourhood should therefore be allowed licensed firearms for their protection. Second, the police needs to be firm in tackling violence against Dalits and ensure that the guilty are speedily brought to justice. Justice and violence are thus two central issues for which the RSM has fought on many occasions, including the Shergarhi incident. The third demand by RSM is that the bureaucracy must tackle the economic problems of Dalits and implement all welfare programmes quickly and effectively.

Since its inception, RSM has launched several struggles and demonstrations in Meerut district based on these demands. The more well known ones include the Bhoopa incident in October 1992, the Shahpur incident in January 1993, the Khaikhera incident in March 1993, the Kumher incident in Bharatpur district of Rajasthan in June 1992, the Papahuda incident in November 1994, and the Shergarhi incident on 30 March 1994. These incidents were related to three main issues: rape, caste-based atrocities and police violence. The RSM also organised demonstrations to demand minimum wages for brick-kiln labourers and against the abolition of small loans of less than Rs 10,000 for Dalits. In keeping with its anti-communal stand, RSM also organised a protest against the demolition of the Babri Masjid on 6 December 1992.[20]

Apart from the rallies held at Shergarhi, the other rallies organised by RSM during the 1990s[21] include the dharna at *tehsil* Sardhana on 1 June 1992, which was held to demand land, stop atrocities against Dalits, writing off of debts, pensions for the elderly, gun licences for self-defence, jobs and help in setting up small businesses; the annual meeting on 6 December 1992 to mark Ambedkar's death anniversary held near his statue outside the court building in Meerut; a rally held in June 1992 at India Gate and in front of the Prime Minister's residence in New Delhi to protest against the atrocities perpetrated on Dalits at Kumher in Rajasthan; a meeting on 20 January 1993 at the *zilla* office in Meerut to protest against the government's refusal to waive small loans and harassment by the local bureaucracy in relation to it; the dharna in front of the Commissioner's office Meerut on 17 March 1994 against the failure of the SP-BSP government to prevent atrocities against Dalits, rise in prices and lack of jobs; and a demonstration in Sikheda village on 22 October 1995 against the destruction of Ambedkar's statue in the local park by caste Hindus. These examples show that the leadership of the RSM was well equipped to play a central role in the Shergarhi incident as, by then, it had already dealt with several issues relating to atrocities against Dalits.

III

The Shergarhi Incident and the Role of RSM

The Incident

The role of the RSM in Shergarhi cannot be understood without a detailed description of the incident that took place there. Shergarhi is a Dalit neighbourhood situated on the outskirts of Meerut city. In the 1990s, it graduated from its status as a village and became a suburb. A key factor in 1994 was the emergence of Shastri Nagar, a housing colony financed by the UP government, close to the area occupied by the Dalits. This raised the value of the land and accelerated the urbanisation of the erstwhile Shergarhi village. While Shastri Nagar soon became an upper-caste/class colony, Shergarhi remained, and still is, a poor and mainly Dalit area.

On 29 March 1994, the residents of Shergarhi installed a statue of Babasaheb Ambedkar in one of their local parks.[22] In the evening of the same day, the local police arrived to 'investigate' the matter. On 30 March, senior city police and bureaucratic officials descended in Shergarhi with a huge attaché of constables. A heated discussion between local Dalit leaders and police officials about the ownership of land ensued, with the policemen attempting to remove the statue.

Officials of the Awas Vikas Nigam, a government housing corporation, who were also present, tried to convince the Dalits that the land belonged to the corporation and was earmarked for building houses. Meanwhile, a very large crowd of Dalits, some armed with lethal weapons, gathered inside the park. The situation soon became volatile, disrupting negotiations between officials and Dalit leaders. The police resorted to a *lathi*-charge and tear gas in order to evict the people from the park; in the resulting chaos, police personnel were surrounded by the crowd and beaten up. According to the police version, the Dalits indulged in stone throwing and even firing. According to the Dalits, there was also firing from a 'third party' to the conflict, i.e., some upper-caste individuals.[23] The crowd had in fact surrounded Shiv Sagar, the chief officer of civil lines, and his bodyguard, Parminder Singh, both of whom were badly beaten. The sight of their colleagues being beaten transformed stunned policemen into a ruthless and reckless force. According to Dalit leaders, the police retaliated by firing 60 to100 rounds at the demonstrators without any warning, killing two and injuring around 60, including women and children. They followed this by violently attacking Dalit homes and property in Shergarhi. In fact, the Dalits allege, the two people officially claimed to have been killed during police firing, were actually killed later, in the course of police brutality in their homes.[24]

It is necessary to mention here that there is much disagreement about 'what led to firing' and 'who was responsible for it'. Most newspaper reports make the point that the firing took place without any warning. The police accused Dalits of having used not only locally made guns but also sten guns and AK-47s, justifying the need to open fire on them. As mentioned earlier, these incidents took place in the presence of senior police and administrative officials—the Additional District Magistrate, City S.P.S. Chauhan; City SP B.P. Tripathi; City Magistrate, Prabhat Kumar Sharma; Commanding Officer, Kunwar Singh; Kotwali, Arun Kumar Gupta; police from different localities and the CRPF. Some media reports pointed to the differences of opinion between the city police head and the other officers on the course of action to be followed, which weakened the police response to the situation, leading to violence. The newspapers also reported the locals as mentioning four deaths, whereas the police confirmed only two.

A second round of police firing took place on 31 March 1994, again in the outskirts of Meerut, near the railway line at Brahampura village, which led to the death of one person and several being injured. This episode proved to be the igniting spark that fuelled protests and demonstrations in the district on a wider and more radical scale. There were aggressive demonstrations all over Meerut and other parts of UP for almost a week. Dalits from other parts of India, particularly Mumbai, also rallied behind the locals. Peace was restored only on 14 April 1994. The protest had lasted for 15 days, during which parts of Meerut were put under curfew. District Commissioner Mohinder Singh ordered a magisterial enquiry.

Two factors made this widespread and organised protest by Dalits against the state and its instruments—the police and the magisterial bureaucracy—possible. The first was the existence of number of Hindi newspapers—mainly *Amar Ujala* (*AU*) and *Dainik Jagran* (*DJ*), but also smaller ones like *Heera Times* and *Saptahik Ganga Yamuna Times*—that had achieved coverage among educated Dalits in villages, which allowed news to travel quickly from the city to the rural areas. The second was the presence of a dense network of Dalit associations in Meerut city and caste panchayats/*mahasabhas* in the surrounding rural areas, which immediately took up the Dalit cause. However, among them, the RSM and the Dalit Sena played the major role.

The relationship between the various associations, particularly these two, was both *competitive and collaborative*. It was competitive because each hoped that by taking up the cause of Dalits, it could gain their support, which, in the prevailing atmosphere of Dalit assertion, could be used for future political gain. This was particularly true of the Dalit Sena and other associations attached to political parties. At the same time, as Dalit associations, they had common interests; this made collaboration between them possible, especially against the violence perpetrated by the police. Many of them jointly formed the Dr Ambedkar Sangharsh Samiti Shergarhi Kand to press their demands upon the government. The protest can be described as one situated within civil society against the use of force by the state, i.e., the police. However, although the local BSP leaders participated at many places, visited the disputed site and made speeches, the top party leadership remained aloof.

The RSM and DS led the other associations in staging a number of protests in and around Meerut, a good example being the dharna on 8 April held in front of the Meerut Collectorate despite the presence of a large police force. In Bulandshahr, at a silent march organised by a community association called Abhiyan, in which all the marchers wore black and red bands, members of the RSM, DS and the Dalit Sauraksha Samiti submitted a joint memorandum to the Collectorate, in which they demanded a law to prevent police firing upon Dalits. The memorandum also demanded that Rs 10 lakh (1 million) be paid to the families of those killed in police firing, Rs 50,000 to those injured, immediate suspension and trial of guilty officials, a judicial inquiry, a white paper on the incident, protection to Dalits, etc. Dharampal Singh addressed the crowd,[25] emphasising that Dalits had now achieved greater awareness and would not tolerate any more atrocities; he condemned the police firing and described the subsequent actions taken by the Meerut administration and the UP government as insufficient for meeting the demands of the Dalits. A few BSP leaders also addressed the crowd— Hafeem Ahmed Quereshi, the Minister for Panchayat Affairs, Rajendra Singh Gautam, Ram Prasad Jataveer, Shiv Shankar (an advocate) and Prem Chand Bharati (*AU* 8 April). With support from the Dalit Sauraksha Samiti, the dharna continued into the third day, with the spirit of unity built up by the RSM and other civil society organisations (CSOs) during the protest contributing in large measure to the assertion of Dalit identity.

For instance, in Dayampur village on 11 April, a statue of Babasaheb Ambedkar was installed at a function jointly organised by Charan Singh, a sitting Member of the Legislative Assembly (MLA) and the Ambedkar Sewa Dal. The constant refrain in the speeches by Dalit leaders was that *'Dalit chetna jagi hai'* (Dalit consciousness has awakened) and that they would no longer tolerate any kind of oppression.

A number of towns in western UP—Bulandshahr, Anoopshahr, Ghaziabad, Simbhavali, Mawana, Sardhana, Kairana and Saharanpur—witnessed dharnas and rallies during which police stations were surrounded, roads blocked, effigies of Mulayam Singh burnt and arrests made on a large scale. In Meerut city itself, the Dalits refused to obey curfew orders, held demonstrations, stopped rail traffic, hoisted black flags on their housetops, and repeatedly *gheraoed* (surrounded) the administration. A Dalit panchayat at Shergarhi issued a 'hit list' that included the names of Commandant Anand Swarup Tyagi and Chaudhuri Gajendra Singh of Shastri Nagar, who were described as police informers.

Although by 1 April, as the situation was slowly brought under control, curfew was lifted in a few parts of Meerut city, the agitation spread into the countryside, with areas like Mawana, Maliana, Modipuram, Daurala and Sardhana being the worst affected. Rallies were held in a number of large villages with substantial Dalit populations, such as Maithena, Nagla Hareru and Machra. Maithena witnessed a massive demonstration, in which about 2,000 to 3,000 people blocked the highway and submitted a memorandum to the local administration. They were organised by local Dalit associations such as the Jatav Mahasabha and the Dalit Sauraksha Samiti. These associations were against the entry of political leaders from other parts of the state or from Delhi, whom they saw as cashing in on the Dalit cause to improve their political image. A common pattern was for the crowd—anywhere between 500 and 2,000 people—to collect and walk towards the district headquarters, where they would stage a dharna and present a memorandum of their demands; or block the highway until the local police/administration assured them that their demands would be considered. These meetings were held either in Ambedkar schools, Dalit panchayat *bhawans* or Ravidas *dharamshalas*, all which have a conspicuous and numerous presence in the western UP. Local BSP leaders addressed the crowds in many places. The demands everywhere were reinstallation of the statue, substantial compensation to the families of the dead and injured and action against police officials for using excessive force.

Protests were also organised by Dalit panchayats against the government. A *jatav mahapanchayat* of 32 villages was held on 7 April at the panchayat *bhawan* of Alipur Morena village close to Meerut (*DJ* 8 April), while a panchayat meeting of 101 villages was held at the Dr Ambedkar Smarak Kanya Pathshala in Durveshpur village on 10 April. While the Shergarhi issue occupied centrestage at the former, other problems that Dalits faced in the region were also discussed. Many local BSP leaders—Naseemuddin Siddiqui (MLA from Banda), Dr Bhagwan Singh and Farath Khan of Hastinapur, Rajendra Prasad Jatav, Bijendra Sewak—also attended the panchayat. A meeting of Dalits was organised by the Rashtriya Ambedkar Wadi Yuva Kalyan Parishad and the Ambedkar Vikas Sangharsh Samiti Kishanpur at Kishanpur Birana village near Meerut, where articles of daily use were collected and sent to Shergarhi (ibid.).

It is important to note that everywhere, agitations against police atrocities under the leadership of Dalit associations rapidly acquired the character of a popular protest against the failure of not only the SP–BSP government, but also of *the Indian state, the police and the magisterial bureaucracy to protect the life and property of Dalit men, women and children, provide them with jobs and economic support as well as the unsympathetic attitude towards a community that was downtrodden and oppressed and denied its cultural right to install a statue of a great leader.* In this, the leadership of RSM, particularly the speeches made by Dharampal Singh, played a key role. He claimed that the disputed site where the statue was erected was *gram sabha* land that belonged to Shergarhi village and had always been used by Dalits for various common activities. The upper castes in the locality were described as colluding with the police to prevent local Dalits from erecting a statue on common village land.

Angry Dalit youth also played an important role in highlighting the failures of the government. On 10 April, at a meeting in the Brahmapura area of Meerut, Dalits demanded that the availability of water and electricity in Dalit *bastis* should be improved with immediate effect. A Dalit in Mawana mustered up enough courage to lodge a complaint with the police when a *jat* in the village called him a *chamar*. Articles of daily use were collected in villages and sent to Shergarhi. There were silent marches and sit-ins, even in Dehra Dun. On 11 April at Siwal Khas, the *Balmikis* under the Dalit Mukti Morcha gathered to criticise the *jatavs* as oppressors of the poorer sections of the community and argued that henceforth reservation be confined only to non-*jatavs*. The BSP was also described as a *chamar* party, unconcerned with the rural poor. At a meeting held in Masoorie village, it was resolved that henceforth, Dalits would arm themselves and not depend upon political parties, the administration or the police to provide them protection. It was also resolved that the unity achieved during the Shergarhi incident be kept alive as the movement was not confined to Meerut district but had spilled over into other areas of western UP. Dalit leaders argued that they had supported the SP and the BSP in the expectation that they would protect the community. However, given the many atrocities perpetrated on Dalits in western UP, the government was characterised as being anti-Dalit.

It is necessary at this point to briefly discuss the role played by the police and the magisterial bureaucracy in order to understand the magnitude of the protest and the passions aroused among the Dalits. A major problem evident from a study of this incident was the *attitude* of these state instruments towards the Dalits, their demands and expectations. The police seemed to believe that poverty bred crime and that

Shergarhi was a crime-infested area. Unfortunately, they also acted on this assumption. A perusal of the affidavit presented by B.P. Tripathi, the head of the city police, S.P.S. Chauhan, the then city magistrate, and other officers who were present when the incident took place on 29 March, testifies to this.[26] They submitted a long list of Dalits residing in Shergarhi who had been arrested in the past for minor offences (though most of them had been later released). They argued that Shergarhi was a trouble spot, where criminal elements from other areas took shelter. They also alleged that the affidavits presented on behalf of the Dalits were distorted and false, and then proceeded to provide what they described as 'real facts'. Distrust of the police was probably the reason why talks held on 31 March between the city magistrate and the Dalit associations broke down, despite the fact that the latter accepted that there may have been lapses on their part. It is worth noting that the main demand put forward by all the demonstrations following the incident was action against the police for brutality and excessive use of force—something that the RSM and other similar associations had been fighting against since their inception.[27] The affidavits presented by the police also differed in significant ways from those submitted on behalf of the Dalits by Dharampal Singh and Vijaypal Singh. The police affidavits claimed that there was no statue already installed, that the crowd behaved in an extremely aggressive fashion, snatching rifles and sten guns from the policemen, that the police did not enter Dalit homes and that the two persons killed died during the firing on the disputed site.

The media, which play an important role in the formation of public opinion on issues dealing with the lower castes, also need to be briefly mentioned. Unlike the national, English-language dailies, which spared little space for something that happened in a provincial area, local Hindi newspapers provided the incident extensive coverage. However, they relied mainly on police reports, with little *independent investigation* on their part. A condescending attitude and frequent use of the term 'harijan', which was banned in 1991 through an executive order of the central government and which is disliked by the Dalits in western UP, characterised most of the reportage. According to one newspaper, the Dalits 'showed their low mentality by fighting the police at Shergarhi' (*DJ* 8 April). Some newspapers conjectured that a land mafia had been involved in the incident.[28] Some argued that the attack on the police by the Dalits was due to hesitation on the part of the administration and the police force in putting down caste-based violence after the formation of the SP–BSP government (*Hindustan* 2 April). The new government had pressured the administration to use 'soft methods' of persuasion and negotiation; consequently the police could not deal with violent crowds and rallies with any effectiveness. A number of instances were quoted in the press of incidents where the 'guilty' (read Dalits in most cases) were dealt with too leniently; as a result of this, 'bad elements' in Meerut had become very bold. The police were also described as having a 'compromising mentality' and allowing the mafia 'free play'. While the papers carried several photographs of Dalits attacking the police, there were very few of the police beating up Dalits.

However, in this context mention must also be made of reports by a small group of concerned citizens, comprising mainly professionals and academics in Meerut city, which appealed to all parties in the dispute to resolve the problem without using violence, and tried to pressure the state into finding a fair solution.

Role Played by the RSM

As has been mentioned earlier, of all the Dalit associations involved in the Shergarhi protest, the role played by the RSM was a key one. While it collaborated with other associations in holding rallies and demonstration under the Shergarhi Kand Samiti, it went beyond the others in upholding the interests of the Dalits in Shergarhi. Vijaypal Singh, who lives close to the disputed site, was present during the police firing on 30

March. He did his best to prevent the removal of the statue, arguing about the ownership of the disputed site with senior police officers and officials of the Awas Nigam who were present during the incident. He also tried, unsuccessfully, to pacify the crowd and prevent it from turning violent. He was injured during the police *lathi* charge and the subsequent firing. In the sworn affidavits presented before the Commission of Inquiry, Dalit leaders alleged that Vijaypal was badly treated by the police because in the past, he had defended Dalits against whom the police in Shergarhi had registered cases, most of which had eventually proved false. Led by Vijaypal and other Dalit leaders, local Dalits had demonstrated before the Meerut Collectorate to draw the District Magistrate's attention to some of these cases and had succeeded in getting them withdrawn. On 30 March, senior police officers were rude to Vijaypal and he was pushed, threatened and surrounded by the policemen present. He argued in his affidavit that he had not encouraged the crowd to misbehave nor had he incited them to violence. Although he was put in a van, he managed to escape and evade arrest when the city legislator Haji Aklak arrived on the scene. He was able to visit the homes of the Dalits and claimed that he was present when the police removed Rishipal's dead body, not from the disputed site, but from the latter's house.[29] It was the rude and crass behaviour of the police[30] that pushed the crowd into becoming violent and aggressive.

RSM leaders also took the lead in negotiating with the government. Shergarhi Salakar Samiti (negotiation committee) was set up in Meerut under the leadership of Dharampal Singh and comprised representatives of all major Dalit associations. The Samiti went to Lucknow to meet the Chief Minister and Mayawati. However, although a number of such visits were made, exhaustive discussions were not possible. The Samiti made five major demands: judicial inquiry, transfer of officials and their trial under penal code 302, reinstallation of the statue, Rs 5 lakh compensation to the families of those killed and Rs 1 lakh to those who were wounded (*DJ* 7 April).

The RSM also played a constructive role in settling the vexed question of whether the annual procession to celebrate Ambedkar Jayanti on 14 April should be held in the prevailing situation. The city administration felt that rather than a procession, which might cause violence, seminars/meetings at various locations on Ambedkar's life and ideology, combined with cultural programmes, might be a better bet. However, opinion among major Dalit associations in the city was divided. The Dr Ambedkar Uthhan Parishad and the Ambedkar Sewa Dal were against a procession, while the others favoured it, although they said it should be held without black bands or weapons. However, some associations like the Shoshit Mukti Morcha and the Mukti Vahini were adamant and wanted to go ahead with the procession with or without the permission of the city administration. A meeting of about a 100 leaders and members of various Dalit associations was held under the leadership of Dharamplal Singh on 7 April at the Ambedkar Higher Secondary School, Subhas Nagar. Here, it was decided the annual procession would indeed be held, but that there would be no violence or slogan shouting. Dharampal Singh was elected to head the organising committee (*DJ* 8 April). Since Dharampal knew that a procession was inevitable as a large number of Dalits were expected to converge in Meerut on 14 April, he realised that banning it would only make more trouble.

However, the most important thing that RSM did, in which other Dalit associations did not participate, was presenting the case of the Dalits before the Commission of Inquiry held by S.I. Jafri, a sitting judge of Allahabad High Court. They provided the commission with details of the incident in affidavits presented by them on 19 November 1994. They tried to show that police allegations of the Dalits being armed and of firing on the police were incorrect, that the police had not used tear gas but had fired on them without warning, injuring them on the upper parts of their bodies, and that they had entered Dalit homes in the Shergarhi area and used force upon men, women and children. Further, the RSM claimed that since the statue was already been in place before 30 March, the question of it being stealthily installed did not arise. They also brought to the commission's notice that two upper-caste individuals, Anand Swarup Tyagi and his son, who were residents of Shastri Nagar, had fired on the crowd.

In addition, the RSM was also able to introduce evidence that the disputed site of about 1,800 m, on which the statue was erected, did not belong to the Awas Nigam but was part of the common land of Shergarhi village. It once used to be a pond that the villagers had filled up for their common use about 12 years ago. It had subsequently been used by villagers to tie up their cattle, build common structures, access mud for building houses, and so on. It had never belonged either to the government or any individual and the villagers thus had every right to erect a statue on it.

The officials of Aawas Vikas Nigam had supplied the commission with maps and plans showing that disputed site, which lay between the Meerut–Garhmukteshwar and Meerut–Hapur highway, had been acquired by the government in 1967.[31] They also claimed that 200 yards (183 m) from where the incident occurred, a statue of Ambedkar was already in place and that the Dalits were now attempting to grab land that rightfully belonged to the Nigam. RSM leaders argued that the plans introduced applied not to the disputed site but to the portion of land on which the Shastri Nagar complex stood.

RSM leaders were also able to submit affidavits on behalf of 15 Dalit residents of Shergarhi, some of whom had been hospitalised for over a month and others who were still in jail. These affidavits supported all the arguments and evidence put forward by Dharampal Singh and Vijaypal Singh regarding police brutality.[32] Through various affidavits and counter-affidavits, the police had presented a fairly strong case to the commission. If the RSM had not represented the Dalits, they would not have been able to counter this with an equally strong alternative case. The threefold action by the RSM—its attempt to defend them against police brutality, the leadership it provided during the subsequent demonstrations and rallies and the demands made to the government, and the case it presented to the inquiry commission—clearly shows that it was an association that worked to protect the interests of the Dalits. It is doubtful if the Dalits, handicapped as they were with low levels of literacy, inexperience in dealing with the official machinery and their lack of contacts, would have been able to pressure the government into agreeing to their main demands.

RSM was able to play this positive role mainly because Dalit protest following the Shergarhi incident created unity and cohesion both *within* it and *between* the associations in Meerut region, making concerted action against state repression possible. However, this unity proved to be shortlived, and once the incident was over, the RSM went into decline. A number of factors were responsible for this. One was the failure of the state government to make public the findings of the Jafri Commission. This is despite the fact that following the failure of the SP-BSP coalition, a government headed by Mayawati came to power with the backing of the Bharatiya Janata Party (BJP). Both the RSM and the Dalits of Meerut felt let down by the BSP, which they identified as a party only interested in capturing power. The second was the emergence of BSP as a strong Dalit party in UP during the mid-1990s, as a result of which many RSM members joined it in the hope of capturing seats in the assembly. This contributed to the decline of many Dalit associations in Meerut. Dalit assertion through grassroots CSOs, which had shown an upward swing in the mid-1990s, dropped sharply. Dharampal Singh is a rather disillusioned man today. He is thinking of rejoining the CPI(M). But this would require disbanding the RSM, which he is reluctant to do. His dilemma mirrors that faced by other leaders of grassroots associations, who wish to organise movements against the state but cannot sustain them except when some incident takes place.

III

Response of the State Government

Before examining the state government's response to the demands made by Dalit associations, it is necessary to understand that it was a coalition government comprising two parties. Formed by the SP and the BSP following the 1993 state assembly elections, it was prompted by the desire to establish a *bahujan samaj* based social justice. However, the interests of the two parties were contradictory. The SP represented the BCs and OBCs, whose interests ran counter to those of the Dalits: in rural areas the former were landowners and employed the latter, who are mainly landless, as labour; in urban areas the educated sections of these communities were competing for jobs. Problems had arisen between the two partners even before the Shergarhi incident (Pai 2000b). Moreover, instead of bringing the *bahujans* together, the 1993 election was paradoxically marked by a new assertiveness by the Dalits in the countryside, who wanted to carry forward their own independent movement. This is reflected in the massive participation (for the first time) of Dalits in parts of the state, and their consolidation behind the BSP on a large scale, in the election (ibid.). As a result, from a party that led agitations against, and was very critical of, the state and mainstream parties, particular the Congress in the 1980s and early 1990s, the BSP became part of a coalition government that had to deal with violent confrontation between the city administration in Meerut and the Dalits who formed its primary support base. Also, many of the prominent residents of Shastri Nagar were BCs and resented the new assertiveness by Dalits that led them to 'grab' land and set up a statue in an area where they lived.[33] These reasons underlay the inability of the government to deal consistently and effectively with the problems thrown up by the violence that followed the Shergarhi incident.

The response of the state government constantly shifted during the fortnight in which the protests took place. The government, particularly Chief Minister Mulayam Singh Yadav, was initially supportive of the law and order machinery and the Awas Vikas who claimed that it was their land on which the statue was erected. Curfew was imposed, compensation announced and an inquiry initiated. This enabled the police to bring the situation under control. But the BSP, as a Dalit-based party, had a greater stake in the situation and Dalits in Meerut and elsewhere followed its actions very carefully. The party, however, was keen to continue the coalition and allowed the SP, particularly Mulayam Singh, to take a tough stand and initially did not take much interest even though this was the first major incident involving Dalits after they came to power. Both parties presented themselves as being 'responsible' rather than partisan, keen to maintain the rule of law and order. Mayawati, who did not visit Meerut until 12 days after the incident, insisted that the BSP cadres were not involved, that the incident had been blown out of proportion by the press, that the statue should not have installed on disputed land and the government could take action only after an inquiry into the incident (*DJ* 11 April). A week after the incident, Kanshi Ram demanded the transfer of the officials involved. He pointed out that he was not asking for the reinstallation of the statue, but if the Dalits of the area wanted this, then the land would have to be acquired by the government before this could be done. In early April, despite the growing violence in the region, Mayawati declared that the BSP was satisfied with the working of the coalition and agreed with Kanshi Ram that Mulayam Singh should be allowed some time to solve the problem without being pressured. This cautious approach was dictated by the need to maintain the SP-BSP coalition and the impending by-election in the Hastinapur (reserved) assembly constituency where a BSP candidate—the Minister for Women and Welfare in the coalition—was being fielded, and four other assembly seats due on 28 May 1994. By April 1994, the relationship between the two partners had already run into trouble and the BSP was keen to avoid any statement or action that might precipitate collapse. This was in contrast to the stand taken by local BSP leaders who, being far more conversant with the situation, were worried that they would lose Dalit support in the region. A number of them visited Shergarhi on 7 April, joined in the ongoing agitations and demanded the reinstallation of the statue.

However, the entry of other political parties and their Dalit associations[34] on the scene, particularly the role played by JD's Dalit Sena under the leadership of Ram Vilas Paswan and the escalation of the agitation by the Dalits, forced the BSP to reconsider its stand. Apprehending trouble, the police did not allow Paswan to enter Meerut on 31 March and sent him back from Partepur thana. He made a second attempt on 3 April but was arrested at Moradnagar while travelling from New Delhi to Meerut. However, with the help of some of his partymen, he did manage to enter the city on 6 April. He immediately offered support to the demonstrating Dalits, visited those who had been hospitalised and imprisoned, described the incident as a case of 'deliberate firing by the police amounting to murder' and criticised the government for being unsympathetic to their needs (*DJ* 7 April). The hospitalised and jailed Dalits provided him with details of the atrocities that the police had perpetrated in their homes and complained about the land mafia in Meerut, accusing them of having designs on the disputed site. All this was given prominent coverage by local newspapers, embarrassing the government. Paswan's statement that the government was anti-Dalit, pointing to the large number of atrocities perpetrated on them during its term, was widely appreciated by the Dalits in Meerut. Paswan also demanded that a special court be set up to look into the incident and accused the government of using delaying tactics and being unconcerned about the needs of the poor and the oppressed.

Due to these developments, the BSP began to put pressure on Mulayam Singh from the second week of April. It now focused on the use of force by the police upon an already oppressed community and the need to reinstall the statue of a great leader. Mayawati demanded the transfer of the city's Assistant District Magistrate and City Magistrate of Meerut, threatening to withdraw support if the demand was not fulfilled. The visit by Paswan and the extensive coverage given to it by the local press, the change in the stand of the BSP and the pending by-election, politicised the entire issue and the government unable to deal with the deluge of protests going on announced its major decisions on 8 April. These were to acquire the land and build an Ambedkar park around it at its own cost, reinstall the statue, transfer all police officials involved, provide high levels of compensation to the families of those killed or injured and set up a commission of inquiry headed by a judge of the Allahabad High Court (*AU* 8 April). These measures were announced after extensive talks between the SP and BSP, where both agreed that it was necessary to protect their vote banks against Paswan.[35]

Mayawati visited Meerut on 11 April and met with those who had been injured during police firing. She also made a number of statements designed to regain Dalit support, publicly putting pressure on Mulayam Singh. She alleged that the removal of the statue was part of a conspiracy of *sawarna* leaders and officials, who were now criticising the government and spreading false rumours. At one Dalit meeting, she also claimed that some of the officials were closely linked to the land mafia, which comprised the *jat* and the *tyagi* castes. She said there was nothing wrong with Dalits putting up statues of great leaders, pointing out that several temples had been constructed on unauthorised land but no action had been taken in their case because they belonged to high caste people. She also alleged that the police and magistrates did not have the right to remove the statue without a court order and demanded that it be reinstalled immediately. The city officials and police were disappointed by her statements, which they felt were part of the politics between the two coalition parties.

Mayawati and Raj Bahadur were expected to visit Shergarhi and reinstall the statue on 14 April, Ambedkar's birthday. However, much to the disappointment of the local *jatavs*, it was reinstalled only on 15 April by city legislator, Haji Aklaq. Local Dalit leaders, while happy with the reinstallation, remained critical of the BSP. Consequently, the Dalit Sena became a major player in the region's Dalit politics, while the BSP lost support as it was viewed as being more interested in winning the Hastinapur by-election, and as being more concerned with upsetting its partnership with the SP than protecting the life and property of Dalits.

The shift in the government's policy had an immediate impact on Meerut's police force. While initially supportive of police action, in the changed situation the government ordered the transfer of all police personnel, right down to the Thana (station) heads, on 16 April 1994, without waiting for even a court of inquiry to be set up. In fact, it obtained special permission from the Chief Election Commissioner to do this, as a by-election was due in Hastinapur assembly constituency on 28 May. The transfers affected police morale and the media carried reports that the police felt that they had been let down despite having discharged their duty of maintaining order in Meerut, which has a long history of communal and caste conflicts. At a meeting on 22 April, senior police officers decided that in future they would insist on written orders from the district magistrate before opening fire on the public. They argued that if they did not use force, they were criticised for being 'soft', while if they did take action, they were accused of using violence. The magistrates promised to take up the issue at the All-India State Civil/Administrative Service Officers meeting scheduled to be held in Bangalore on 3 May (*DJ* 22 April).

The reinstallation of the statue and the construction of an Ambedkar Bhawan in the park caused a lot of strife between the Dalit and non-Dalit residents of Shergarhi. The city administration began construction on 10 April, the day after curfew was lifted. The local non-Dalit residents protested against it and formed an Adarsh Sudhar Samiti as they were concerned about the demarcation of the boundary between the park and the housing colony. They criticised the government's decision to build a park as being part of BSP's vote bank politics. While the Dalits wanted the statue installed on the non-housing land facing the park and claimed 1,500 sq m for it, the UP Awas Vikas officials argued that only 900 sq m had been earmarked for the site. At a meeting called by the district magistrate with local Dalit leaders, led by Dharampal Singh, to resolve the issue amicably, it was decided that work would begin only in the area that was not under dispute. Today, the park is a neglected piece of land surrounding the statue; there is no Ambedkar Bhawan and little effort is made by the local administration to even keep it clean.

Conclusion

In the light of the empirical data just presented, it is now possible to discuss the nature of civil society and its interface with governance in the Indian context. A major finding from our study is that a democratic polity does exist in India, which is tolerant of dissent and allows space for protest and contestation against the state. This is evident enough from the two weeks of widespread and intense protests launched by the Dalits in Meerut region after the Shergarhi incident, which the state did not try to crush through the use of force. As far as possible, all attempts were made to negotiate and reason with the leaders of the movement. However, an appraisal of the incident and role played in it by various groups indicates that unlike in the West, civil society in India is a deeply divided and hierarchically structured domain, exclusive of the lower castes. It is not a democratic space that all citizens can access. Rather, it is a conflict-ridden arena with little consensus, particularly over issues like social justice, dignity, self-respect, rights and inclusion of oppressed sections. The reasons for this, as has already been pointed out, is the historically different path taken by Indian society, leading to lack of social transformation and the continued existence of traditional values, which are now being aggressively questioned by the lower castes.

Such experiences are not limited to India. The attempt made by countries in Eastern Europe and Latin America to overthrow authoritarian/military regimes in the late 1980s, show a similar trajectory. In the former, the people rejected both reform of state power from above and political revolution from below, but found that the civil society they had created was an unequal society in which disadvantaged sections were at the mercy of capitalists, corporate bureaucracies and ethnic majorities. In the latter, the fall of military regimes also brought disappointment because, instead of pushing the process further, political parties that had spearheaded the revolt against authoritarian states split the anti-military movements in the region. Post-military regimes led to civilianisation but not democratisation: the new regimes did not respond to the democratic aspirations that the idea of civil society had evoked (Schneider 1995). Hence, civil society in societies outside Western Europe is not a harmonious space where citizens associate with each other to influence public policy; rather, it is a site for contestation among different groups, as much against each other for their rightful place and for the benefits of development, as against the state.

The lesson that emerges from these examples is that in segmented and hierarchical societies, *the path to the democratisation of civil society lies in contestation and struggle by disadvantaged and marginalised groups* seeking an equal space within civil society. Civil society can provide both the site and the values that help to fight the inequities within itself. It is this process that we witnessed in western UP. Dalit protest during the Shergarhi incident was a revolt from below that raised fundamental issues of democratic governance. It was a product of Dalit assertion based on the issue of identity and mobilisation that had been taking place over a long period of time, and recent militant demands by a new, educated and politicised generation for improved economic status, removal of social disabilities and a share in political power.

Our study also points to the limitations of the state in fostering and helping in the establishment of civil society. In the absence of an equal society, Dalits and other disadvantaged group had hoped that, after independence, the Indian state would protect them and look after their special needs. The state was thus given a much larger space than civil society and was expected play an interventionist and redistributive role in helping the poor and underprivileged, protecting their lives and property and guaranteeing them equal rights as citizens. It also assumed the responsibility for the management of conflict between various social groups. Through negotiation and bargaining between groups, it was hoped that conflicts would be resolved, hierarchies questioned and broken, and new and more egalitarian equations between segments established—all of which would help in building a cohesive, democratic order. Initially, the relationship between the state and civil society was not adversarial; in fact, the former encouraged and supported many civil society initiatives that were meant for the poor, such as Bhoodan. The Dalits also supported the state and looked up to it. In the 1960s, Dalit leaders in UP decided to leave the Republican Party of India and join the Congress party, which, until the 1980s, was supported by a large mass of Dalits. It was seen as a party that would help Dalits occupy their rightful place in society. However, since the 1980s, with increasing politicisation and greater awareness of their identity, the Dalits began to revolt against the state, which, they felt, had failed not only to protect them, but also guarantee their rights or improve their socio-economic position vis-à-vis the upper castes/classes. They realised that the state was an illiberal one, manned and controlled by the upper castes/classes, from which they could not expect justice. While the formal, institutional conditions of democracy were present, there was no real or substantive democracy. As the RSM leaders pointed out, in such a situation, even the formation of a government comprising lower-caste parties failed to change the situation of Dalits. Once in power, the BSP proved incapable of taking decisions that would help the Dalits and allowed the Shergarhi incident to be politicised. This is a reflection of the undemocratic civil society in which the state is embedded. It points out that 'only a democratic state can create a democratic civil society; only a democratic civil society can create a democratic state' (Walzer 1998: 24).

The impact of this pattern of development on governance is clear. Our study shows that at best RSM, which provided leadership to the Dalit protest, achieved limited success in its attempt to promote democratic governance. It succeeded in getting the statue reinstalled, a number of police personnel implicated in the incident transferred and a judicial inquiry initiated. Much of this, however, must also be attributed to the strident criticism of the government and the mobilisation of Dalits by the Dalit Sena under Paswan. The RSM did not succeed in making the state address the issue of violence against Dalits and justice for them. During the Shergarhi incident, the instruments of the state, namely, the police and the bureaucracy, failed to protect the lives and property of the Dalits in Shergarhi, which led to disillusionment, alienation, distrust and finally violence against the government. Governance is therefore not sensitive to Dalit issues. The attitude of the senior police and magisterial officers and the press towards the Dalits was condescending, biased and unhelpful. As result, the Dalits of Shergarhi completely lost faith in the Meerut police—a critical factor that undermined the cohesiveness of civil society, perpetuating injustice and violence, especially as it convinced the Dalits to adopt undemocratic and illegal means to hit back. The Dalits point out that they are still denied the right to life and protection of property, which remain key issues. Their demand for licences to carry firearms is another indication that the police practices discrimination. Dalits also point to the continued practice of untouchability and discrimination against them in all spheres and the failure of the state to check these practices. This is because political interference in state institutions, which are under the control of the better-off sections of society. The capacity to provide adequate governance has therefore declined.

Our study also shows that RSM cannot be considered a civil society association. Based on the notions of caste/community, it fosters primordial values, promotes the interests of only a section of society and mobilises along caste lines. Internally, it lacks a second line of leadership, is dependent upon a single individual and its associational abilities and agenda are geared towards dealing with the immediate needs of the Dalits. There is also the question of sustainability. During the Shergarhi incident, the RSM provided leadership to the struggle and created greater cohesion between Dalit associations in Meerut and the surrounding areas. Despite their differences, this led to the formation of a Sangharsh Samiti to fight against state repression and resist attempts by the upper castes to manipulate the incident. The Shergarhi incident certainly generated a new level of awareness and reinforced the idea of Dalit solidarity and identity. However, once that struggle was over, the RSM disintegrated due to factionalism and lack of interest among the Dalits. While communication channels among Dalit associations are strong in Meerut district, enabling them to unite quickly when atrocities occur, once a particular incident is over and the movement loses momentum, they fall apart. In the Indian context, many such associations have emerged recently and are struggling to survive. Members of such association are also easily coopted by political parties, or attracted by administrative posts within the state. In this instance, political society, which the BSP represented, was stronger than civil society, and since it was more interested in acquiring power, it curbed the development of grassroots associations. The Shergarhi incident shows that associational life among the Dalits, which could have exerted pressure upon the state, was weak.

Yet in the absence of class-based mobilisation, associations such as the RSM, which are syncretistic—combining both traditional and modern values in their methods and outlook, could play a central role in strengthening civil society. They have the advantage of having been thrown up from the grassroots and not imposed from above. Even before the Shergarhi incident, the RSM was functioning as a pressure group, articulating the needs of and protecting the interests of the Dalits. It was this that won it their trust and enabled it to play a central role, a role that we have already discussed in detail, in the Shergarhi episode. Throughout the struggle, the RSM functioned as a bridge between the Dalits and the government. At the same time its methods were democratic and non-violent; it tried to ensure that the protest was peaceful and did not spin out of control, particularly during the celebration of Ambedkar's birthday soon after the incident. The leadership of RSM—unlike that of many other associations—also did not try to politicise the incident for personal gain, such as increasing their own popularity. They were also aware of the need to promote democratic rather than sectarian values. As a result, the Dalits of the region have acquired the ability to pressure and influence state policies; this can only be described as a legacy of the Shergarhi incident. A number of factors facilitated this process. The existence of an autonomous press as an institution of civil society, providing communication links among the Dalits, was a significant development. The capture of power by the BSP in 1993 also encouraged Dalit associations to make strident demands on the state.

All this suggests that in highly segmented societies like India, that are undergoing rapid social transformation, state-society interaction and its implications for governance are not the same as in other societies. Drawing upon a number of case studies on the working of civil society in different countries, Hann and Dunn (1996) argue that everywhere civil society is different due to the socio-cultural and economic context in which it is placed. In India, civil society is still in the process of being formed through the conflicts among different social groups. Relationships between caste/class groups remain fluid and are yet to crystallise, and the interplay between economic development, social transformation and political action creates patterns that are different from those in Western Europe. The main task of civil society is to bridge the gap between formal institutions and substantive democracy. But the role of the state in this process cannot be minimised, for it can either encourage or inhibit the development of civil society. And it is only if it provides the institutional framework within which civil society can flourish, and guarantees freedom, rights and equality to the citizens, that democratic governance for all citizens can become a reality.

Notes

1. For a detailed delineation of these two aspects and an analysis of civil society in India, see Neerja Gopal Jayal, 2001, 'India' in Yamamoto Tadoshi and Kim Gould Ashisama (eds) *Governance and Civil Society in a Global Age*, Japan Centre for International Exchange, Tokyo: 116–53.
2. In a recent study, Kaviraj (1996) has argued that this is the only form in which civil society exists in India.
3. In our study, this applies particularly to Mayawati, an important Dalit leader within the Bahujan Samaj Party (BSP) who was a minister in the ruling coalition when the Shergarhi incident took place. As a Dalit leader, she had openly encouraged Dalits to grab land and set up statues of Ambedkar as a gesture of defiance; as a minister she had to deal with an incident that created riots in Meerut.
4. While studies mention the rise of modern civil society associations in the nineteenth century influenced by Western values such as the Brahmo Samaj and Prarthna Samaj, which attempted to reform Indian society, their reach and influence remained limited (Jayal 1999).
5. Lying in the centre of Meerut division, Meerut district has an area of 3,911 sq km and consists of four *tehsils:* Meerut, Mawana,

Baghpat and Sardhana. Dalits comprise about 15 to 20 per cent of the population of Meerut district. For a recent study of the district, see Jagpal Singh 1992.

6. UP has 66 Scheduled Caste (SC) groups listed in the census, although only about eight are numerous enough to be of importance. The *chamars* are the most dominant and numerous (Mukherjee 1980). In the 1930 Census, they succeeded in changing their name to *jatavs*.

7. For more details on Maithena and Dalit-majority villages in the area, see Sudha Pai and Jagpal Singh (1997).

8. Mohinder Singh's study shows that Dalits in the western districts were able to gain more employment, enjoyed higher wages, were better fed and educated that their brethren in eastern UP, who were very poor in comparison, with most of them serving as harwahas under a landlord (Singh 1947). After independence, these districts benefited from the Green Revolution, which increased yields and wages benefiting all sections of the agrarian population (Pai 1993).

9. For the changing relationship between the Dalits and the traditionally dominant, landowning groups, see (Sudha Pai 2000a).

10. See (Sudha Pai 2000b).

11. See Mendelsohn.

12. The idea of setting up statues was first suggested during the 1980s by Radhey Lal Boudh, a leader of the Dalit Panthers. He argued that by doing so, Dalits could propagate an Ambedkarite iconography, which would generate a kind of pan-Indian, *bahujan* 'imagined community' apart from asserting their control over land. It was also meant to provoke riots polarising the upper and lower castes and thereby building a stronger lower-caste identity (Mukerji 1994: 60). There is little doubt that the latter objective has been achieved.

13. Literally meaning 'all land that belongs to the government belongs to us'. Mayawati's intention was to mobilise and instill confidence in the Dalits vis-à-vis the upper castes and the government which, she argued, represented the interests of the latter.

14. Such associations began to be formed in the 1980s to deal with atrocities perpetrated by caste Hindus, particularly by the middle castes, who did not like the new assertiveness among the Dalits. This was mentioned by Dharampal Singh, leader of the RSM.

15. Mentioned and described in *Amar Ujala* and *Dainik Jagran* while reporting on the Shergarhi incident between 29 March and 30 April.

16. This information was provided by Vijaypal Singh, an RSM leader.

17. The SP and the JD were both offshoots of the BLD/LKD and the JD saw the Shergarhi incident as an opportunity to improve its image vis-à-vis the SP.

18. All information about the RSM in this and other sections in based on a series of interviews with Dharampal Singh and Vijaypal Singh at the former's residence during September, October and December 1999.

19. A brief look at the life of Dharampal Singh is instructive as he represents the 'new, educated Dalit class' that was active in the region. Singh was educated in the immediate post-colonial period, when there was great emphasis on educating harijan children in Meerut, and ended up becoming a lawyer. During his high school/college days, he was inducted into the CPI, which was active in Meerut. As a successful lawyer, Singh and his family moved into an elite locality of the town but found that, despite his economic success, he was shunned by his caste Hindu neighbours. This led to a new awareness of his Dalit identity and he moved to Subhas Nagar, where he now lives among his own community and is active in helping them to obtain employment and providing them legal aid when necessary.

20. From the literature provided by RSM leaders and interviews with Dharampal Singh.

21. These are based on the pamphlets and leaflets that RSM generated to announce the rallies. They were widely distributed throughout Meerut district and pasted on all available hoardings.

22. The narrative of the incident is from two Hindi newspapers—*Amar Ujala* (*AU*) and *Dainik Jagran* (*DJ*)—dating from 29 March to 22 April 1994, and interviews with Dharampal Singh and Vijaypal Singh.

23. Anand Swarup Tyagi and Chaudhuri Gajendra Singh, both residents of Shastri Nagar.

24. This is the version given by Dalit leaders during interviews and also in the sworn affidavits given to the one-man Judicial Inquiry Commission comprising S.I. Jafri, then a judge in Allahabad High Court. The police version is given later.

25. This was because Vijaypal Singh went 'underground' to avoid arrest by the police. Hence, during this phase of the struggle, the lead role was played by Dharampal Singh.

26. These comments are based on the sworn affidavits presented by B.P. Tripathi and other police officers and magistrates on 9 November 1994. The court papers were provided to us by the RSM leaders.

27. On 1 April, an unknown assailant fired at the house of district S.P.S. Chauhan, who had given the order for the firing in Shergarhi. It was widely believed that this was done by some Dalit youth unhappy with the police and magistrates' handling of the situation. The assailant was not caught and his identity was never discovered.

28. *Saptahik Ganga Yamuna Times* 10–16, 1994. This magazine printed a story that the installation of statues is closely related to the activities of Mayawati who, in collaboration with the land mafia, was busy amassing property worth crores of rupees and at the same time ensuring political mileage by putting up Ambedkar's statutes. The magazine did not back this statement with any corroborative evidence.

29. Affidavit presented to the Court of S.I. Jafri, November 1994.

30. While the affidavit does not provide details, Dalit leaders allege that police officials told Vijaypal that they 'would teach the harijans a lesson'. Interview with Dharampal Singh and Vijaypal Singh.

31. It had been acquired vide 32(1) of the government rules in 1965 for 'Housing Accommodation and Street Scheme', according to the gazette dated 7 January 1967.

32. Affidavits presented on 19 November 1999 by Dharampal Singh and Vijaypal Singh (court papers of the RSM).

33. As already stated, the Dalits held that there had been firing by a third party and they were suspicious of Tyagi and his son, who had widespread support in the area.

34. During the first week itself, all political parties had realized the importance of the incident and sent their leaders and Dalit wings to Meerut. The important ones were the Sewa Dal of the Congress, JD's Dalit Sena and BJP's Anushochit Jati Morcha (*DJ* 8 April 1994).

35. 'Harijan Rajniti of Paswan and Mayawati', *DJ* 8 April 1994.

9

A View from the Subalterns

The Pavement Dwellers of Mumbai

Bishnu N. Mohapatra[*]

Long years ago we made a tryst with destiny, and now the time comes when we shall redeem our pledge, not wholly or in full measure, but very substantially.... The service of India means the service of the millions who suffer. It means the ending of poverty and ignorance and disease and inequity of opportunity.... To the people of India, whose representatives we are, we make an appeal to join us with faith and confidence with this great adventure. This is not time for petty and destructive criticism, no time for ill will or blaming others. We have to build the noble mansion of free India where all her children dwell.

—Jawaharlal Nehru 1947

[*]I am grateful to the members of Society for the Promotion of Area Resource Centres (SPARC), the National Slum Dwellers Federation (NSDF) and Mahila Milan for their support and help. My special thanks to Sheela and Sunder for giving me an insider's point of view that was so crucial for my research. Geetanjali and Indu collected much of the data.

My father came down the sahyadaris
A quilt over his shoulder
He stood at your doorstep
With nothing but his labour.

My father withered away toiling
So will I, and will my little ones?
Perhaps, they too face such sad nights
Wrapped in coils of darkness.
My ear wells up,
Seeks an outlet;
For it was my father
Who sculpted your epic in stone.

—Narayan Surve [1]

Ai dil hai mushkil jina yahan
Zara hatke, zara bachke
Ye hai Bombay meri jaan.

(*My heart, it is difficult to live here*
Move a little, watch out
This is Bombay my love.)

—Hindi Film: *CID*

This chapter explores the problematic link between civil society and governance in India. How should the relationship between the two be framed? Does the existence of civil society alone ensure good governance? How do we make sense of the myriad activities that go on within the sphere of civil society? How does the 'civil society argument' appear in specific contexts? While the main inspiration for the study comes from these large questions, these questions only make sense when they are appropriately modified in particular contexts. Before I lay out the context for this study, I would like to state some of the assumptions or biases that inform the exploration. The first is our belief in the capacity of people to transform the character of the state and society through collective action and the politics of mobilisation. Here, a large area of possibility and agency lies between the cynical acceptance of the status quo and the violent destruction of the state and society. The other bias is of a radical kind. The efficacy of civil society should be judged from the vantage of poor and marginalised groups. How do the poor use civil society for their benefit? How are they, in turn, constituted by it? How do they influence the policies of the state? Although important, the state is not the only thing the subalterns wish to transform; they also want to alter the character of civil society by making it more democratic and egalitarian.

The fundamental question that the present study asks is: how does a group of subalterns, say, pavement dwellers, feature in the civil society argument? Being the most deprived and the most marginal among the urban poor, how do they relate to the urban space and the politics of the city? Are they truly citizen-like agents or are they merely the object/target of state policy? By focusing on the lives of pavement dwellers in Mumbai, this study contextualises notions such as citizenship and civility and their constitutive links with the process of governance. Several organisations in Mumbai are involved in enhancing the agency of the pavement dwellers vis-à-vis the state, a process that was and still is full of challenges and possibilities. In this context the role of SPARC, an organisation that works primarily for the urban poor in Mumbai, assumes vital importance.

Contexts and Questions

There are several ways in which the idea of civil society can be explored. We can locate it in history and uncover how its meaning has changed over a period of time. We can also examine the internal coherence of the concept and explicate the idea through the writings of its main articulators: Hobbes, Ferguson, Hegel, Marx and Gramsci, to name just a few. I have chosen not to follow this course. This is not an exercise in the history of ideas. The fundamental objective here is to project the ways in which the concept/idea of civil society is mobilised in different contexts. The study is thus primarily about the 'reception' and 'domestication' of a powerful idea. Concepts or ideas are often mobilised not by following any predetermined trajectory; the people who employ them do not bother too much whether a particular use of the concept is consistent with its canonical understanding. The underlying assumption is that, in different contexts, people make different uses of civil society. For instance, in the American context the civil society argument is employed in order to underline the need to promote and strengthen a network of solidarity among citizens who are otherwise passive and individualistic. It is in the realm of civil society, as has been argued, that depletion of 'social capital' can be checked (Putnam 1995). In contrast, the idea of civil society in Eastern Europe is invoked to counter the state and to celebrate citizenship values and individual rights (Seligman 1992). What are the questions or problems that are raised in post-colonial/third world societies within the grid of civil society? How do these societies create a discursive space around civil society?

This study hinges fundamentally on the distinction between state and civil society. The distinction between the two has a long history in Western political theory. In the late sixteenth and seventeenth century political thought, the term civil society (*societe civile, societas civilis*) was used to denote a realm of stable political order distinct from the city of God (Colas 1997). As a matter of fact, contractualists like Hobbes saw in the establishment of a 'lawful state' a victory of 'civility' over uncontrolled desire, a triumph of order over chaos. According to this thinking, there was very little distance between civil and political society. However, by the early nineteenth century the term civil society came to represent a sphere that is distinct from that of the state. The separation and the tension between the two continue to resonate in our times. The tension between civil society and the state has been interpreted in several ways. For some, civil society is the domain in which the interests of individuals and that of society are reconciled (Ferguson 1995). For others, it is the sphere in which interdependent individuals tend to pursue their freedom (Hegel 1991; Taylor 1975: Chapter XV). Civil society is usually linked to two kinds of function. First, it is seen as a domain of self-regulating activities,[2] a realm defined by intersubjective communication and solidarity (Cohen and Arato 1992). In this sense, it comes closer to Habermas' idea of 'life-world' (*Lebenswelt*). Second, it is viewed as an amalgam of activities whose objective is to reform/transform the state (Keane 1998, 1988a, 1988b). It is not surprising, therefore, that the attitude of contemporary literature towards civil society is by and large celebratory. Its positive role is often highlighted against the backdrop of a non-performing and overbearing state. In this context, it is worth exploring the question of how the civil society argument is articulated in India. How do we map the multiplicity of discourses concerning civil society?

As soon as we undertake this task, a conceptual dilemma crops up. There are many who equate civil society with the entire non-state sphere in India. In so doing, the category becomes a residual one. Yet, there are others who designate only the 'modern' institutions within the non-state realm as civil society. We thus get hopelessly caught between these two definitions: one that contains too much and the other too little. I think that if we adopt too broad a definition, the concept of civil society becomes analytically imprecise and empirically less helpful. In contrast, if we include only the modern/ civic institutions within the sphere of civil society, too many crucial social and political realities are left outside its orbit. Though analytically precise, a restrictive definition makes it too insignificant for understanding Indian democracy and politics. I think it is possible to get out of this problem by altering the questions altogether. Instead of asking what remains within and what falls outside it, or where does its boundary lie, we can view civil society in terms of a set of dynamic social and political processes. Seen thus, the civil society argument can lead to a different level of analysis. It is also likely that by adopting this approach, the descriptive as well as normative dimensions of the civil society discourse can be brought together. It is futile to presume that the tension between the two dimensions of civil society can ever be fully resolved. But by seeing it as a process, one can locate it in the realm of history and explore its relationship with other aspects of society. Nevertheless, the question remains: how do we evaluate a particular civil society when the most marginal section of the population does not find a niche for itself within it? This takes us to the heart of the relationship between the civil society and governance.

The term 'governance', like 'civil society', is much overused today. In the discourses of multilateral agencies, both terms feature within a single package. Either it is employed in a technical sense, made up of a list of indicators by which the state constitutes itself, or it refers, narrowly, to the output functions of a political system. In fact, civil society is seen as an important contributor to good governance. Etymologically, the term governance refers primarily to the action or manner of governing, or 'steering conduct' of public/legal/constitutional institutions (Jessop 1998). In its contemporary usage, a distinction is often drawn between 'governance' and the two related terms 'governing' and 'government'. Whereas government refers to a network of institutions and rules, and 'governing' to the act of governing itself, 'governance' points to 'patterns that emerge from governing activities of social, political and administrative actors' (Kooiman 1993: 2). In one sense, there is nothing new about the issue of governance per se. It articulates or refers to the old theme of the state and the nature of its activities. However, the resurgence of this term since the 1980s has to be understood as a part of a larger intellectual and political move recast the relationship between state, society and development.

In its new avatar, the theme of governance is intimately linked to the issue of development. This shift in its usage was clearly manifest in the World Bank's 1989 report *Sub-Saharan Africa: From Crisis to Sustainable Growth*. According to the report, 'underlying the litany of Africa's development problems is a crisis of governance' (World Bank 1989). A detailed discussion of this report is beyond the scope of this essay. Yet it is necessary to point out the connection the report highlights between democracy and development, between state and society. According to it, the term 'good governance' encompasses values such as greater accountability and transparency of public institutions. It also lays emphasis on a minimal state, better public sector management, encouragement of private enterprise and finally, on a neo-liberal economic agenda.

Several scholars have noted the limitations in the Bank's understanding of 'governance'. According to the critics, the Bank's usage of 'governance' is more management oriented than political in spirit (Beckman 1992). Some view the underlying notion of democracy in governance discourse as too instrumental and severely limited (Jayal 1997; Guhan 1998). Yet others argue for a need to rescue the term governance from its technical use that is devoid of ethical significance (Kothari 1987). At the empirical level, the prescriptive value of the 'governance' perspective is also subject to serious scrutiny. It is argued that in a society fractured by deep inequalities, a minimal state cannot bring about social justice. Similarly, the attack on the welfare state by this perspective is seen as anti-poor. This is not to say that the issue of 'governance' is not important. As a matter of fact, issues like corruption, accountability, transparency and so on raised by the Bank and other multilateral agencies are vital. Hence, there is a need to bring the idea of governance closer to the concerns of democracy and equity.

Here, I have tried to define the word 'governance' from a normative point of view and particularly from the angle of the most disadvantaged in the society. According to this understanding of 'governance', the issue of 'economic benefit' is as important as that of 'dignity' and of being counted in a polity. The idea of governance, I would like to suggest, is not a technical concept; nor should it be treated purely as an empirical category. It is best seen within the context of contesting politics and values, as it is often caught in the web of hegemonic and counter-hegemonic politics in societies. The second element that needs to be emphasised is that 'governance' should be disentangled from the larger, neo-liberal agenda. There is no doubt that state is quite important and that it plays a crucial role in the lives of ordinary people in most post-colonial societies. Yet, the impetus of governance issues is not confined in this sphere. Once this is recognised, reconfiguring society becomes as much an important agenda of good governance as transforming the state.

The link between a vibrant civil society and democratic governance is widely noted by scholars and policy-makers in recent times. Here the vibrancy of civil society is conceived minimally in terms of its capacity to reflect the interests of the people living within it. In other words, it is conceived as a crucible of 'interests'. Issues like who represents whom and how effectively are quite crucial within the sphere of civil society. Interest-group theorists assume that individuals, motivated by rational calculation, form groups or associations in order to realise their goals. The Scottish moralists viewed group solidarity as a product of 'natural sentiments' among individuals caught in a system of commercial transactions. Whether collective lives are a product of individual self-interest or of a need for recognition that people acutely feel in a mutually dependent world is a question that is beyond the scope of this study. However, it is essential to recognise that the theme of collective life or agency is a crucial component of the civil society argument in its new incarnations. In fact, one can clearly detect Tocquevillean echoes in the argument.

Reflecting on American democracy, Tocqueville observed that a rich, associational life was crucial for its growth and vitality. He also attributed the success of democracy in America to the widespread civic engagement present in American society. This insight regarding American democracy has achieved wide recognition in the writings on civil society in recent times. According to this line of thinking, a rich, associational life is considered a sign of and contributes to a vibrant civil society. The more people are part of a dense network of associations, it is argued, the more likely they are to play the role of active citizens. Are all groups in civil society equally capable of forming associations? What about people who are not in a position to form associations or networks to ensure that their interests are regarded as legitimate? What happens when the state refuses to even recognise a particular group of people? Do these people belong to the sphere of civil society? In the literature, interest-based associations are seen as important components of social and political order. This positive link between civil society and associations may intuitively appear to be correct, but my research among pavement dwellers has compelled me to view it as a problem. Even during the early phase of my research I could see that the formal associational aspect of the civil society argument would not be able to capture the life-world of the pavement dwellers in Mumbai. In fact, the initiatives of the pavement dwellers and those of other organisations working with them can be interpreted as an attempt to secure them a place within the sphere of civil society.

The relationship between civil society and governance, as I have hinted earlier, should be seen in the larger context of social relationship and coordinates of power within a specific setting. It is quite important to also pay attention to the modes in which the poor and deprived sections of society engage with the state and other structures of power and authority. In a situation where the state views pavement dwellers primarily as intruders or encroachers of public space, the relationship between them and civil society acquires a new meaning. Since their identity as citizens is not recognised, how would we describe their engagement with the state and other institutions of governance? I strongly believe that the case of pavement dwellers stretches the civil society argument to its logical limit. In fact, it throws the limitations of the civil society argument into sharp relief. In this context, it would appropriate to mention some of the methodological points that inform this study.

First, the present study does not claim to be a comprehensive study of pavement dwellers in Mumbai. The case of the pavement dwellers is taken as a context within which the problematic link between civil society and governance can be meaningfully explored. Second, apart from the secondary sources, evidence for the study has come largely from interviews with the pavement dwellers and other people involved with them. Like most dialogues or conversations, these interviews are suggestive but inconclusive, and they carry the imprint of numerous 'contingencies' and of an ongoing engagement with the 'present'. Finally, a study like this is deliberately open-ended because any attempt to do otherwise will derecognise the fluidity of the situation.

As I have remarked earlier, understanding specific historical and political contexts is quite essential for the study of civil society. Depending on the context, the civil society argument tends to highlight a particular set of issues. For instance, in the East European countries, the civil society argument was/is often employed to highlight the negative elements of an overbearing state. The emphasis in these societies was on dismantling the authoritarian state. However, in many of the post-colonial societies the argument is not directed against the state as such; rather, it is deployed against the state being controlled by a dominant elite. The idea is that it is civil society that can control, if not entirely transform, the state and press it into the service of democracy and social justice. How can this be done? Are all social forces equally capable of transforming the state? What are the critical factors that enable groups within civil society to influence it? This study addresses these problems (to which I shall return later in the essay).

The Issue of 'Governance'

One of the most pressing issues for pavement dwellers in Mumbai is shelter. Yet it is the most difficult to achieve in the short or medium run, for it requires a great deal of resources (both financial and organisational) and a strong will on the part of the state and the relevant public institutions. A secure home is the dream of every pavement dweller, but it is a dream that they find difficult to fulfil in a hostile environment. What the older people, who have spent decades on the pavements of Mumbai, had to say was an unwieldy mixture of optimism and pessimism. Although important, the issue of alternate shelter gets edged out by the overwhelming pressure of daily life.

The story of the pavement dwellers' survival was, and still is, intimately linked to an ingenious if not sturdy defence of their locations in the city and the incessant struggle to be a part of the entitlement network of the state and other public institutions. Whether it is the facility for drinking water, sanitation, ration card or a demand to be covered by the state's development, these can all be viewed as issues pertaining to 'entitlements'. A significant part of the governance issues, therefore, centres on the 'entitlement concerns' of the pavement dwellers. It is no surprise, then, that organisations like SPARC have always fought for the inclusion of the pavement dwellers in the 'redistributive or entitlement-related schemes' of the state.

The other governance issue relates to the question of 'autonomy' of pavement dwellers. I do not intend to discuss here the debate concerning 'autonomy' that has been so eloquently articulated by the liberal political theorists in recent years. But I would like to point out that it is not important for people merely to be a part of the state's entitlement network; it is equally vital that they play a key role in the fashioning of this network. The autonomy of pavement dwellers consists in their ability to take control of their lives and to increase their agency vis-à-vis the state and other institutions. This takes us to the heart of the debate on citizenship and the state. In this context, it is necessary to discuss the autonomy of pavement dwellers on both the individual and collective level.

Finally, the question of dignity can never be overlooked in a discussion of governance issues. The issue of an alternative shelter for pavement dwellers is not merely about acquiring a space for decent living; it is inextricably linked to the issue of 'dignity' and self-respect. One can clearly detect in their articulations a moral tone, which in turn creates a normative ground for them to evaluate the state, politics and political leaders. According to Samina, who has been a pavement dweller for more than 20 years, 'The person on the footpath is never treated with respect. But a house-owner, even if he does not have one *roti* to eat, is treated with respect.' The moral texture of their perception concerning well-being and quality of life is often overlooked within the official discourse on 'governance'. The moral aspect of 'governance', I would like to argue, should be taken seriously.

The theme of governance thus ought to be explored at different levels. For instance, to bring about changes in state policy is as important as the step pavement dwellers take to cope with daily indignities. The neighbourhood network of pavement dwellers should be studied as seriously as we study their formal, organisational initiatives. For the pavement dwellers in Mumbai, life on the street is a series of tough negotiations. And it is in this process of negotiation that they tend to refashion their relationship with the state, re-imagine their locations in an indifferent civil society, and redefine their attitudes towards the concerned organisations/activists. In some sense, the relationship between civil society and governance is the story of these complex negotiations.

The Underbelly of Modernity

The large presence of urban poor in Mumbai is not a new phenomenon. However, their social locations and the relationship with institutions of governance in the city have always been complex and historically varied. In the late nineteenth century, the city had emerged as the most important commercial centre of British India. Especially during the inter-war years (between the First and the Second World War), the consolidation of the textile industry made it the hub of economic activity of colonial India. After independence, the image of the city as the chief carrier of industrial modernity continued. As a city, Mumbai has always evoked multiple and contradictory structures of feelings. Like most other metropolises elsewhere, it has been portrayed as being simultaneously a land of opportunity, a place of bewilderment and of inhumanity. In the Hindi films of the 1950s and 1960s, the city came to symbolise a destination of material allurement and moral corruption. Against the background of an island of opulence, the poor/subalterns were portrayed as the genuine symbol of fellowship and human warmth. Like most metropolises in the third world, Mumbai lives with its own brand of unevenness and unmanageable contradictions. In the 1990s, the era of globalisation, it increasingly is being defined by the tension that exists between the claims of 'cosmopolitism' and the growing religious/ethnic intolerance, between the global flow of capital and a cesspool of poverty; and finally, between the deepening of democracy and the cold indifference of the state and public institutions towards the plight of the marginalised groups such as the pavement dwellers in the city.

According to one estimate, more than half the city's population lives in slums or is without any home (Patel and Thorner 1995: Introduction). Since the 1960s, the population living in slums/pavements has recorded a dramatic increase. Over the last three decades, the percentage of people living in slums has increased from 10 to 55 (Singh and Das 1995). While it is possible to view this as a consequence of the city's urbanisation pattern, in a very significant sense the issue of shelter reflects the entrenched inequality prevalent in the city. For instance, in 1985 the 'unauthorised slums' occupied only 2,000 (out of a total 40,000) hectares of land in Mumbai (Desai 1985: 38). By the early 1990s, the area covered by slums was not more than 8 per cent of its total area (Patel and Thorner, op. cit.). The inhuman conditions of the slums, among other things, reflect the contradictory character of Mumbai's modernity. Where do the pavement dwellers feature in this?

Although the slum and pavement dwellers together belong to the most marginal section of the city, the difference between the two should not be overlooked. Although patchy, it is still possible to get some data on the slum dwellers. It seems that since 1976 they have been sporadically included in the census with the objective of bringing them into the policy network of the state.[3] In contrast, it has always been difficult (and relatively speaking, still is) to obtain reliable data concerning pavement dwellers (Afzulpurkar 1995: Chapter 30).[4] The state has never included them in any census 'as a matter of policy', because it views them merely as intruders into or encroachers of private/government property. Thus, the state's refusal to recognise them resulted in denying the pavement dwellers their status as citizens. Although living on the pavements of the city, they remained invisible and ignored. In other words, historically, no other group in the city suffers as much from the problem of invisibility as the pavement dwellers. The only way the state approached them was by dislocating them, demolishing their hutments, demonising them and by keeping them away from its network of entitlement and rights.

The treatment meted out to pavement dwellers by the state is symptomatic of a larger crisis that has characterised post-colonial democracy in India. Ironically, while a large majority of pavement dwellers enjoy the right to vote in the elections, their citizenship status has been reduced merely to 'voting'. As pointed out earlier, the absence of other rights has meant that most of the time, their agency is seriously compromised. How do we understand their agency in such circumstances? Can a traditional understanding of the term 'security' capture the experiences of the pavement dwellers? The threat and the actual incidents of demolition[5] and the indignities involved in the process prompt us to raise serious questions about the nature of the state and the imperatives of public policy.

Contexts and Modes of Intervention

In the early 1980s, the issue of pavement dwellers came into the limelight following a large-scale demolition of slums undertaken by the government of Maharashtra. The 'operation eviction' initiated by Antulay's government exposed the anti-poor character of the state and also brought the issue of shelter before the concerned citizenry. It was the state's lack of concern for pavement dwellers that prompted concerned citizens to frame the relationship between the state and the civil society in a new way. How can we protect the interests of people who for decades have lived on the pavement? Should public spaces be retrieved without adequate attention being given to pavement dwellers' right to life and livelihood? How can the attitude of the state and other concerned institutions towards the urban poor be altered?

The immediate reaction of social activists and concerned citizens was to stop the large-scale eviction of the pavement dwellers. For instance, organisations like the Nivara Haka Suraksha Samiti (Das 1995) organised protests against the state's insensitive move. Following this mobilisation, a stay order was obtained from the Bombay High Court against the demolition of slums, including hutments on pavements. In 1983, the Bombay Municipal Corporation challenged the order of the High Court in the Supreme Court of India, whose verdict in 1985 proved to be the turning point for the issue of pavement dwellers. While a detailed analysis of the Supreme Court judgement is not possible here, a brief discussion of the verdict is necessary in order to capture the discursive space or grid that was used to comprehend the problems of the city's pavement dwellers.

The Supreme Court's judgement was ambiguous, to say the least. On the one hand, it permitted the demolition of pavement dwellings in Mumbai; on the other, it recognised the intensity of the problems faced by pavement dwellers. The petitioner on behalf of the pavement dwellers argued that their eviction would deprive them of their livelihood. But the argument concerning the right to life and livelihood, invoking Article 21 of the Indian Constitution, did not prove sufficiently effective. Instead of creatively interpreting it, the Court merely focused on the reasonableness of its application. The Court clearly saw that the pavement dwellers chose 'a pavement or a slum in the vicinity of their place of work, the time otherwise taken in commuting and its costs being forbidding for their slender means. To lose the pavement or the slum [is] to lose the job.'[6] Yet the Court pronounced that the removal of 'encroachers' from footpaths or pavements could not be regarded as 'unreasonable, unfair and unjust' (Cordozo 1985: 39).

The petitioners also argued that the pavement dwellers should not be treated as 'trespassers' as claimed by the Bombay Municipal Corporation. It was further argued that the pavement dwellers had a right to use the footpath for living as the pedestrian had a right to use it for walking and so on. The Supreme Court also rejected the parity between pavement dwellers and pedestrians. According to the judgement:

> footpaths or pavements are public properties which are intended to serve the convenience of the *general public*. They are not laid for *private use*. If used for private purposes, they frustrate the very object for which they were carved out from portions of public streets (emphasis mine) (Venkatramani 1985: 403).

What did the Supreme Court's judgement achieve? The immediate consequence of the judgement was that the demolition was suspended and the Court directed the Bombay Municipal Corporation to carry out the eviction after the monsoon and in as humane a manner as possible. The judgement quite eloquently exposed the callous attitude of the state towards the urban poor. For instance, the Bombay Municipal Corporation argued that the slums or pavement dwellers often indulge in criminal activities. The Court unequivocally rejected this and indicted the state government for harbouring 'prejudice against the poor and the destitute'. In one sense, the Supreme Court judgement for the first time put the issue of pavement dwellers in a broad perspective, against the backdrop of values such as justice, rights and minimal entitlements.

This is one of the significant contexts in which the intervention of civil society organisations in the affairs of the pavement dwellers has to be understood. The immediate task before the civil society organisations was to address the issue of demolition and the cruel indignities involved in the process. These organisations quickly realised that their information on pavement dwellers in Mumbai was quite patchy. The state's ignorance regarding them was equally striking. Following the Court's judgement, attempts were made to generate more information on the pavement dwellers of Mumbai. For instance, SPARC's work among the urban poor took a dramatic turn when it began enumerating pavement dwellers in the city's 'E' ward.[7] Enumeration of groups, as historians of identity politics suggest, has always produced new possibilities for cultural and political mobilisation. Even though it tends to reify social identity, makes it less fuzzy and amenable to manipulations by the elite, its ability to create new discourses of politics cannot be underestimated. If earlier, social activists working among the urban poor in Mumbai highlighted the wretchedness of pavement dwellers, the numbers thrown up by enumeration enhanced its intensity. Such interplay of quality and quantity gave the enumeration conducted by SPARC its political cutting edge. Within a month (30 August to 28 September 1985), it had covered about 6,000 households comprising nearly 27,000 individuals within the 'E' ward of the city. The exercise was conducted by people trained in enumeration and with the full participation of the pavement dwellers living in the area. The exercise also provided SPARC staff a fresh opportunity to strengthen their links with these people. It is no surprise, then, that this enumeration came to be seen as a people's census. People were kept informed of the progress in enumeration at every stage, at the end of which the findings were shared with them.

'*We, the Invisible*' (SPARC 1985),[8] the report SPARC produced following the enumeration, is not a conventional census document. Besides providing basic data on pavement dwellers, it tries to construct a larger picture pertaining to their lives and livelihood. In the process, it has demolished many myths and prejudices concerning the most marginal people in the city. Contrary to the common belief that pavement dwellers are a transient and mobile population, the census pointed out that a majority of them have lived on the pavement for years. Nearly 13 per cent of the heads of pavement dweller households were born in Bombay and around 60 per cent of the total population migrated to the city over a decade ago. Another belief that pavement dwellers are a burden on the city's infrastructure (particularly transport) was also found to be untrue. As a matter of fact, as the census pointed out, most of them walked to their workplaces. It further pointed out that they constituted an important source of cheap labour in the city, as the majority of them worked below the minimum wage level (at that time, Rs 18 per day). The report also put the issue of migration and shelter in a larger perspective. The chronic poverty among pavement dwellers was, and still is, responsible for destitution and vulnerability. Finally, the report tried to contest the middle-class vision of the city and a notion of 'governance' (although the word is not used in the document) that was unabashedly elitist and patently illiberal.

The enumeration exercise helped SPARC to articulate different strategies of intervention for both short- and long-term objectives. As mentioned earlier, frequent demolition of their hutments created a specific set of problems for the pavement dwellers. The municipal authorities would often confiscate their belongings, leading to legal and administrative wrangling. When this happened, SPARC took their complaints to the appropriate administrative authorities as well as to the courts (Bapat 1992). These responses were undoubtedly shaped by and directed towards the immediate needs of the pavement dwellers. However, their impact on the people tended to linger. It was thus easy to foster solidarity not only among the pavement dwellers but also between them and SPARC. Further, taking the authorities to court punctured the idea of their invincibility. There are cases where the municipal authorities had to compensate the pavement dwellers for the loss of their belongings.

However, it was clear right from the beginning (in spite of occasional victories) that the battle between the pavement dwellers and the state authorities was an unequal one. Any attempt to address their issues or problems would involve a critical look at the larger policy environment of the city. Where did pavement dwellers stand vis-à-vis the structure of urban governance? This realisation led SPARC to start the process of intervening in policies of the city/state. There are different ways by which a voluntary organisation can do this. For instance, it can act independently on behalf of these people and put pressure on appropriate institutions, in which case it does not need to mobilise the people except to the extent that it can ascertain, aggregate and represent their true interests. Thus, the people on whose behalf the organisation speaks may not necessarily be active participants in this process. Another way would be for the voluntary organisation to raise the issue of marginal groups by mobilising them and work towards enhancing their agency in the public sphere. In this method of intervention, the emphasis is on the initiatives of the people and their capacity to sustain such initiatives. The role of the voluntary organisations is that of a facilitator and its activities are largely geared towards sustaining the people-led process.

The nature of SPARC's intervention, broadly speaking, has been of the second type. It is important to make the point, however, that this intervention did not happen on its own. Ever since its establishment in 1984, SPARC members had been working with the women pavement dwellers of the Byculla area of Central Mumbai. Many of its intervention strategies can be traced to this early experience. For instance, mobilising women to take a leading role in community affairs and helping them to face the world of public institutions are some of the early lessons that SPARC members learnt. In the initial years, the main objective of SPARC was to initiate a process that could put pavement dwellers, the most marginal and insecure among the urban poor, within the network of rights and entitlements and in the sphere of civil society. Apart from helping them to shed their apathy, it wanted to organise them into a group that could enter the competitive world of lobbying and negotiation.[9] These initiatives have significant implications for the 'civil society argument', which I shall discuss later in the essay.

SPARC's activities can be best understood in the context of its linkages with community-based organisations. In the 1980s, it found itself collaborating with the NSDF, a people's organisation, with a largely male membership, formed in the 1970s. NSDF was primarily involved with securing entitlements for slum dwellers. The organisation was very successful in mobilising slum dwellers. However, due to its 'agitational' politics, it could not establish a synergistic relation with the various institutions of the state. Nevertheless, it had a presence, not only in other cities of Maharashtra but also outside the state.

Another organisation that partners SPARC is Mahila Milan (MM), a federation of women's collectives in Mumbai. It started in 1987 as a network of collectives of women pavement dwellers, but within a decade it had acquired an extensive presence both within and outside Maharashtra. In the early days of its formation, SPARC played a crucial role in helping it to acquire autonomy, which is so essential for sustaining mobilisation and collective action among people. How did MM emerge? While MM's emergence can be seen primarily as a response of pavement dwellers to their daily problems and indignities, this does not explain the timing of its emergence. This is where SPARC's intervention played a crucial role. Interviews with the members of MM brought out this point quite clearly.

In the formative years of its existence, MM's activities were directed towards two things: to prepare the pavement dwellers to collectively face the problems arising out of demolitions, and to increase their collective capacity to address their live-lihood issues, including that of shelter. The formation of a credit and savings network among the families living on pave-ments provided the women with much-needed experience and helped them to create a sense of solidarity that was earlier absent. The fact that MM helped families to obtain ration cards and open bank accounts, and provided them with emer-gency loans, contributed towards it popularity among the pavement dwellers. MM not only helped people to cope with the problems of everyday life, it also provided the women pavement dwellers with an entry point into the world of public institutions. Conventional understanding does not adequately recognise the role of experience in collective practice. People's experiences are often seen as mere instinctive reactions, far removed from the sphere of reasoned reflection. Our evidence suggests that the experiences of collective action and the sharing of common problems at an emotional level helped the pavement dwellers to criticise existing knowledge and create a new epistemic orientations towards the larger world in which they lived. According to Lakshmi, a MM leader who has lived on the pavement all her life:

> Making one organisation has made a big difference. The municipal-ity used to come and demolish (our huts) everyday. Now that is stopped since we formed our Mahila Milan. Earlier they did not make ration cards for us, they said the person living on footpath does not have any right to a ration card. After we came into Mahila Milan, we got our ration cards. We used to feel scared when we saw the police and we were afraid to go to the police station. Now, after coming into Mahila Milan, we have become brave. Now we talk to the senior, to the inspector, everyone in the police station. We have learnt this after Mahila Milan came. *Because all came together we gained strength and by staying with these people, we began under-standing things that are difficult to understand* (emphasis mine).[10]

Over the years, the activities of MM have gone beyond the running of a savings and credit network among the pavement dwellers. It has also now taken up the issue of shelter. Through running the organisation and the exposure this has given them, the capacities of the women in MM have increased dramatically. The leadership of MM is now familiar with the intricacies of house construction and the vexed issue of finance to undertake it. Once again, SPARC's intervention in this process has been and continues to be quite significant. In this context, it would useful to look at how MM sustains itself as a collective. One might say that common interest acts as the glue for collective bonding among the women pavement dwellers. It is also possible to argue that members of the credit and savings association do not default in repayment of loans because of the presence of a collective moral pressure or due to the fear of being ostracised by the neighbours and friends. However, it is equally likely that the credit and savings networks among the pavement dwellers work reasonably well because the process of interaction and cooperation generates a lot of trust among the people (Patel and D'Cruz 1993). In other words, such voluntary interaction is sustained by a strong presence of, to use a popular phrase, 'social capital' or what, in a different context, Albert Hirschman calls 'moral resources'.

The resources that pavement dwellers use for their betterment are often generated within the sphere of collective action. However, the efficacy of such actions depends on several factors, including the larger environment that includes the state and other political/public institutions. This has led SPARC and its partner organisations, the NSDF and MM, to take the issue of the slum and pavement dwellers into the larger arena, with the aim of altering the policies of the state towards the urban poor. In several ways the relationship between SPARC and NSDF is symbiotic. As an organisation of professionals, it has been able to articulate and sharpen the agenda of the NSDF. As discussed earlier, the pavement dwellers were primarily seen as 'encroachers' of public spaces and hence removed in order to reclaim these spaces for the citizenry. They remained, by and large, invisible. To make them visible needed a fresh look at their status, aspirations, and above all, the policies of the state.

Policy Matters

Until 1995, the pavement dwellers were not even treated at a par with slum dwellers. A decade after the Supreme Court judgement brought the issue of pavement dwellers into the limelight, the state of Maharashtra constituted a study group to look into the issues of slum rehabilitation in Mumbai. And for the first time, pavement dwellers were included by this study group in its discussions. The findings, published as the Afzulpurkar Report[11] (named after the chairperson of the study group) were a product of deliberations involving 18 members comprising civil servants, architects, engineers, NGO representatives, property developers and bankers. The group recommended that by 1 January 1995, people living in slums (including on pavements) be made eligible for free housing in Mumbai. It further recommended that the electoral rolls of 1 January 1995 be considered as the evidence for eligibility. Some of its key provisions were:

1. All people living in slums and pavement settlements as of 1 January 1995 be eligible to be a part of the Slum Redevelopment Scheme.
2. Pavement dwellers be considered fully eligible and relocated on nearby vacant land.
3. Legal title (long-term lease) of land to be transferred to cooperative societies and organisations of slum dwellers rather than individuals.
4. All households be allotted 225 sq ft units, free of cost.
5. One unit be allotted per existing household regardless of the number of people in the household.
6. As far as possible, slum dwellers be rehabilitated on existing site.
7. If rehabilitation on site is not possible, then new sites be located within 20 km of existing slum.
8. Redevelopment schemes to move ahead as long as at least 70 per cent of households in a slum agree to participate in them.

The study group also recommended the participation of the slum/pavement dwellers in the process of rehabilitation and redevelopment. The role of NGOs was also stressed. There is no doubt that this occasioned a significant turn in the policy of the state towards the pavement dwellers in the city. The recognition of pavement dwellers' specific needs also gave a new impetus to the collective mobilisation of groups in the area of shelter. Finally, at least in the realm of policy if not in actual practice, pavement dwellers' distinct identity was acknowledged.[12] The acceptance of the report by the state led to a series of discussions, debates and follow-ups. At the time of writing, SPARC was involved in the process of rehabilitating and relocating[13] 7,000 pavement dwellers by October 2000.

Inevitably, responses to the Afzulpurkar Report and to the new policy of rehabilitations/redevelopment were mixed. Some argued that the report failed to take 'its implications to their logical conclusion' (Singh and Das 1995). They also saw in the scheme a lack of strong commitment on the part of the state to resolve the issue of housing for the urban poor. There was also the fear that powerful builders/property developers in the city may take advantage of this programme. However, SPARC and other organisations like it viewed the new policy as providing fresh opportunities for mobilisation and new contexts for intervention. They saw its enabling aspects and hoped to utilise its provisions for the betterment of pavement dwellers. The magnitude of the problem that the report outlined was indeed daunting. It estimated that rehabilitation would involve the construction of 11 to 11.5 lakh dwelling units (including transit tenements but excluding the tenements of the free sale components) with a rough outlay of Rs 15,900 crore (159 billion) (Afzalpurkar Report 1995: 87).

How do we evaluate the change in policy? As recommended by the study group, the Maharashtra government was quick to establish the Slum Rehabilitation Authority (SRA), a nodal agency for the slum rehabilitation programmes in Mumbai. Yet, the construction of houses did not follow the pace envisaged in the report. Between 1992 and 1997, the government was able to provide houses for only 33,000 people.[14] If one were to judge the new policy in terms of its actual performance, then the balance sheet does not appear to be impressive. Yet I think it is too early to dismiss the impact of this policy. Further, the process set into motion by the policy should be taken into account while passing judgement on the functioning of SRA. The inclusion of pavement dwellers within the framework of the policy, as mentioned earlier, is itself a significant achievement. How did this happen? Although the evidence is not sufficiently robust to link any single initiative in the civil society sphere with the policy outcome, the persistent campaigning by SPARC and its partner organisations for the welfare and rights of pavement dwellers and its impact on the policy environment cannot be underestimated. Their unflinching engagement over the years with the issues of pavement dwellers has given their interventions potency and character. To enable a group of people to achieve visibility in the policy environment is a significant step in the right direction. For the issue of governance and social and economic justice can be addressed only once this minimal condition of inclusion in the 'public sphere' has been met.

Implications for Civil Society and Governance

The central concern here has been to explore the problematic link between civil society and governance through the study of a concrete context. Much of the contemporary literature treats the positive link between the two as *a priori*. It is argued that a vibrant civil society contributes naturally to good governance, which in turn enhances the democratic capacity of the state. The case of Mumbai's pavement dwellers suggests that it is analytically unhelpful and empirically incorrect to essentialise civil society as 'good'. The nature of any civil society depends upon several factors, including the power relations among contending groups living within it. The sphere of civil society, like that of the state, is shaped by the inequalities prevalent in the society. A romantic understanding of civil society as a repository of positive values is historically flawed and politically naïve. However, this is not to deny the transformatory potential of a civil society that is democratic in nature and is informed by egalitarian values.

With the inauguration of the Constitutional Republic in 1950, political equality was introduced as a key feature of the Indian polity. It was also hoped that in time and with the help of other institutions and social engineering, the state would transform the principle of formal equality enshrined in the Constitution into a substantive aspect of Indian society. The competitive, democratic politics, it was believed, would create new stirrings that would undermine, if not entirely eliminate, the social hierarchies. Fifty years on, the narrative of Indian democracy is being written in terms of the wide gap that persists between its declared ideals and their blatant violation in every sphere of the society. By the late 1970s, the signs of institutional decline were quite visible in India. The students of Indian government and politics had also detected a proportional decline in the capacity of the state to govern India. Much of the recent literature (Manor 1983: vol. 18; Kothari 1990: vol. II; Kohli 1991; Saberwal 1996; Mohapatra 1997; Varshney 1998; Mitra 1999) on Indian government and politics highlights the growing erosion of institutional values in Indian society. At the same time, scholars of Indian democracy also speak of a growing democratic upsurge in recent decades. The increasing self-assertion of people that hitherto were peripheral to the political processes is central to this upsurge. Much of the recent democratic stirrings are taking place in the realm of civil society. It is important to note that the Indian state has not been able to adequately engage with such stirrings. As a result, there are several groups/classes those who still survive at the margins of the policy processes of the Indian state.

Collective efforts to influence state policies, as some scholars point out, may be self-generated or influenced by intermediaries.[15] The case of Mumbai's pavement dwellers clearly suggests that a group of people who are economically poor and socially marginal find it difficult to make their mark on state policies, even the ones that directly influence their life-chances. Here, mediation by voluntary organisations is of crucial significance. These organisations devote their energies to bring marginal groups under the 'policy-gaze' of the state. Although significant, making the poor visible is not the ultimate goal of voluntary organisations. The aim is to help marginal sections of society develop appropriate skills to aggregate their interests by themselves and to mobilise adequate resources to engage with the state. The role of SPARC, as far as the pavement dwellers are concerned, encompassed both objectives. Most of SPARC's interventions are geared towards helping the pavement dwellers to achieve autonomy.

Although there has been a significant shift in the policy of the Maharashtra government towards pavement dwellers, we cannot deduce from this that the latter have really become autonomous. Achieving autonomy is not a one-shot affair, but a long and arduous process. How far the pavement dwellers will succeed in influencing state actions cannot be judged *a priori*. History tells us that the struggle is likely to be tough. Where the issue of shelter for pavement/slum dwellers is concerned, SPARC believes that it is possible to achieve a synergistic relationship between civil society organisations and the state. Behind this belief is the faith that state can be transformed, the leviathan can be tamed. One the basis of this study, it is possible to argue that the effectiveness of interventions by voluntary organisations depend as much on their strategies as on the responsiveness of the state. And specific conjunctures and constellations of social forces contribute a great deal towards the effectiveness of civil society vis-à-vis the state.

Current interest in civil society coincides with a great deal of disaffection with the state and state-related institutions.

The forces of liberalisation and the decline of old-style social-ism have given this disenchantment an added force. With the state's capacity to achieve social justice in doubt, civil society is seen by many as a true substitute. I do not hold any brief for a state that does not articulate the aspirations of the people. Not do I think that in the years to come, political imagination can never transcend the state. Yet, in the context of most post-colonial societies, it is difficult to abandon the project of the state in the name of civil society. The objective should be to make it more democratic, more responsive to the needs of the poor and socially excluded. Where societies are fractured by segmentation and structural inequality, the state can play the role of a protector of the disadvantaged individuals and groups. The aim should therefore be to make the state as well as the civil society more democratic in India.

The relationship between civil society and governance in India, as I have already pointed out, is best seen in the larger political and institutional context of society. There are several ways in which the political context can be interpreted. One way is to acknowledge, as the pavement dwellers case shows, the contradiction between the project of citizenship and the hegemony of the state in post-colonial democracy. According to some scholars, the relevance of the civil society argument in the context of democracy is quite limited. This is because a large number of marginal people do not use the principle of 'liberal citizenship'—a characteristic of civil life—to engage with the state. Instead, they use an imaginative combination of the 'language of community' and the 'emancipatory rheto-ric' of autonomy and equal rights' to fight for their survival. Their engagement with the state often does not follow the standard trajectory of associational politics but operates within a complicated terrain of 'political society' (Chatterjee 1998). It is true that the pavement dwellers of Mumbai tend to use the 'language of community' as a vital resource for fostering solidarity. However, the activities of SPARC can be seen as attempts at introducing the 'language of civil society' to the process of collective mobilisation. But it is difficult to imagine all the possible uses to which Mumbai's pavement dwellers will put this language in the future.

I have pointed out that the civil society argument comes in different guises and secretes different values. It can be informed by egalitarian values, but it can also be undemocratic and exclusionary. Two cautionary notes are in order here. First, we should not excessively burden the term civil society with analytical tasks that it cannot perform. Second, the functioning of civil society needs to be analysed in the concrete contexts involving the political and social relations among people and between people/groups/class and the state. Depending on the context, the civil society argument is used by the subalterns in India to create a universal order of law and citizenship. It is also employed as a category that highlights their particular interests and aspirations that can only be realised by respecting their differences vis-à-vis others. As the pavement dwellers' case suggests, the civil society discourse in India is not only focused on the state but also on itself.

Notes

1. Translated from the Marathi by M. Kulkarni, J. Wagle and A. Sardesai.
2. The uncoerced aspect of human association is often linked to the notion of civil society. See Michael Walzer (1992).
3. A.R. Desai and S.D. Pillai's *A Profile of an Indian Slum* (1972) makes us aware of the problem of data regarding the slum dwellers of Bombay. Evidence used for the 1960s in the book is computed largely from data supplied by the Bombay Municipal Corporation. The report prepared by Dinesh K. Afzulpurkar (Programme for the Rehabilitation of Slum and Hutment Dwellers in Brihan Mumbai) in 1995 mentions the 1976 census of slum dwellers in the city.
4. According to a study undertaken in 1959 by the Bombay Municipal Corporation, there were around 20,000 pavement dwellers in the city.

5. Interviews with pavement dwellers clearly point to the tragic impact of demolitions. They also highlight the psychological impact of demolition, including the intense humiliation they suffer at the hands of officials. Studies also indicate that repeated demolitions also cause an adverse nutritional impact on children living in slums (*The Times of India* [Bombay], 2 March 1999).

6. The 1985 Supreme Court Judgement quoted in Nicky Cardozo (1985), p. 39.

7. The Nirmala Niketan College of Social Work had undertaken an enumeration (on a small scale) of the pavement dwellers in Mumbai. This was done as a response to the large-scale demolition undertaken by the Bombay Municipal Corporation in 1981. Nirmala Niketan College of Social Work (1985).

8. See also Meera Bapat's review of *We, the Invisible: A Census of Pavement Dwellers* (SPARC: 1985) in *Economic and Political Weekly*, 12 October 1991.

9. A reflection on SPARC's early experience is summarised in Meera Bapat and Sheela Patel (1993).

10. Quoted from the report prepared by SPARC in 1999: Between Squalor and Hope: Pavement Dwellers and Slum Dwellers Along the Railway Tracks in Mumbai.

11. Report of the Study Group appointed by the Government of Maharashtra for the Rehabilitation of Slum and Hutment Dwellers Through Reconstruction (1995).

12. The Afzulpurkar Report (1995), see Chapter 20.

13. Interview with Sheela Patel, Director, SPARC, August 1999.

14. Reported by the Minister for Housing Development in a meeting of SRA held in January 2000.

15. For an excellent discussion on democracy and participation see Mark Robinson (1998).

10

Land Distribution for Kol Tribals in Uttar Pradesh

B.K. Joshi[*]

This case study deals with the distribution of land *pattas* (titles) to Kol tribals in Chitrakoot district of southern Uttar Pradesh. A local civil society organisation, the Akhil Bharatiya Samaj Sewa Sansthan (ABSSS), played a leading role in implementing the government's programme to provide land titles to the poor and socially disadvantaged sections of society, mainly the scheduled castes and tribes in the district. The focus here is on the role of the ABSSS and its contribution to governance in the context of this programme.

The Kols are a tribal group who inhabit large tracts of land in central India, comprising Madhya Pradesh (MP) and the adjoining areas of southern Uttar Pradesh (UP), i.e., the districts of Allahabad, Chitrakoot (which formed part of Banda district until 1997), Varanasi, Mirzapur and Sonebhadra. They are a proud people with a long, though unrecorded, history of

*The author wishes to acknowledge the help provided by Sachindra Sharma and Vasudev during data collection, tabulation and for the critical insights they brought in to the study.

living in harmony and communion with nature and the environment. They trace their lineage to the legendary Shabari of the Ramayana, who has been revered by generations of Hindus for her devotion to Lord Rama during his exile. She is best remembered for having fed him berries after first tasting them to make sure they were sweet. Interestingly, while the Kols are included in the list of Scheduled Tribes (STs) in MP, they have not been accorded the same status in UP, where they are classified as Scheduled Castes (SCs). They have been demanding ST status in Uttar Pradesh as well, but with little success. The ABSSS has played an important role in articulating this demand on their behalf.

During the last century, the Kols have been treated very harshly by the dominant sections of the region, especially in the southern districts of UP. They suffer high levels of exploitation, immiseration and marginalisation at the hands of feudal landlords, who combine economic exploitation with social discrimination. Needless to say, these feudal landlords belong to the upper Brahmin and Thakur castes; they find it easy to victimise and exploit the Kols by dispossessing the tribals of their lands. They do this mainly through subterfuge and in collusion with the local administration, whose members belong to the same social, economic and caste groups as themselves; and when this fails, they use brute force. Because the concept of private ownership and legal title is alien to tribal society, the Kols have been unable to establish legal ownership to the land that they have cultivated for generations. In the face of relentless exploitation by feudal interests, the Kols have had only two options or survival strategies available to them—retreating into the forest to eke out a living through their intimate knowledge of the forests and their wealth, or becoming bonded labourers in the service of the very same feudal landowners who exploit them.

The first of the two options is becoming increasingly unavailable to them due to the extension of state control over forests and the recent tendency to close forest areas to any kind of human activity in the name of environment protection—a process began in the middle of the nineteenth century, when the colonial government extended its control to cover forests as well. As the post-colonial government through its forest department expanded its control to cover more and more forest areas, it tended to look upon forest dwellers, in this case the Kols, with increasing suspicion and sought to evict them, declaring them to be encroachers or squatters. Today, forest officials consider the Kols to be the main destroyers of the forests as they are engaged in cutting fuel-wood and selling it in nearby urban centres. They forget that for generations these people have not only lived in harmony with the forests, but have also been responsible for their preservation. If today they are forced to carry headloads of fuel-wood for sale in urban areas, it is only because of the compulsions of survival.

In the post-independence era, the Kols have been displaced from the forests due to two main reasons: (*a*) the construction of major projects like dams and hydro-electric and large thermal power stations in areas inhabited by them, such as Sonebhadra district, and (*b*) the establishment of sanctuaries and wildlife parks in forest areas, such as the Ranipur Wildlife Sanctuary that was created in 1978 and extended over 23,000 hectares of forest land. They have thus become victims of the forces of modernisation, development and progress, and more recently, of programmes for environmental preservation and conservation that, ironically, seek to improve the lives of ordinary people like them.

The Kols of Chitrakoot district thus live a life of abject poverty, exploitation and almost complete subjugation by feudal landowners, locally known as *Dadus*. The *Dadus* not only exploit the Kols economically by keeping them in bondage, but also treat them in the most inhumane way imaginable. They see Kol women as objects of sexual gratification and subject them to all manner of humiliation, including rape. And as if this were not enough, they routinely use brute force, either directly or through hired gangs of musclemen, to ensure that the Kols remain in a state of abject servility.

Chitrakoot district falls in a region known as *Patha*, which is characterised by rocky terrain, poor, gravelly soil, semi-arid conditions and a chronic shortage of water for both irrigation and drinking. In addition to Chitrakoot, the region includes parts of Allahabad and Banda districts. The harsh *Patha* terrain only serves to exacerbate the chronic poverty of the Kols, because the highly unequal and exploitative feudal social structure ensures that they are relegated to land that is of the poorest quality and denied access to even safe sources of drinking water. Having to make do with whatever is available, they suffer from chronic malnutrition and are prone to all sorts of illnesses. With no medical care available, especially in remote rural areas, their condition can only be described as miserable. Adding to their misery is the absence of schools for their children: literacy levels among the Kols are extremely low. The Kols thus seem condemned to live a life of deprivation, with little expectation of upward mobility in the foreseeable future. In recent years, their only ray of hope has come from the ABSSS.

I

Akhil Bharatiya Samaj Sewa Sansthan

The Kols' abject poverty, structured and maintained by the prevailing feudal order in cahoots with the local political and administrative system (which flourishes due to the apathy and neglect, if not tacit approval, of the higher echelons of political power and administrative authority), deeply affected one Gaya Prasad 'Gopal', a young schoolteacher in Banda district, who had also worked as a journalist for a few years. He had travelled extensively in the *Patha* area of Banda (now Chitrakoot) district where the Kols lived, and was well aware of their situation, living conditions and problems. He was moved by a strong desire to do something concrete to improve their life, and it was out of this desire that the ABSSS was born on 23 March 1978. It may be recalled that the year 1978 fell in the immediate aftermath of the Emergency, when democracy had been re-established in the country and voluntary activity had found fertile soil. The Emergency, in spite of all its shortcomings, had at least helped in focusing attention on the plight of bonded labour in the country. It was only natural for ABSSS to take on the liberation of bonded labour, in this case the Kols of the *Patha* region, as one of its major programmes.

Before launching its programmes, ABSSS conducted a survey of 5,000 Kol households in five *nyaya* panchayats—Umari, Rampur-Kalyangarh, Unchadih, Kihuniya and Saraiya—of Manikpur block in Banda district. The aim was to gather accurate and reliable information and data on the living conditions and the problems faced by Kols in order to design programmes that would be of relevance to them. Since the information ABSSS had about the region was largely anecdotal and based on personal observation, there was clearly a need for collecting more authentic evidence. The ABSSS survey identified the following major problems as afflicting the area:

- Prevalence of bonded labour.
- Severe shortage of drinking water.
- Subjection of Kol women to sexual exploitation, including rape.
- Lack of education and general awareness.
- Indiscriminate felling of trees and the prevalence of a contractor system in forestry operations.
- Illegal occupation of land belonging to the Kols, reducing them to landlessness.
- Large number of Kols being falsely shown as having borrowed money.
- Ill health and malnutrition.
- Widespread misappropriation of funds during implementation of government programmes.

Based on these findings, ABSSS adopted a multipronged approach to simultaneously address three sets of issues that

it felt were crucial for improving the lot of Kols. These were:
(*a*) creating awareness among the Kols about their situation
and the need for organised effort to break the shackles of
feudal exploitation; (*b*) creating awareness in the wider society,
including the government machinery at the district and state
levels, about the grinding poverty, misery and exploitation
suffered by the Kols; and (*c*) taking up specific development
programmes and lobbying with the government to ensure that
the benefits of development and welfare programmes actually
reached the people for whom they were intended. The
methods it used to do this included

- Extensive travel in Kol-dominated areas.
- Personal contact with the people.
- Organising meetings, seminars and discussions with the
  people.
- Contacting government agencies like the Terai Anusuchit
  Jati Evam Janjati Vikas Nigam (Terai Scheduled Castes
  and Tribes Development Corporation), and individual
  officers both at the district and state headquarters.
- Establishing links with journalists at the state and na-
  tional levels and asking them to tour the Kol areas and
  report on the condition of the people living there.
- Setting up Kol organisations—Patha Kol Adhikar Manch
  (Patha Kol Rights Forum) and the Uttar Pradesh Adivasi
  Vikas Manch (Uttar Pradesh Tribal Development Forum)—to mobilise the Kols on the issue of their rights.

During the past two decades of its existence, the ABSSS has
notched important achievements to its credit in all three areas
of its chosen activity. Thanks to its success in inviting journalists from the national press to tour the area and write about
it, there is fairly comprehensive documentation available on
the conditions of the Kols and on the programmes undertaken
by ABSSS on their behalf. It would be no exaggeration to say
that if today, the Kols are able to see a glimmer of light at
the end of the proverbial dark tunnel, it is largely due to the
efforts of ABSSS.

In this case study we take a close look at one important and pioneering initiative of the ABSSS, i.e., assisting the Kols to gain possession of the land allotted to them by the state government of Uttar Pradesh under its programme of giving land *pattas* to landless persons belonging to Scheduled Castes and Scheduled Tribes.

II

Distribution of Land *Pattas*

The *Patha* region is characterised by severe inequality in the pattern of land ownership. The Kols own very little land while the *Dadus* control most of it. Much of the land that the *Dadus* control has been illegally acquired from the former. Again, while the better-quality, irrigated land is in the hands of the upper castes, the Kols are relegated to barren and rocky tracts. Over 50 per cent of Kol households were found to be without any land when the ABSSS began its work. In the 1960s and 1970s (especially after 1975, i.e., during the Emergency period), the government had undertaken a major programme of allotting Kols with rights to the *gaon sabha* (village community) land. Much of this was supposed to be ceiling-surplus land vested in the *gaon sabha*. The distribution of *pattas* was done according to Sections 195 and 198 of the Zamindari Abolition and Land Reforms Act, 1950. The impetus for this programme, as for the imposition of ceilings on landholdings during the 1960s and 1970s, came largely from political compulsions—to keep the landless rural poor satisfied in order to prevent them from succumbing to the radical ideas, including armed struggle, that were being espoused by the extreme left groups in many parts of the country. In the mid-1970s, the desire to impart a pro-poor ideological flavour to the Emergency gave the programme added urgency.

Whatever the political or ideological compulsions, like the law imposing ceilings on landholdings this programme, too, remained largely an exercise on paper. This was especially true of UP, and within it, of districts like Banda, where the feudal structure was still all-powerful. The implementation of the ceiling law and the land *patta* allotment programme were almost completely frustrated by the *Dadus* acting in league with the local administration. They were able to retain possession of land in excess of the specified ceiling by transferring it either in the names of their relatives (who included even their domestic animals!) or their Kol servants or bonded labourers without the latter even being aware of what was happening. The *Dadus* frequently appropriated loans that they persuaded the Kols to take from official agencies in their names (as ostensible owners of the land that had to pledged as surety for the loan) by falsely promising to repay the loans on their behalf. But since the land was recorded in the name of the Kols, it was they who were held responsible for repayment of both the principal and interest thereon. When they failed to do this, they lost their not only their meagre possessions but also their freedom, as they often ended up either in jail or as bonded labour of the very *Dadus* who had hoodwinked them into taking these loans.

Similarly, the *pattas* given to the Kols remained as entitlements on paper only. They were seldom given physical possession of the land. In many instances, they were not even aware that land had been allotted to them. In addition, much of the allotted land was of very poor quality. Located on hill slopes, it was rocky, difficult to irrigate and uncultivable. Further, large tracts of land allotted to them in the 1960s were under litigation, with the Forest Department claiming ownership rights. For instance, a major portion of the 23,000 hectares earmarked for the Ranipur Wildlife Sanctuary had belonged to the Kols for generations. But because they had no documentary proof of ownership, they not only lost possession of this land, they received no compensation for it either. Local revenue officials, too, used wily tactics to ensure that several of the *pattas* given to the Kols were open to question. In some cases more than one person was allotted the same piece of land, which inevitably led to dispute and even litigation.

The ABSSS decided to intervene on behalf of the Kols to ensure that they actually got physical possession of the land to which they were entitled. Based on the findings of the survey it conducted soon after its inception, this was one of the many programmes that it undertook to better the lot of the Kols. The ABSSS became active simultaneously on several fronts in order to tackle the Kols' land rights issue. Apart from carrying out an intensive awareness raising campaign among the people, its activists travelled extensively in the villages and organised meetings with panchayats and the villagers in general, providing them with detailed information about the land distribution programme, their rights and how they could organise themselves to fight for them. Periodically, development seminars were held, providing the Kols with a platform where they could come together and exchange ideas. Government officials, political leaders, academics, journalists and other opinion-makers were also invited to these seminars in the hope that they would disseminate information about the injustice being done to the Kols and thereby create a broad alliance for the protection of their rights. Among the more prominent people invited by the ABSSS to tour the Kol areas of Banda and attend these seminars were Rajmohan Gandhi, Swami Agnivesh, Pran Chopra, Prem Bhai, Mahendra Singh Tikait, Rajendra Kumari Bajpai (Union Minister) and a number of Members of Parliament (MPs) from different parts of the country.

A third form of activity that ABSSS undertook involved agitations, dharnas and mass mobilisation. These were organised with the help of the Patha Kol Adhikar Manch (Patha Kol Rights Forum) whenever the administration filed false or misleading reports about the distribution of land *pattas*. This also helped in focusing attention on the skewed pattern of land ownership in the region and the denial of justice to the Kols by the administration. A fourth activity involved organising legal aid camps to educate the Kols about their legal rights and provide them with assistance to contest the various cases filed against them by landowners in order to frustrate the land allotment programme.

The Patha Kol Adhikar Manch was formed in November 1987 at the initiative of Gaya Prasad Gopal. Some publications of the ABSSS describe it as a sister organisation, and it is true that several ABSSS workers played an active role in the formation of the Manch. Legally, however, the Manch is not a part of ABSSS and has a separate organisational identity with a distinct membership and its own office-bearers. In terms of activities and programmes, however, there is close interaction and cooperation between the two. The Manch has a membership in excess of 10,000 and, over the years, has emerged as a major force for awareness generation among the Kols as well as for organising and mobilising them around issues that have a bearing on their lives. It has also served as a nursery for leadership among the Kols and all its office-bearers and functionaries are from the Kol community. About 50 young men are intimately involved in its day-to-day activities. ABSSS provides it guidance and support, encouraging the Kols to be at the forefront of all struggles, agitations, dharnas, demonstrations, etc.

The battle that ABSSS was fighting was decidedly unequal as it had to take on the combined might of the entrenched feudal interests, who had for generations dominated and exploited the Kols, and the local-level administration that shared class and caste affinities with the former. Inevitably, therefore, the progress of its work was far from smooth. Positive results were achieved whenever there was a sympathetic and sensitive district administration. At other times, not only were there no results, the ABSSS workers and functionaries also had to face the wrath of the *Dadus* and the local administration. Intimidation tactics employed by the *Dadus* against the ABSSS workers and the Kols included threats, violence and implication in false criminal cases. In 1989, even Gopal Bhai, the Director of ABSSS, was falsely implicated in a case of dacoity.

He was finally acquitted after nine years in 1998 (see Box 10.1).

ABSSS' efforts to help Kols get possession of the land for which they had been issued *pattas* were quite successful. By the end of 1997, 2,500 poor Kol families of Mau and Manikpur had acquired possession of 10,000 acres of land valued at Rs 2 crore (20 million). For a short span of two decades, this was a truly remarkable achievement, particularly in view of the prevailing social environment—feudal oppression backed by a pliant and conniving local administration that had no hesitation in using brute force to retain dominance—in which it has been achieved without a drop of blood being shed.

Box 10.1
The Clout of the *Dadus*

Bhagirath Kol of Chureh Kesharuwa village, Karwi Tehsil, had 46 bighas of land in his name. In the year 1969 (Fasli) Gungai Seth alias Hiralal of Manikpur connived with the local *Lekhpal* and *Qanungo* and gained possession of the land. Bhagirath Kol filed a case to regain possession of this land, which went up to the Allahabad High Court. On 21 May 1970, the Court decided in favour of the widow of Bhagirath Kol (the latter having died in the meantime) and ordered that possession of the land be given to her. In total disrespect of the Court's order and with the support of the local administration, Seth Hiralal alias Gungai continued to hold possession of the land, while the widow of Bhagirath Kol and her relatives continued to be oppressed by him. When they tried to harvest the crop on their land, they were accused of dacoity, arrested and jailed. On 22 December 1989, Shri Gopal Bhat, the Director of ABSSS, was also accused of the same dacoity. He was charged under Section 395/09 of the Indian Penal Code with being armed and with abetting and instigating the forcible harvesting of the *jowar* crop. He was ultimately acquitted of the charge in February 1998.

Source: ABSSS (nd): 30–31.

III

The Case Study

The main objectives of this case study have been to

- Analyse the role played by a civil society organisation (CSO) in promoting good governance, especially in influencing the state and its agencies (in this case the district administration) to act in accordance with its explicitly stated policies and programmes.
- Understand the various ways in which the CSO attempted to influence state action to promote good governance and the methodology it followed to achieve this.
- Assess the results achieved by the CSO in its effort to promote good governance.

In the context of this study, good governance would mean the proper implementation of the state's programme for allotting land *pattas* to the Kols. This, in turn, would imply not merely the allotment of *pattas* and submission of a compliance report to the higher authorities (state headquarters), but actually handing over the title deed and physical possession of the land to the allottees. And this, in turn, would involve demarcation and measurement of the land allotted as well as the removal of encroachments on it. Clearly, then, fraudulent allotments, which have frequently occurred in the past, would not qualify as proper implementation.

Given this definition of 'proper implementation', what we mean by 'contribution of the CSO to good governance' also becomes clear. It would cover the steps taken by it to educate those affected about their rights vis-à-vis the land allotted to them, motivate them to organise and jointly pressure the state machinery to act according to its stated policies and programmes, and work with the state machinery, where necessary, to identify cases where either possession of land has been denied to the lawful allottees, or the land allotted to them has been forcibly occupied by others. Ensuring good governance in this instance would also undoubtedly include taking on the might of the vested interests and preventing them from frustrating the implementation of the land allotment programme.

The methodology adopted by this study involved the following steps:

1. In the first stage, secondary material pertaining to the ABSSS and its activities was scanned to obtain a general idea about the work in which it is involved. Special emphasis was given to its efforts to empower the Kols to get possession of the land allotted to them. A preliminary field trip to the area by the research team was made for this purpose.

2. Based on this initial survey, issues were identified for detailed investigation. According to our preliminary findings, ABSSS had been working with Kols in 233 villages, with 5,894 Kol families, covering two blocks, i.e., Mau and Manikpur. It was decided to collect information from 20 villages—12 from Manikpur and 8 from Mau. In each village, five households that had been allotted *pattas* would be contacted for collecting information. The investigation would not be restricted to the Kols but also include other SC *patta* holders. Thus a total of 100 *patta* holders from 20 villages in two blocks formed our information resource pool.

   Two instruments for data collection were devised in Hindi—one for village-level information pertaining largely to the general features, locale, availability of various facilities in the village, etc.; and the other for collecting information from the respondent households, who were the primary units for obtaining data collection through structured interviews based on a checklist of items on which information was required.

3. The actual collection of data was done in two phases between August and October, 1999 with a gap of about two weeks between the two phases, as the parliamentary elections intervened during this period. Incidentally, elections in this area are characterised by high levels of violence caused by incidents of booth capturing and the intimidation of poor voters by the *Dadus* and their musclemen.

4. The data were analysed partly on the basis of the quantified information that emerged from the study and partly on the basis of discussions and interviews conducted with the people.

Characteristics of the Study Area

Manikpur and Mau, the two development blocks chosen for the study, fall under the Karvi and Mau *tehsils* respectively. As mentioned earlier, the study was conducted in 12 villages of Manikpur block and eight of Mau block. The villages covered in Manikpur block were: Chheriha Khurd, Tikaria, Mangawan, Doda Mafi, Barah, Kihunia, Itwa, Kusumi, Markundi, Amchur Nerua, Chheriha Buzurg and Sarhat; the Mau block villages comprised Jamira Colony, Semra, Goiya Khurd, Lodhaura, Kotawa Mafi, Kataiya Dandi, Bargadh and Kalchiha.

All these villages are quite remote from the district, *tehsil* and block headquarters, with their average distance from Chitrakoot, the district headquarters, being 59 km. The villages in Manikpur are at an average distance of 25 km from the block headquarters, while those in Mau are about 22 km away from the block headquarters. Manikpur, Bargadh and Majhgawan are the nearest towns/markets that cater to the needs of these villages. Seven villages are close to Manikpur, eight to Bargadh and five to Majhgawan. The average distances of the villages from Manikpur, Bargadh and Mahgawan are 21, 6 and 14 km respectively.

The remoteness of these villages can be gauged by the fact that only nine of them are situated near a road; the remaining are at a distance of between 2 and 15 km from the nearest road. Table 10.1 shows the situation regarding the availability of other facilities such as transport, communications, health and education by charting the distribution of villages in terms of average distance from the various facilities.

As can be seen, the primary school is the only facility available in all the villages. Other facilities available in some villages are a bus station (four villages), a junior high school (two villages) and a high school (one village). Among these, the only ones available within 3 km of the villages are the bus station, primary school and junior high school. Others, like the post office, the PHC, CHC and AHC, are located at distances exceeding 3 km. Certain facilities like the telegraph office, public telephone, high school (except in one village) and intermediate college are only available at a distance of 5 or more km. The last column of the table, which shows the maximum

Table 10.1   Distribution of Sample Village According to Average Distance from Various Facilities

(Distance in km)

Facility	0.0	0.1–2.0	2.1–3.0	3.1–5.0	>5	Total	Highest Value
Bus Station	4	2	4	–	10	20	7
Post Office	2	–	–	14	4	20	15
Telegraph Office	–	–	–	–	20	20	54
Public Telephone	–	–	–	–	20	20	39
PHC	–	–	–	7	11	18*	21
CHC	–	–	–	4	16	20	25
AHC	–	–	1	5	14	20	7
Primary School	20	–	–	–	–	20	–
Junior High School	2	3	5	2	8	20	9
High School	1	–	–	–	19	20	8
Inter College	–	–	–	–	20	20	25

Notes: PHC–Primary Health Centre; CHC–Community Health Centre; AHC–Animal Husbandry Centre.
*Information not available for two villages.

distance at which facilities are available, is particularly revealing. In specific cases, this distance can range from 7 km (bus station and AHC) to 54 km (telegraph office).

A survey of the land-use pattern in the villages (Table 10.2) shows certain marked similarities and some equally major differences between the two blocks. The similarities are in terms of the extent of the forest area and barren land. Forests constitute just over 26 per cent of the area occupied by the villages in Manikpur block and about 21 per cent in Mau block; barren land comprises about 31 per cent and 28 per cent respectively of the areas that the sample villages cover in the two blocks. The extent of irrigated land is also roughly the same—about 40 per cent in each of the two groups of villages. The differences between the two blocks are apparent mainly in two land-use categories: areas not available for cultivation and areas that are being cultivated. The first category constitutes almost 19 per cent of the total area in Manikpur and only 6 per cent in Mau, while the second category has a share of only 23 per cent of total land in Manikpur and 42 per cent in Mau. In addition, there is the obvious difference between the total areas occupied by the villages in the two blocks, with that in Manikpur being more than four times that of Mau. It is obvious, then, that a large chunk of land, especially in

Table 10.2   Land-use Pattern in Sample Villages

Land-use Category	Manikpur Block (12 Villages)		Mau Block (8 Villages)	
	Hectares	Per cent Share	Hectares	Per cent Share
Total Area	21,536	100.0	5,236	100.0
Forest Area	5,729	26.6	1,084	20.7
Barren Land	6,773	31.4	1,480	28.3
Area Not Available for Cultivation	4,010	18.6	436	8.3
Cultivated Area	5,022	23.3	2,236	42.7
Irrigated Area as Per cent of Cultivated Area	39.9		40.3	

Manikpur, is either barren/uncultivable or under the control of the Forest Department. Moreover, irrigation is available in only a small part of the cultivated area. Given the nature of the terrain and the generally poor quality of the soil, the non-irrigated land is bound to be infertile. These conditions explain the *Dadus'* intense desire to control as much of the land, especially good quality land, as possible and use whatever means available to retain this control, including patently illegal methods to prevent the Kols from taking possession of the land allotted to them by the state. Further, ownership of land gives rise to the need for labour to cultivate it. Unwilling to employ wage labour at market-determined rates (given the uncertain returns from agriculture), the *Dadus* resort to bonded and other kinds of cheap labour.

Characteristics of Sample Population

Although we had planned to select five *patta* holders from each of the 20 villages to give us a total sample of 100 households, we were able to access only 91 households. Of these, 60 were from the 12 Manikpur block villages and 31 (as against the 40 planned) from the 8 Mau villages. The shortfall occurred because the requisite number of *patta* holders was not available in the Mau villages selected for study. However, no great significance need be attached to this shortfall since the sample size and study design was not intended to draw any inferences (statistical or otherwise) about a larger population. The aim was to obtain a wide cross-section of opinion among the *patta* holders regarding the implementation of the land distribution programme and the role of ABSSS in it.

Ninety per cent of the households (82 out of 91) were Kol households, while the remaining 10 per cent (9) belonged to other Scheduled Castes. The total population of these households was 716, comprising 379 males and 337 female members. The sex ratio of the sample population worked out to 889 females per 1,000 males, which is slightly higher than the 1991 figure for Uttar Pradesh (879) and significantly higher than that for Banda district in the same year (841). Where literacy is concerned, we found that 59 per cent of the population was illiterate and 18 per cent barely literate, i.e., they could just about sign their names. Thus, for all practical purposes, over three-fourths of the population was non-literate. The remaining (23 per cent) can be classified as literate with some education. Of them, 73 per cent had studied up to the primary level (Class V), 12 per cent up to the upper primary level (Class VIII) and 15 per cent up to high school or further. It is noteworthy that the proportion of people with a high school or further education was significantly higher in the Mau block villages (26 per cent) than that in Manikpur block (3 per cent). Both literacy and levels of education, especially among adults, seemed to be related to the poverty syndrome—a combination of economic hardship, exploitation, social deprivation, inequality and lack opportunities together with the remote nature of the villages and their lack of access to facilities and infrastructure. As seen in Table 10.1, the villages of Mau block are relatively less remote and better served by social and economic infrastructure. This fact is reflected in better access by villagers to educational facilities, especially high school, as compared to those in Manikpur block, where the villages are more isolated.

The situation is much brighter where the education of children is concerned. In our sample, 62 households reported that their children were in school as against only 17 per cent who said that they were not; the remaining 12 per cent either did not have children or any children of schoolgoing age. The credit for this must largely go to ABSSS, which has a major programme of establishing primary schools in the backward, Kol-inhabited villages of Manikpur block, and to the large number of private schools in Mau block. The government's efforts in this crucial area of human development have been minimal.

As noted earlier, all 20 villages in our sample have a primary school located within the village. In fact, many have more than one school. Thus the villages in Manikpur have 32 primary schools while those in Mau have 24. It is interesting to note that in Manikpur block, 24 of these 32 schools are run by ABSSS, three are private and only five are government schools. In Mau, on the other hand, there is only one government primary school, with the rest being privately owned. The primary education system in the area is therefore predominantly non-governmental—dependent on a non-governmental organisation in one block and on private initiative in the other.

Information on the economic status of the households revealed widespread prevalence of poverty among the people. Household incomes are slightly higher in Mau villages as compared to those in Manikpur, but on average, the majority of households fall below the officially defined poverty line.

The main occupations of the people in the sample villages are collection of forest produce, agricultural labour, agriculture and non-agricultural labour. Since none of these activities can by itself provide enough to sustain the family, most people engage in more than one activity. Table 10.3 shows the distribution of households and individuals engaged in various occupations. As can be seen, most of them are in the four

Table 10.3 Main Occupations of Sample Households and Individuals

Occupation	Households		Individuals	
	No	%[a]	No	%[b]
Agricultural Labour	73	80.2	174	24.3
Non-Agricultural Labour	72	79.1	162	22.6
Collection of Forest Produce	71	78.0	175	24.4
Agriculture	66	72.5	163	22.8
Non-Agricultural Work	21	23.1	29	4.1
Other Work	7	7.7	9	1.3

Notes: [a] Per cent of all households.
[b] Per cent of all individuals.

occupations just listed. This fact only confirms the picture of the region as an underdeveloped one, dependent on primary activities, especially forestry and agriculture.

A final characteristic of the sample households relates to the high incidence of bonded labour among. During our inquiries, 47 households—more than half the total—admitted to one or the other member as having been in bonded labour at some point during the past, with the duration of bondage varying from 2 to 60 years! Most, however, had been in bondage for a period ranging from 10 to 20 years. In almost all cases, the reason for being in bondage was indebtedness, even though the loans taken were often very small—a few hundred rupees or a few kilos of grain. The masters were invariably the dominant landowners, several of whom were also the local (political) leaders.

Box 10.2
All for a Few Rupees

Lakshmi's bondage to Prem Narain Tripathi, a local leader of the Bharatiya Janata Party, was inherited. His father, Kuber, had taken a loan, both in cash and grain, from Tripathi, and for this he ended up in bonded labour. When he died, his son had to continue to discharge his father's obligation till he won his freedom in 1994 after he had paid off the debt.

Ram Bhawan spent three years as a bonded labourer in the service of Keshni Pandit for failure to repay a cash and food grain loan valued at Rs 500.

Bachha remained in bondage for 20 years after taking a loan of Rs 6,000 for a wedding in the family. He got his freedom in 1992 after he repaid the loan with help from ABSSS.

Buddha of Doda Mafi ended up in bondage for a paltry Rs 100 that he had borrowed from a local leader.

Maia Deen remained in bondage for 20 years in lieu of a loan taken by his father.

Allottment of Land Pattas

The legal basis for allotting land to specific categories of people was provided by the Uttar Pradesh Zamindari Abolition and Land Reforms Act, 1950. As is well known, the Act vested all estates in the state and to redeem the promise of land to the tillers made by the Congress Party during the freedom struggle, abolished all intermediaries (variously known as *zamindars*, *taluqdars*, etc., in different parts of the state) between the actual cultivators and the state. The cultivators were thus brought into direct relation with the state and the land tenures, which had become highly complicated under the *zamindari* system as a result of constant sub-infeudation, were considerably simplified. Section 117 of the Act provided that the state vest certain lands in the *gaon sabhas* (village communities consisting of all adults in a village), to be managed by the *sabha*'s Land Management Committee (LMC), a statutory body constituted under the UP Panchayat Raj Act, 1947. Further, under the UP Imposition of Ceiling on Land Holdings Act, 1960, the *gaon sabhas* and their LMCs also came into possession of some ceiling-surplus lands. Section 195 of the UP Zamindari Abolition and Land Reforms Act authorised the LMCs to admit any person as a title holder with non-transferable rights to any land vested in them. Section 198 of this Act gives the following order of preference in admitting persons to such land:

(*a*) Landless widow, sons, unmarried daughters or parents residing in the circle of a person who has lost his life by enemy action while in active service in the Armed Forces of the Union;

(*b*) a person residing in the circle, who has become wholly disabled while in active service in the Armed Forces of the Union;

(*c*) a landless agricultural labourer residing in the circle and belonging to a Scheduled Caste or Scheduled Tribe;

(*d*) any other landless agricultural labourer residing in the circle;

(*e*) any other landless agricultural labourer belonging to a Scheduled Caste or Scheduled Tribe not residing in the circle but residing in the *nyaya* Panchayat Circle referred to in Section 42 of the UP Panchayat Raj Act, 1947.

While the legal basis for the grant of land *pattas* was quite clear, the process for doing this turned out to be far from simple. Since ownership and control of land is still the main instrument of domination in rural society, the landed interests are willing to go to any lengths to prevent alienation of the land held by them. They also do not favour the idea of a more egalitarian distribution of land. Implementation of measures like imposition of ceilings on land holdings and distribution of land to the landless poor has therefore been largely frustrated. The situation is particularly serious in areas—such as Bihar and UP—where the pressure on land is high and feudal values and attitudes, along with caste-based oppression, reign supreme. However, land distribution programmes can only be subverted through collusion with the administrative machinery, especially at the local level. The role of the political system and higher administration has also been rather dubious, as they have seldom put their full weight behind the implementation of these programmes, which they themselves have formulated and drafted and which they unceasingly and vociferously support at the level of rhetoric.

Distribution of land involves three important steps: distribution of land *pattas*; entry of the *patta* holders' names in the village land records; and actual possession of the land by the *patta* holders. Our investigations show that land *pattas* have been distributed fairly regularly to the landless poor since the 1950s. Among the households we contacted, six had received *pattas* between 1954 and 1959, 14 during the 1960s, 26 each during the 1970s and 1980s, and 14 during the 1990s (Table 10.4). The names of the *patta* holders had also been entered in the *patwari*'s land records with almost the same regularity.

Table 10.4   Progress of Land Distribution Cases in Chitrakoot
District: 1954–1999

Period (Year)	No. of Pattas Given	No. of Pattas Recorded	No. of Patta Holders Given Possession of Land
1954–59	6	4	3
1960–69	14	16	3
1970–79	26	23	6
1980–89	26	28	20
1990–99	14	15	53
Total	86	86	85
Backlog	—	—	1

There is little evidence of undue delay at this stage, except in isolated instances. Even in these instances, the delay that occurred was at the most of one year. But where getting possession of the land is concerned, the story has been entirely different. In this area, progress has been very tardy, especially during the 1950s, 1960s and 1970s. It is only during the 1980s and 1990s that the majority of land allottees (73 out of 86, or 85 per cent of all allottees) managed to get possession of their land—20 during the 1980s and 53, representing 62 per cent of all *patta* holders, during the 1990s. This period, it needs to be remembered, coincides with the formation of the ABSSS and its decision to take up the cause of *patta* holders who had been unable to get possession of the land allotted to them.

However, ensuring this has not been an easy task for the ABSSS. It has had to struggle hard and it is only during the last five years that it has achieved a notable degree of success. This is borne out by the fact that in more than half the cases (47 out of 85, or 55 per cent), possession of the allotted land has been possible only after 1995. On the whole, however, there is little doubt that the ABSSS has achieved remarkable success in its efforts in this direction. This can be judged from the fact that at the time of our field study, possession of land had been given to all but one of the *patta* holders.

From the point of view of the *patta* holders, the assistance provided by ABSSS has been absolutely crucial in acquiring possession of the land. It is hardly surprising, then, that most of the people we talked to (70 of the 85 who had got possession of their land) acknowledged the help they received from ABSSS, which included petitioning the concerned authorities, providing legal aid when necessary, keeping track of the cases in the courts and providing moral and material support to people in distress (Box 10.3).

The ABSSS has also helped in indirect, less visible ways by building an environment favourable to the protection of the

---

Box 10.3
Lending a Helping Hand

Sattilal was given a *patta* for a piece of land in 1969, though he remained unaware of this fact for many years. The land allotted to him was being cultivated by one Khelwan Yadav. When he learned of this, he approached ABSSS and with its help, petitioned the District Magistrate to get possession of his land. With continued support from ABSSS, he was finally successful in 1998—a full 29 years after he received the *patta*.

Ram Biswas got possession of the land allotted to him after 17 years, again through the intervention of ABSSS. One Jola Yadav was forcibly cultivating his land. However, he still has to get possession of a half-hectare of the land he was allotted, as the *patwari* has been demanding a bribe of Rs 1,000 for measuring the land.

Bhola's land, on the other hand, was not occupied by any other person as it is rocky and of poor quality. Yet, for 30 years he did not get possession of it, as the *patwari* would not demarcate the land. It was only when ABSSS intervened that he was finally able to get his land measured and demarcated, and take possession of it.

In the case of Badlu, the delay occurred because instead of his land, the *patwari* measured and demarcated land belonging to someone else. The mistake was corrected only after ABSSS took up Badlu's case and the other person whose land was affected also raised a hue and cry.

Kols' rights and against the injustices perpetrated on them. It has done this by periodically holding seminars and discussions, by building alliances with other CSOs and by inviting influential persons, journalists and opinion- and policy-makers to tour the area and check the condition of the Kols for themselves. It has also used forums like the Patha Kol Adhikar Manch to organise and mobilise Kols to fight for their rights.

A unique feature of the approach adopted by the ABSSS has been the extensive use of the media to spread information about the widespread poverty, exploitation and miserable living conditions of the Kols in the *Patha* region. It has been successful in persuading correspondents and reporters of various newspapers, magazines and news agencies to visit the *Patha* region and report on the conditions prevailing there. The ABSSS also publishes a newsletter in Hindi called *Gaon ki Ore* (Towards the Village), whose circulation includes the villagers, the panchayats, district-level government offices, other NGOs, etc. It provides information on the activities of the ABSSS, reports on government programmes, publishes news about the region and provides general awareness about issues that are of importance to the locals. It is worth noting that in its use of the media, ABSSS has focused not only on the negative aspects of the feudal social structure and the malfunctioning of the government at the grassroots level—of which, unhappily, there are countless examples—but has also not hesitated in bringing to light instances of positive responses from the government and individual officials to the problems of the region and its people.

In spite of the support and assistance from the ABSSS, a large number of *patta* holders have had to face intimidation from dominant landlords, who illegally occupied and cultivated the land allotted to the Kols and refused to vacate it. In some cases they forcibly harvested the crops grown by the Kols on their own land. The arrogance and high-handedness of the *Dadus* has been such that even the presence of the ABSSS and its public espousal of the Kol cause has not deterred them from using intimidating tactics (Box 10.4).

Box 10.4
High-handedness of the *Dadus*

Tunaia of Mangawan village has not been able to get possession of half an acre of land that belongs to him. It is under forcible occupation by Bachaua Pandit of Bambiha village. All efforts to regain possession have been futile.

Hirmaniyan of Doda Mafi village had been given a *patta* for over 1.2 hectares of land. He has been able to acquire possession of only a third of it. The rest is occupied and is being cultivated by one of the most powerful persons in the village.

Brijpal Pandit of Bambiha village forcibly harvested the crop raised by Shiv Pal of the same village on his own land.

Saman is not able to till his land, which is illegally occupied by Ashok Pandit. Some years ago, Saman had taken a loan Rs 75 from Pandit, who now wants 75 tolas (800 gm) of gold valued at over Rs 3,30,000 to vacate the land!

Unfortunately, gaining possession of their land does not mean that their woes are at an end. The Kols have to deal with two further problems. If the land is at all cultivable, there is a strong likelihood that the *Dadus* will try to dispossess them of it. The Kols are then faced with the prospect of becoming labourers on their own land or even reverting to bondage under the *Dadus*. An overwhelming majority (four-fifths) of the *patta* holders we spoke to reported that attempts had been made by the dominant groups to dislodge them from the land allotted to them. And they had invariably turned to ABSSS for help in resisting these attempts. It was quite clear from our discussions with them that ABSSS is the only agency to which they turn for support when threatened and intimidated by the *Dadus*. The ABSSS has always stood by them, even though is has not always been successful. Interestingly, attempts to dislodge the Kols from their land were made both by the dominant sections of the rural society as well as by local political leaders. This is hardly surprising because the local power structure is almost completely under the control of large landowners who belong to the upper castes. The *Dadus* are also the local leaders and active in all political parties. In such a situation, the attitude of the local administration can at best be indifferent, if not downright hostile, to the plight of the Kols.

The second problem that confronts *patta* holders relates to the quality of land. Almost 50 per cent of them complained that soil was gravelly and lacked irrigation facilities. Agriculture is thus mainly rain-fed. The main crops grown are paddy and *kodon* (a millet) during the *kharif* season (monsoon) and wheat, barley, gram and mustard during the *rabi* season (winter). A majority of people said that they cultivated their land only during *kharif.* The poor quality of land is reflected in its low productivity. Rough estimates show that the yield obtained by the people we spoke to was only about 4.5 quintals per hectare during both *kharif* and *rabi*, as compared to the 1997 yield of these crops in Banda district: 7.4 quintals per hectare during *kharif* and 10.9 during *rabi*!

The poor quality of the land and the virtual absence of irrigation and other infrastructure mean that agriculture alone cannot provide the people with a secure livelihood. In the case of *patta* holders, the problem is compounded by the fact that area allotted to them is very small. The average area of a *patta* is 1.25 hectares and seldom exceeds 1.5 hectares. An overwhelming majority of land allottees informed us that their land could not meet even their basic food requirements. In fact, more than 80 per cent of those who cultivated their land said that it barely yielded them six months' requirement of food and they had to depend on the market for the rest. Sadly, the Public Distribution System (PDS) does not reach the really poor and needy despite all the official rhetoric about targeting tribal areas. Less than 10 per cent of our sample made use of fair price shops for their food grain requirement. This means that the poor need a second source of income that would enable to buy food for the rest of the year. The only secondary occupations available to them in this remote and backward region are wage labour—both agricultural and non-agricultural—and the collection and sale of forest produce.

Since for generations the Kols have been living in close harmony with the forests and have a good knowledge and understanding of its various products, they have been using this knowledge to supplement their income. The main items of forest produce collected and sold by them include *tendu* leaves (used to make *bidis*), firewood, *amla* (a small fruit used for medicinal purposes and for making pickles and preserves), honey, *mahua* (a flower used for distilling liquor) and *chiraunji* (a small seed used for flavouring sweets and confections).

Other Activities of the ABSSS

Although best known for helping Kol *patta* holders to get possession of their land and for liberating bonded labourers, ABSSS' other work in the *Patha* region is no less important, even if not as well known outside the region. It is true that possessing even a small plot of land that they can call their own is very important for restoring the dignity and self-respect of the Kol community. At the same time, merely providing land and ensuring that the Kols get possession of it are not enough to lift them out of poverty and put an end to the conditions that in the past have been responsible for their becoming bonded labourers. The ABSSS has therefore launched several programmes designed to improve the economic conditions of the Kols. These include:

- Land improvement through soil conservation, contour bunding, construction of check dams and gully plugging.
- Natural resource management, especially conservation and management of water resources.
- Social forestry.
- Women's self-help groups.
- Education and literacy.

Of these, two deserve special mention: water conservation and management, and education.

The *Patha* is a drought-prone area and suffers from severe shortage of water, both for drinking and irrigation. The worst sufferers are the poor Kols as the few sources of water available in the area have been cornered by the *Dadus*. In order to overcome this problem and provide water to the Kols, ABSSS launched a programme for water conservation and harvesting using traditional knowledge and practices. Under this programme, the ABSSS took up the task of constructing dug wells, reservoirs, shallow ponds, locally known as *chohras*, for collecting water in low-lying areas, check dams and small earthen dams. All these were designed to store and retain rainwater *in situ* and to improve the ground water recharge.

The first three reservoirs were constructed by ABSSS between 1982–83 and 1983–84 at Harijanpur, Sukhrampur and Parmhans. The impact of these reservoirs on water availability was so great that it generated tremendous enthusiasm among the people, especially when they reaped a bumper harvest for the first time in their life. People from other areas were also enthused and wanted similar programmes in their villages. In 1987–88, ABSSS took up the construction of five wells, 13 *chohras* and four reservoirs with assistance from Council for Advancement of People's Action and Rural Technology (CAPART) and Oxford Committee for Famine Relief (OXFAM). Thereafter, the programme really took off and by 1997 ABSSS had completed the construction of 22 wells, 26 *chohras* and 18 reservoirs in 66 villages.

Allied to water harvesting was a programme for soil conservation, with particular focus on building contour bunds on the lands of the poor Kols. The programme was first taken up in 1988–89 and by 1997 had covered 1,488 acres of land belonging to 554 families. It, too, has resulted in considerable gains in agricultural productivity and improvement in the living conditions of the affected families.

Apart from improving land productivity, ABSSS also took up other programmes for improving the economic condition of the Kols. For instance, it has been helping people to organise and demand higher wages from the landlords on whose fields they work as agricultural labourers. The traditional wage in the region has been a meagre 1.25 kg (*paanch pav*) of grain for a day's work. ABSSS has also been successful in negotiating higher prices for the collection of *tendu* leaves. The replacement of contractors by the UP Forest Corporation as the collection agency in 1982 clearly helped the Kols to get better rates for *tendu* leaves and checked many of the earlier malpractices indulged in by contractors, and more recently, the forest corporation workers. In addition, ABSSS has been running various income-generation and micro-credit programmes for the Kols.

The importance of education for Kol children was recognised by ABSSS from the very beginning. Education is not just an important means for awareness raising and upward mobility; it also lays the foundation of leadership among the people. The lack of education among Kols is probably responsible for many of their problems. Absence of any leadership among them has meant that there has been no one to intercede on their behalf or articulate their problems to the political administrative system at either the district or state level. The government system of primary education is largely non-functional; and where it does function, tends to discriminate against the Kols as the teachers are drawn from the same section of society as the feudal interests that control the economic life of the region. Instead of teaching the few Kol children who attend such schools, the teachers make them work in their homes.

Confronted with this grim picture of education in the *Patha* region, ABSSS decided to do something about it in 1988–89. It was well aware of the shortcomings of the existing education system, especially its alienation from the life of people in rural areas, particularly the rural poor. It wanted to make education relevant to and intimately linked with their lives. At the same time, it believed that education should have a strong ethical foundation. According to ABSSS, the aim of education was to instil the individual with proper values—of creativity, or respect for other individuals, curiosity, self-reliance and discrimination. Needless to say, it found all these values absent in the dominant, state-supported school system.

Inspired by these ideals, ABSSS began its educational activities in 1989 by setting up 15 primary schools under the umbrella of Bharat Mala Shiksha Sanskar Kendra in various *Patha* villages. The teachers in these schools are known as *gram pals* (keepers of the village), implying that they are responsible for the well-being of the entire village and not just the education of children under their charge. The success of the primary school education programme can be judged by the huge demand it generated for opening such schools in other villages of the region. By 1997–98, ABSSS was running 40 primary schools where 2,169 children—1,279 boys and 890 girls—were enrolled.

In addition to running primary schools, ABSSS is also involved in providing adult literacy and has been running a number of centres for this purpose. It also operates 100 non-formal education centres under the Mahila Samakhya project, a programme for the education and empowerment of women.

State and National Linkages

The work of ABSSS on the land issue, however, has remained restricted to Manikpur and Mau blocks of Chitrakoot district. Failure to give possession of the land allotted on pattas is not specific to Chitrakoot. From all available evidence, it is a feature that is common to the whole of UP, indeed, the entire country. But the ABSSS has not linked up with any other organisation, either within the state or in other parts of the country, which is working for the same cause. Neither has it attempted to undertake a state- or national-level campaign on the issue of land rights for the poor and landless tribals. By linking up with similar struggles elsewhere, it might have made greater headway in forcing the administration to take note of the issues involved. For in the absence of a larger—state- or national-level—campaign, it has been easy for the administration and political leadership to dismiss the issue as a local one. It has therefore not been given the importance it deserves in the policy framework for poverty alleviation at the state and national levels. Instead of providing access to the one basic, productive asset, i.e., land, which is what really matters in an agrarian economy, state action has remained predicated on either transfer of limited resources like money (through employment schemes), or subsidised food grain (through the PDS) or some income-generation schemes (like the Integrated Rural Development type programmes).

But where the ABSSS *has* extended the scope of its intervention and advocacy to the state and national levels, it has achieved remarkable success. Take, for example, the issue of oppression and exploitation of Kol women by the *Dadus* with the active support of the local administration. In May 1997, ABSSS organised a seminar on the status and condition of women in the *Patha* region, inviting the Chairperson of the National Commission on Women (NCW) to be the chief guest. In this seminar, about 300 women, mainly from Shankergarh, Majhgawan and Manikpur blocks, narrated harrowing tales of the exploitation they had suffered. Moved by their stories, the Chairperson of NCW wrote to Ms Mayawati, the Chief Minister of Uttar Pradesh, asking that steps be taken to protect the rights of women in the region. At about the same time, the press, too, reported on the piteous condition of *Patha* women. The result was that the state government ordered an inquiry, setting up a committee that toured the region extensively and found that most incidents of exploitation, harassment and abuse—which included instances of women being pawned, made bonded labourers, raped and attributed with fraudulent loans—that had been narrated by the Kol women during the seminar were true.

As a follow-up to the seminar and government inquiry, ABSSS, in association with NCW, organised a public hearing on the problems of *Patha* women in Delhi on 4 November 1997. The objective was to ensure justice for them. The jury for this public hearing comprised Justice (retd.) V. Krishan Iyer, Capatin Lakshmi Sehgal, Swami Agnivesh, Ms Asma Jehangir (Chairperson, Human Rights Commission, Pakistan),

Ms Mohini Giri (Chairperson, NCW) and Ms Padma Seth (Member, NCW). Representatives of both the national and international press and television were also present, as were the Superintendent of Police, Chitrakoot district (then known as Shahuji Maharaj district), Superintendent of Police (City) of Banda, and the Secretaries of the Social Welfare and Basic Education Departments of the UP government. Thirty-two Kol women deposed before the jury, as a result of which concerned officials were ordered to provide an immediate explanation of their behaviour.

The upshot of this hearing was that the administration came under considerable pressure and was forced to take action and arrest the persons who were known to be exploiting women but had thought themselves immune from any kind of punitive action. The public hearing and the subsequent arrest of the guilty parties provided a tremendous boost to the self-confidence of Kol women, who for the first time in their lives felt that they could come forward, confront their oppressors and demand justice for themselves.

IV

Conclusion

This case study on the role played by the Akhil Bharatiya Samaj Sewa Sansthan in helping the Kol tribals of Chitrakoot to acquire possession of the land for which they had been allotted *pattas*, brings into sharp focus some very important issues. First, it points to the tremendous odds with which any programme of economic uplift and empowerment of the poor and the oppressed, especially in a tradition-bound, feudal social and economic order, has to contend. The study clearly brings to the fore the clash between the philosophy of social justice and commitment to the uplift of the poor and the oppressed that is enshrined in the Constitution, and the actual implementation of legislations and programmes formulated to translate these constitutional directives into reality. That vested landed interests would oppose a programme for distributing land to the rural power is understandable, especially in remote, tradition-bound and backward regions like southern UP, even when, as in the present case, the land distribution programme does not challenge their economic power. It is pertinent to mention here that the distribution of land *pattas* does not involve the confiscation of land from the large landowners, except that which they have illegally or fraudulently occupied. What is distributed comes from the lands vested in the *gaon sabhas*. At the same time, the average area of the distributed land is so small that it has little impact on the overall pattern of land distribution in a village. Moreover, the land given to the poor through *pattas* is generally of such poor quality that it cannot bring about any significant improvement in the living conditions of the *patta* holders. As we have seen, at the most they can get only six months' requirement of food grain from the land; for the rest, they have to rely on some secondary occupation like wage labour and the collection and sale of forest produce.

The real significance of the land distribution programme is symbolic and lies in the challenge it poses to the feudal power structure in rural areas. Once the Kols acquire land, they are likely to reclaim their self-respect and dignity that for generations has been crushed through bondage and other forms oppression, including sexual exploitation and the rape of women. With the return of self-respect and dignity, it is likely that the Kols would stand up for their rights and challenge their exploitation at the hands of the *Dadus*. When this happens, the *Dadus* would be unlikely to get labour at exploitative wages, which in turn would affect their economic status. Ultimately, their social domination, which is partly caste-based and partly relies on their economic status, would also be threatened. In this threat, perhaps, lies the explanation for the concerted attempts made by dominant groups to frustrate the programme of land distribution to the Kols.

What is not so easy to understand is the failure of the state-level political leadership and higher-level administration to provide the requisite support for the implementation of a programme that they themselves have initiated and about which they never tire of waxing eloquent. The wide gulf between rhetoric and action points to the lack of commitment and sincerity on the part of all major political parties and of the state-level administration towards poverty alleviation and the social uplift of the poor, particularly when it means challenging the dominant power structures at the local level.

With little or no support from the macro level, working for the rights of the downtrodden and exploited in a socio-economic environment characterised by brutal domination and suppression at the micro level is surely a daunting task. But as our analysis shows, by adopting a multipronged approach, ABSSS has accomplished it with remarkable success. At one level, it has sought to make the Kols aware of their legal rights, especially to the land for which they have received *pattas*, and their exploitation at the hands of the dominant feudal interests. It has helped in uniting and organising them under the banner of the Patha Kol Adhikar Manch, which is the main instrument of organised action and struggle by the Kols. It has also pursued cases filed in court against or by the Kols vis-à-vis *patta* land and provided them with legal assistance through legal aid camps. At another level, it has pressured the administration at the subdivision, district and state levels to implement the land distribution programme in both its letter and spirit. Whenever it found sympathetic officials at the local level, it has sought their support and assistance to get justice for the Kols. At a third level, it has helped to spread information about the condition of the Kols in the *Patha* region and built alliances not only with CSOs in other parts of the country, but also with influential leaders, and opinion- and policy-makers. The ABSSS has organised seminars and discussions on the problems of the Kols, which has helped in spreading awareness about them. It has invited journalists to tour the area and report on the conditions prevailing there. This has helped to disseminate information about the plight of the Kols to the world at large.

These efforts have served three purposes. First, by making public the inhuman oppression of the Kols, it has helped to create some degree of fear among the *Dadus*. Second, by persuading influential persons from the larger society to express solidarity with their cause has helped to build self-confidence among the Kols, which will stand them in good stead in their struggle for land and other rights. Third, the Kols have slowly but surely started to assert themselves, questioning the existing order and organising for the protection of their rights.

The road ahead is far from easy, but the first few steps have been taken. One strategy that ABSSS has not used, and which perhaps might have brought it greater success, is conducting state- and national-level campaigns on the land question and linking up with other organisations and movements working on the same or related issues. After all, the land issue is not unique to southern UP; similar programmes have been taken up in many other parts of the state and country. Were the ABSSS to link up with these other organisations and orchestrate a wider and larger campaign on the issue of land distribution to the rural landless and the government's inefficacy in implementing the programme, its efforts might achieve better results. As the example of the public hearing shows, state-level political and administrative systems may react quite differently to such a campaign. It might jolt them out of their apathy and force them to respond in more positive ways.

The activities of ABSSS among the Kols of Chitrakoot have not been restricted to helping them get possession of the land for which they have been issued *pattas*. As we have seen, this only one of the many issues it has taken up. Its other activities include action for the identification and abolition of bonded labour, abolition of the contractor system for the collection of *tendu* leaves, mobilising people for the protection of their rights and ending exploitation, especially sexual exploitation, of women, running primary schools in remote, Kol-inhabited villages, watershed management and setting up water harvesting systems to meeting drinking and irrigation needs, setting up income-generation and self-help groups to improve the economic condition of the Kols, providing them with health education, basic health care and immunisation services and working towards raising women's awareness and their empowerment.

The multipronged approach adopted by ABSSS to help *patta* holders get possession of their land has meant that it has used a variety of strategies for achieving its objectives: mobilisation and organisation of the affected people, lobbying with the administration and government, using the print media to spread awareness and information about the condition of the Kols and building alliances with other organisations and influential persons. The confluence of these strategies probably has a lot to do with ABSSS' success.

References

ABSSS (undated) *Akhil Bharatiya Samaj Sewa Sansthan: A Profile—1990–91.* Akhil Bharatiya Samaj Sewa Sansthan, Manikpur, Banda.

Afzulpurkar, Dinesh K. (1995) Programme for the Rehabilitation of Slum and Hutment Dwellers in Brihan Mumbai Report.

Agarwal, Anil (1985) Ecological Destruction and the Emerging Patterns of Poverty and People's Protest in Rural India. *Social Action*, 35.

Ambedkar, B.R. (1969) *Thus Spake Ambedkar*, Volume II. Compiled by Bhagwandas. Bhima Patrika Publication, Jullundur.

Aron, R. (1970) *Progress and Disillusion: The Dialectics of Modern Society.* Praeger, New York.

Artha and Sankhya Prabhag (1996) *Uttar Pradesh ki Arthik Sthiti ke Abhigyan Hetu Zilewar Vikas Sanketak—1995.* Rajya Niyojan Sansthan, Uttar Pradesh.

Bardhan, Pranab (1984) *The Political Economy of Development in India.* Oxford University Press, New Delhi.

———. (1988) 'Dominant Proprietary Classes and India's Democracy' in Atul Kohli (ed.) *India's Democracy: An Analysis of Changing State–Society Relations.* Princeton University Press, New Jersey.

Bapat, Meera (1992) Bombay's Pavement Dwellers: Continuing Torment. *Economic and Political Weekly*, 10 October.

Bapat, Meera and Sheela Patel (1993) Shelter, Women and Development: Beating a Path towards Women's Participation. *Economic and Political Weekly*, 13 March.

Baviskar, Amita (1995) *In the Belly of the River: Tribal Conflicts over Development in the Narmada Valley.* Oxford University Press, New Delhi.

Beckman, Bjorn (1992) 'Empowerment or Repression? The World Bank and the Politics of Adjustment' in Peter Gibbon (ed.) *Markets, Civil Society.*

Bhatt, Chandi Prasad (1991) Chipko Movement: The Hug that Saves. *The Hindu Survey of the Environment.*

Brass, Paul R. (1968) 'Uttar Pradesh' in Myron Weiner (ed.) *State Politics in India.* Princeton University Press, New Jersey.

Cardozo, Nicky (1985) Slums: Myths, Law and Court. *Mainstream,* 2 November.

Chandhoke, Neera (1995) *State and Civil Society: Explorations in Political Theory.* Sage Publications, New Delhi.

Chatterjee, Partha (1997) Beyond the Nation? Or Within? *Economic and Political Weekly.* 32.

———. (1998) Community in the East. *Economic and Political Weekly.* 7 February.

Chilika Aquatic Farms Limited (1991) Integrated Shrimp Farm Project Report.

Chilika Bachao Andolan and Krantadarshi Yuva Sangam (undated) *Chilika: Voice of the People.*

———. (1993) *Maa, Mati, Chilika* (in Oriya).

Citizens and Governance (1999) *Civil Society in the New Millennium.* The Commonwealth Foundation, London.

Cohen, Jean L. (1982) *Class and Civil Society: The Limits of Marxian Critical Theory.* Martin Robertson, Oxford, UK.

Cohen, Jean and Andrew Arato (1992) *Political Theory and Civil Society.* MIT Press, Cambridge.

Colas, Dominique (1997) *Civil Society and Fanaticism: Conjoined Histories.* Translated from the French by Amy Jacobs. Stanford University Press, California.

Coleman, James (1988) Social Capital in the Creation of Human Capital. *American Journal of Sociology.*

Das, B.B. (undated) *Chilika: The Nature's Treasure.* Orissa Krushak Mahasangh.

———. (undated) *Chilika Lake: Will it be Allowed to Die.* Orissa Krushak Mahasangh.

Das, P.K. (1995) 'Manifesto of a Housing Activist' in Sujata Patel and Alice Thorner (eds.) *Bombay: Metaphor for Modern India.* Oxford University Press, Bombay.

Desai, A.R. (1985) *Trends of Urban Development in India and the Proliferation of Slums and Squatting.* C.G. Shah Memorial Trust Publication, Bombay.

Desai, A.R. and S.D. Pillai (1972) *A Profile of an Indian Slum.*

Dhanagre, D.N. (1987) Green Revolution and Social Inequalities in Rural India. *Economic and Political Weekly*, 22

Duncan, Ian R. (1979) Levels, the Communication of Programmes and Sectional Strategies in Indian Politics, with Reference to the BKD and the RPI in UP State and Aligarh District. Unpublished PhD thesis. University of Sussex.

Dutta, Madan (1992) The Deathless Patriot. *Frontier*, 1 February.

Ferguson, Adam (1766, 1966) *An Essay on the History of Civil Society.* Edited by D. Forbes, UP Edinburg, Edinburg.

Fernandes, Walter (1991) Power and Powerlessness: Development Projects and Displacement of Tribals. *Social Action*, July–September.

Fisher, J. (1993) *The Road from Rio: Sustainable Development and Non-Governmental Movement in the Third World.* C.T. Praeger, Westport.

Foucault, Michel (1980) *Power/Knowledge: Selected Interviews and Other Writings 1972–1977.* Pantheon, New York.

Fukuyama, Francis (1992) *End of History and the Last Man.* Penguin Publishers, UK.

Gadgil, Madhav and Ramchandra Guha (1994) Ecological Conflicts and the Environmental Movements in India. *Development and Change*, 25.

Government of Maharashtra (1995) Report of the Study Group Appointed by the Government of Maharashtra for the Rehabilitation of Slum and Hutment Dwellers through Reconstruction. Government of Maharashtra, Bombay.

Gowalkar, M.S. (1939) *We or Our Nationhood Defined.* Bharat Prakashan, Nagpur.

Goyal, S. (1992) 'Social Background of the Officers of the IAS: Appendix II' in Francine Frankel and M.S.A. Rao (eds.) *Dominance and State Power in Modern India: Decline of a Social Order.* Volume I. Oxford University Press, New Delhi.

Gramsci, Antonio (1971) *Selections from the Prison Notebooks of Antonio Gramsci.* Edited and translated by Quaintin Hoare and G.N. Smith. Lawrence and Wishart, London; International Publishers, New York.

Guha, Ramchandra (1989) New Social Movements: The Problem. *Seminar*, No. 355, March.

———. (1991) *The Unquiet Woods: Ecological Change and Peasant Resistance in the Himalaya.* Oxford University Press, New Delhi.

Guhan, S. (1998) World Bank on Governance: A Critique. *Economic and Political Weekly,* 33:4, 24 January.

Hann, Chris and Elizabeth Dunn (eds.) (1996) *Civil Society: Challenging Western Models.* Routledge, London.

Havel, Vaclav (1997) Speech to the Parliament of the Czech Republic. 9 December.

Hegel, Georg Wilhelm Fredrik (1942) *The Philosophy of Right.* Translated by T.M. Knox. Oxford University Press, Oxford.

High Court of Orissa (1993) Report of the Fact Finding Committee on Chilika Fisheries.

Honneth, Axel (1993) Conceptions of Civil Society. *Radical Philosophy,* 64, Summer.

Issac, Jeffrey (1993) Civil Society and the Spirit of Revolt. *Dissent,* Summer.

Jagran Research Centre (1998) *Jagran's Uttar Pradesh at a Glance 1998.* JRC, Kanpur.

Jayal, Nirja Gopal (1997) The Governance Agenda: Making Democratic Development Dispensable, *Economic and Political Weekly,* 33:4, 24 January.

———. (1999) Consolidating Democracy and Governance in Civil Society in India. Paper presented at the Global Thinknet Paris Conference at the Institute Francais des Relations Internationales, Paris, 18–1 9 March.

Jessop, Bob (1998) The Rise of Governance and the Risks of Failure: the Case of Economic Development. *International Social Science Journal,* March.

Keane, J. (1988a) *Democracy and Civil Society.* Verso, London.

———. (1988b) *Civil Society and the State.* Verso, London.

———. (1998) *Civil Society: Old Images, New Visions.* Polity Press, Cambridge, UK.

Kohli, Atul (1987) *The State and Poverty in India: The Politics of Reform.* Cambridge University Press, Cambridge.

———. (ed.) (1988) *India's Democracy: An Analysis of Changing State-Society Relations.* Princeton University Press, New Jersey.

———. (1991) *Democracy and Discontent: India's Growing Crisis of Governability.* Cambridge University Press, Cambridge.

Kooiman, Jan (ed.) (1993) *Modern Governance.* Sage Publications, London.

Kothari, Rajni (1986) Masses, Classes and the State. *Economic and Political Weekly,* 21.

Kothari, Rajni (1987) On Humane Governance. *Alternatives*, XII.

———. (1988) *State against Democracy: In Search of Humane Governance.* Ajanta Publications, New Delhi.

———. (1990) *Politics and People*, Vol. II, Ajanta Publishers, Delhi.

Kuh, Thomas (1962) *Structure of Scientific Revolutions.* University of Chicago Press, Chicago.

Lynch, Owen (1969) *Politics of Untouchability, Social Mobility and Change in a City of India.* Columbia University Press, Columbia.

Manor, J. (1983) Anomie in Indian Politics: Origins and Potential Impact. *Economic and Political Weekly*, 18:19–21.

Melucci, Alberto (1988) 'Social Movements and the Democratisation of Everday Life' in John Keane (ed.) *Civil Society and the State.* Verso, London.

Mill, J.S. (1910) 'Considerations on Representative Governments' in *Utilitarianism, Liberty, and Representative Government.* J.M. Dent, London.

Milner, Andrew (2001) Civil Society: Towards a New Definition. Unpublished Draft. The Commonwealth Foundation, London.

Mitra, S.K. (1999) Effects of Institutional Arrangements on Political Stability in South Asia. *Annual Review of Political Science*, Vol. 2.

Mohanty, Ranjita (1995) Environmental Movement in the Context of Development: A Sociological Study of the Movement against Sardar Sarovar Project. Unpublished PhD thesis. Jawaharlal Nehru University, New Delhi.

———. (1999) Civil Society and State: Theoretical Explorations in the Indian Context. Paper presented at the Asian Third Sector Research Conference, 20–22 November, Bangkok.

Mohapatra, Bishnu N. (1997) The Problem. *Seminar*, No. 456, August.

Monteiro, Vivek (1998) 'Hang Together or Hang Separately' in *On a Rainbow in the Sky*. The Chhattisgarh Mukti Morcha. Centre for Education and Communication, New Delhi.

Mukherjee, A.B. (1980) *The Chamars of UP: A Study in Social Geography.* Inter India Publishers, New Delhi.

Narayan, Ram (1996) The Making of the Scheduled Caste Community in Uttar Pradesh: A Study of the SCF and Dalit Politics 1946–48. Unpublished M.Phil thesis. University of Delhi, New Delhi.

Nirmala Niketan College of Social Work (1985) *A Census of Pavement Dwellers in Greater Bombay.* Nirmala Niketan College of Social Work, Bombay.

Niyogi, Shankar Guha (undated) 'Mines, Mechanisation and People' in Anil Sadgopal (ed.) Sangharsh aur Nirman.

———. (undated) 'What is the problem of Iron Ore Mines in Dalli Rajhara' in Anil Sadgopal (ed.) op. cit.

Niyogi, Shankar Guha and Anoop Singh (undated) 'Alternative Industrial Policy' in Anil Sadgopal (ed.) op. cit.

O'Donnell, Guillermo and Philippe C. Schmitter (1986) *Transitions from Authoritarian Rule: Tentative Conclusions about Uncertain Democracies.* John Hopkins Press, Baltimore.

Omvedt, Gail (1993) *Reinventing Revolution: New Social Movements and the Socialist Tradition in India.* M.E. Sharpe, New York.

Oommen, T.K. (1990) *Protest and Change: Studies in Social Movements.* Sage Publications, New Delhi.

———. (1996) State, Civil Society and Market in India: The Context of Mobilisation. *Mobilisation: An International Journal,* 1:2.

———. (1999) Dalits and Production of Knowledge, Parts I and II, *The Hindu,* 13 and 15 September.

Pai, Sudha (2000a) New Social and Political Movements of Dalits: A Study of Meerut District. *Contributions to Indian Sociology,* 2.

———. (2001) 'From Harijans to Dalits: Identity Formation, Political Consciousness and Electoral Mobilisation of Scheduled Castes in Uttar Pradesh' in Ghanshyam Shah (ed.) *Dalit Identity and Politics.* Sage Publications, New Delhi.

Pai, Sudha and Jagpal Singh (1977) Politicisation of Dalits and Most Backward Castes. Study of Social Conflict and Political Preferences in Four Villages of Meerut District. *Economic and Political Weekly,* 7 June, pp. 1358–61.

Patel, Sheela and Celine D'Cruz (1993) The Mahila Milan Crisis Credit Scheme: From a Seed to a Tree. *Environment and Urbanization,* 5:1, April.

Patel, Sujata and Alice Thorner (eds.) (1995) *Bombay: Metaphor for Modern India.* Oxford University Press, Bombay.

Pathak, Akhileswar (1994) *Contested Domains: The State, Peasants and Forests in Contemporary India.* Sage Publications, New Delhi.

Pelcynzski, Z.A. (1988) 'Solidarity and the Rebirth of Civil Society' in John Keane (ed.) *Civil Society and the State.* Verso, London.

Pirez-Diaz, Victor M. (1993) *The Return of Civil Society.* Harvard University Press, Cambridge.

Population Foundation of India (1991) *District Profile: Uttar Pradesh.* PFI, New Delhi.

PRIA (1993) Forms of Organisation—Square Pegs in Round Holes. Mimeo. Society for Participatory Research in Asia, New Delhi.

Rai, Manoj et al. (2001) The State of Panchayats—A Participatory Perspective Summary. Samskriti Publications, Delhi.

Putnam, Robert D. (1993) *Making Democracy Work: Civic Traditions in Modern Italy.* Princeton University Press, Princeton, New Jersey.

———. (1995) Bowling Alone: America's Declining Social Capital. *Journal of Democracy*, 6:1.

———. (1997) 'Democracy in America at the Century's End' in Axel Hamilton (ed.) *Democracy's Victory and Crisis.* Cambridge University Press, Cambridge.

Rosenau, James N. (1992) 'Governance Order and Change in World Politics' in James W. Rosenau and Ernst-Otto Czempiel (eds.) *Governance Without Government: Order and Change in World Politics.* Cambridge University Press, Cambridge, UK.

Salmon, L.M. (1994) The Rise of Non-Profit Sector. *Foreign Affairs*, 67:4.

Schneider, C.L. (1995) *Shantytown Protest in Pinochet's Chile.* Temple University Press, Philadelphia.

Seligman, Adam (1992) *The Idea of Civil Society.* Princeton University Press, New Jersey.

Sethi, Sunil (1997) When Dalit Women Find Their Voice. *Times of India*, New Delhi, 28 July.

Singh, Gurbir and P.K. Das (1995) Building Castles in the Air: Housing Scheme for Bombay's Slum Dwellers. *Economic and Political Weekly.* 7 October.

Singh, H.D. (1998) *543 Faces of India.* Newsman Publication, New Delhi.

Singh, Jagpal (1992) *Capitalism and Dependence: Agrarian Politics in Western Uttar Pradesh 1951–91.* Manohar Publications, New Delhi.

Singh, Mohinder (1947) *The Depressed Classes and their Economic Condition.* Hind Kitabh, Bombay.

Tandon, Rajesh (1991) Civil Society, the State and Roles of NGOs, Mimeo. PRIA, New Delhi.

———. (1999) Profile of Civil Society in India. Draft Paper. Society for Participatory Research in Asia, New Delhi.

———. (2000) Civil Society in India—An Exercise in Mapping. Mimeo. PRIA, New Delhi.

SPARC (1985) *We, the Invisible: A Census of Pavement Dwellers.* Society for the Promotion of Area Resource Centres, Bombay.

SPARC (1999) Between Squalor and Hope: Pavement Dwellers and Slum Dwellers Along the Railway Tracks in Mumbai. Report prepared by the Society for the Promotion of Area Resource Centres, Bombay.

Taylor, Charles (1975) *Hegel*. Cambridge University Press, Cambridge.

———. (1991) 'Civil Society in the Western Tradition' in E. Groffier and M. Paradis (eds.) *The Notion of Tolerance and Human Rights: Essays in Honour of Raymond Klibansky.* University of Carleton Press, Ottawa.

Tocqueville, Alexis de (1956) *Democracy in America,* Volumes I and II. Knopf, New York.

———. (1990) *Democracy in America.* Translated by H. Keene. Volumes 1 and 2. The Colonial Press, New York.

Touraine, Alain (1983) Triumph or Downfall of Civil Society. *Humanities in Review*, 1.

Van Til, J. (1988) *Mapping the Third Sector: Voluntarism in a Changing Social Economy.* The Foundation Centre, New York.

Varshney, Ashutosh (1998) India Defies the Odds. *Journal of Democracy*, July.

Venkatramani, S. (1985) The Supreme Court Judgement and Some Implications for the Pavement Dwellers. *Social Action*, 35:4, October–December.

Walzer, Michael (1992) 'The Civil Society Argument' in Chantal Mauffe (ed.) *Dimensions of Radical Democracy.* Verso, London.

———. (1998) 'The Concept of Civil Society' in Michael Walzer (ed.) Towards a Global Civil Society. Berghahn Books, Providence, Oxford.

World Bank (1989) *Sub-Saharan Africa: From Crisis to Sustainable Growth.* Oxford University Press, Oxford.

———. (1991) *Managing Development: The Governance Dimension.* Washington, D.C.

———. (1992) *Governance and Development.* Washington, D.C.

———. (1994) Governance: The World Bank's Experience. Washington, D.C.

Zelliot, Eleanor (1998) Dalit Traditions and Dalit Consciousness. Revised version of paper presented at the international seminar on 'Challenges to Indian Democracy: State Market and Politics of Identity' organised by the SIDA Project Members on Democracy and Social Capital in Segmented Societies, Jawaharlal Nehru University, New Delhi, August.

About the Editors and Contributors

The Editors

Rajesh Tandon is currently the president of PRIA, a non-profit development organisation he founded in 1982 to provide support to the grassroots initiatives in India. A renowned scholar and practitioner on participatory research, training and development, he has published extensively on various aspects of development, role of the voluntary sector, civil society and citizen participation. His recent books include *Participatory Research: Revisiting the Roots and Voluntary Action, Civil Society and the State.*

Ranjita Mohanty currently heads the academic linkage and research programme of PRIA. She has published on various dimensions of collective action relating to natural resource management, people's participation in development, the interface between civil society and the state on issues of public policy and the dynamic relationship between civil society and the democratic state in India. *Civil society and Governance* is her recent publication which she authored with Rajesh Tandon.

The Contributors

Neera Chandhoke is currently Professor and Head, Department of Political Science, University of Delhi. Her academic interest covers a wide range of issues such as grassroots social movements, secularism and minority rights, and theoretical understanding of civil society and the state, on which she has published extensively. *The Conceit of Civil Society* is her most recent publication.

T.K. Oommen is former Professor, Study of Social Systems, School of Social Sciences, Jawaharlal Nehru University, New Delhi. His academic interest includes social movements, political sociology, agrarian relation and social transformation on which he has published extensively in the form of journal articles and books. *Pluralism, Equality and Identity: Comparative Studies,* is his most recent publication. Prof. Oommen has been awarded the V.K.R.V. Rao Prize in Sociology (1981) and the G.S. Ghurye Prize in Sociology and Anthropology (1985).

Bishnu N. Mohapatra is Associate Professor at the Centre for Political Studies, School of Social Sciences, Jawaharlal Nehru University, New Delhi and has currently joined as a programme officer in the New Delhi Office of the Ford Foundation. He has published on various aspects of social capital, civil society and democracy.

Harsh Mander, a social activist, writer, and former civil servant, is currently the country director of Action Aid, India. He is closely associated with social causes and movements, important among them is the Right to Information movement in Rajasthan. *Unheard Voices: Stories of Forgotten Lives* is his recent publication.

Jayaprakash Narayan, a former civil servant, now works closely on issues related to constitutional and administrative reforms including electoral reforms, transparency and accountability of public institutions. To advance this cause he founded a non-profit, non-partisan organisation called Foundation for Democratic Reforms, and *Lok Satta*, a grassroots movement aimed at reforming the fundamental structures of Indian governance.

Sudha Pai is Professor, Center for the Study of Political Studies, School of Social Sciences, Jawaharlal Nehru University,

New Delhi. She has published extensively on issues of party system, electoral politics in India and Dalit assertion. *Dalit Assertion and the Unfinished Democratic Agenda: The BSP in Uttar Pradesh,* is her recent publication, While continuing her interest in issues of Dalit politics, she is at present also interested in issues of governance in India.

Ram Narayan is a senior research scholar working on the issues of socio-historical aspects of Chamars struggle for identities in Uttar Pradesh. He is also the recipient of Sephis Grant for his research work.

B.K. Joshi is former Professor and Director, Giri Institute of Development Studies, Lucknow and former Vice Chancellor, Kumaon University, Nainital. Currently he is working as an independent consultant on development policy, primary education and development-related problems in Himalayan region. He is also closely associated with various NGOs in different capacities.

Index

Abhiyan, 260
academia, 11
accountability, 36, 39, 46, 57, 61, 68, 71–75, 88, 119, 121, 123, 146, 150, 160, 171, 172, 208, 231; instruments of, 112–15
activism, 79, 83, 145
Adarsh Sudhar Samiti, 275
Adivasis, 199, 201, 217
administration, administrative, 204, 236, 336; efficiency, 13; failure, 349; hostility, 206; incompetent, 173; inefficiency, 171; politics in, 203; quality, capacity and process, 171, 173–74, 201; reforms, 172; system, complexity, 108
Africa: authoritarian regime, 169, 172
Afzulpurkar report, 307–8
Agnivesh, Swami, 346
Akhil Bharatiya Jankalyan Ambedkar Sudhar Samiti, 253
Akhil Bharatiya Samaj Seva Sansthan (ABSSS), 23; land to Kol tribals, role in, 315, 316, 318–21, 323–25, 327, 331–33, 337–40; other activities, 342–45; state and national linkage, 345–47
Aklak, Haji, 266
Alberuni, 79
All India Trade Union Congress (AITUC), 203, 211, 212–13, 226
altruism, 126
Amar Ujala (*AU*), 259

Ambedkar Sangharsh Samiti Shergarhi Kand, 260
Ambedkar Sewa Dal, 254, 261, 267
Ambedkar Sudhar Samiti, 253
Ambedkar Utthan Parishad, 253, 267
Ambedkar Vikas Sangharsh Samiti, Kishanpur, Meerut, Uttar Pradesh, 262
Ambedkar, B.R., 115, 138, 244, 248, 250–52, 256–57
anarchy, 78, 108
Andhra Pradesh: government employees, 87; populist programmes, 103–4
anti-communal groups, 56
anti-corruption law, 153, 161
anti-liquor movement, 216, 237, 240
Antulay, A.R., 299
Anusuchit Jati Morcha, 254
Argentina: assertion of civil society, 32; military dictatorship, 60, 169
Ashok Mining Company, 226
Associated Cement Company (ACC), 204, 215
associational life, 33, 38, 40, 43, 47, 48, 50–51, 52, 53–54, 208, 244, 245
associational politics, 312
associations, 61, 62, 63; and civil society, 293
authoritarianism, authoritarian regimes, state, 16, 54, 77, 99, 109, 170, 172, 244, 294; rebellion against, 60